Pitt Series in Policy and Institutional Studies

Public Spirit in the Thrift Tragedy

Mark Carl Rom

University of Pittsburgh Press

Pittsburgh and London

Published by the University of Pittsburgh Press, Pittsburgh, Pa.
15260
Copyright © 1996, University of Pittsburgh Press
Manufactured in the United States of America
Printed on acid-free paper

Designed by Jane Tenenbaum

Library of Congress Cataloging-In-Publication Data

Rom, Mark C., 1957–

    Public spirit in the thrift tragedy / Mark Carl Rom.

       p.   cm. — (Pitt series in policy and institutional studies)

    Includes bibliographical references and index.

    ISBN 0-8229-3943-6 (cloth : alk. paper). — ISBN 0-8229-5600-4

(pbk. : alk. paper)

    1. Thrift institutions—Government policy—United States.

2. Savings and loan association failures—United States.   3. United

States. Federal Home Loan Bank System.   4. United States. Federal

Home Loan Bank Board. I. Title. II. Series.

HG2152.R65   1996

332.3'2'0973—dc20   95-48261

                                                      CIP

A CIP catalogue record for this book is available from the British Library.
Eurospan, London

With love to Elizabeth Lynch Rom

Contents

Acknowledgments

My parents, Meg and Roy Rom, taught me at an early age that it is good to help other people and not just myself. My wife, Lisa, asks me in disbelief, "Do some scholars really believe that people act solely in their own self-interest?" To her, at least, it is obvious that people often do things because they are seen as the right thing to do and not just the expedient thing. My attempts to develop a "public spirit" view of political behavior stem largely from the wisdom of these family members.

Other scholars and institutions have helped me shape and articulate these thoughts. My special thanks go to the scholars in the Departments of Politics at the University of Arkansas (especially Conrad Waligorski), the University of Wisconsin (John Witte in particular), the Brookings Institution (most notably Paul Peterson), and the faculty in the Department of Government and the Graduate Public Policy Program at Georgetown University. All of these fine institutions have provided me financial support, supportive colleagues, and congenial homes. Thanks also to the fine staff of the University of Pittsburgh Press.

I wish there were no errors in these pages, but regrettably I must have made some. Those who want to promote a better understanding of politics and policy will undoubtedly find them.

Public Spirit in
the Thrift Tragedy

1

Public Spirit in
the Thrift Tragedy

THE FEDERAL HOME LOAN BANK SYSTEM (FHLBS) failed spectacularly
during the 1980s. The savings and loan associations that belonged to
it went bankrupt in record numbers at extraordinary cost. More than
twelve hundred thrifts failed between 1980 and 1990, while another
six hundred were broke but remained open for business.[1]

More important for the taxpaying public, the Federal Savings and
Loan Insurance Corporation (FSLIC), which insured savings deposits
at thrifts, went massively bankrupt, suffering "the largest [deficit] ever
reported by a public or private corporation."[2] FSLIC's failure could cost
taxpayers about $180 billion, give or take $15 billion.[3]

How did this tragedy happen? The financial causes are now well
established. Savings and loan associations became insolvent because
they paid out too much interest and received too little, because they
made bad loans, and because they engaged in fraud. In other words,
thrifts went broke from interest losses, asset losses, and criminal activity.

Until the 1980s, thrifts had a tradition of investing primarily in
long-term, fixed-rate home mortgages while borrowing short-term
money from depositors. When interest rates increased, thrifts began
to pay more to borrow money than they were earning on their mortgages. As one financier noted, "You didn't need to be a genius to

understand that if you were borrowing money at 16 percent and lending it out at 8 percent, you wouldn't remain in business very long."[4] These interest rate mismatches caused the vast majority of thrift industry losses through 1982.

Many thrifts then attempted to achieve profitability by lending for or investing in a wide range of "nontraditional" ventures, including commercial real estate, land, junk bonds, and other ventures. Thrifts lost money whenever these loans went into default or the investments dropped in value. Even if you lend at 16 percent, it turns out, you will not stay in business very long if your loans are not repaid. Bad investments on nontraditional assets caused most of the thrift industry's losses after 1982.

There have also been implications of fraud in a large number of thrift failures.[5] Thrifts lost money whenever someone—owner, director, employee, or customer—stole it. It does not really matter what interest rate the thrift is charging to those who have no intention of paying interest. Criminal activity at savings and loans was widespread throughout the 1980s.

Fraud provoked most of the publicity, but interest rate losses and bad investments caused most of the damage. The interest rate losses that thrifts experienced before 1983 account for roughly 50 percent of the total cost of resolving thrift failures. Another 25 percent of the price may be assigned to bad real estate loans and investments, made primarily between 1983 and 1985. All other factors—including fraud, losses on other assets (including junk bonds), excessive operating costs, and Bank Board delays in handling insolvencies—account for the remaining 25 percent of FSLIC's losses.[6]

It might be tempting to personalize FSLIC's losses by means of three stereotypes. Criminals (Charles Keating and his ilk) stole much less than a quarter of the money that FSLIC lost. Aggressive developers (Donald Trump types, had Trump owned a thrift) who went bankrupt cost FSLIC an additional 25 percent. And well-intentioned thrift managers (such as Jimmy Stewart in *It's a Wonderful Life*), who made those beloved low-interest home mortgages, account for fully half of FSLIC's losses.

Stereotypes, however, can be misleading. Some thrift operators were saintly, some rapacious, and others were quite simply dishonest.

Yet many failed thrifts, it turns out, had operators with all three attributes. In a typical case, a thrift initially got into trouble by making fixed-rate home mortgage loans and developed even worse problems as it attempted to grow out of its troubles; it engaged in fraud only in a last-ditch effort to cover up the fact that it was bankrupt. Deception usually did not cause the failure but rather followed it.

It is thus instructive to look below the surface fraud to determine the deeper financial causes of FSLIC's losses. The depths are murky, however. Even with a clear metric—the dollar—it has been difficult to attribute accurately the financial causes of the massive losses FSLIC incurred because each dollar lost can have "several overlapping causes."[7] Only by examining the thrift industry broadly and deeply could these causes be identified.

Political Causes of the Thrift Tragedy: Conventional Views

As the financial bases of FSLIC's failure have become better understood, attention has increasingly been drawn to the political causes. The conventional wisdom can be easily summarized: "The savings and loan bankruptcies give sordid evidence of immoral financial buccaneers, incompetent regulators, and compliant legislators."[8]

According to the popular view, corrupt politicians are largely to blame for the thrift mess.[9] Some of the major villains include Speaker of the House Jim "Money Talks" Wright, House Banking Committee Chair Fernand J. "The Stooge" St. Germain, Senator Alfonse "Senator Shakedown" D'Amato and, of course, "The Keating Five."[10] These politicians, along with other key members of the banking committees and the congressional leadership, did receive lavish campaign contributions from the thrift industry.[11] S&L interests donated at least $11.6 million to congressional candidates and political party committees during the 1980s.[12] Charles H. Keating Jr. and other officials of Lincoln Savings and Loan contributed $1.3 million to the Keating Five senators who intervened with S&L regulators on Lincoln's behalf.[13] In the popular view, these campaign contributions were little more than legal bribes; the recipients were virtually bought by the thrift industry. According to Common Cause, Congress "contributed to the worst financial scandal in American history and . . . the corrupt campaign finance system . . . allowed it to happen."[14]

Similarly, the common consensus is that the bureaucrats failed to prevent FSLIC's losses, even though they could and should have done so. Charges of incompetence at the Federal Home Loan Bank Board (FHLBB, the agency that regulated the thrift industry) are so numerous and diverse they are not easy to summarize. A few are worth quoting. First, meet the leadership. Richard Pratt, Bank Board chairman at the beginning of the 1980s, was "the angel of death for the thrift industry. . . . If you had to pick one individual to blame for what happened to the S&Ls and to some hundreds of billions of dollars of taxpayer money, [Pratt] would get the honor without even campaigning."[15] And Pratt's successor, Edwin Gray: "He knew no law; he knew no accounting; he knew little economics. Even worse, those who knew him in the White House . . . variously described him as a nincompoop, a fool, and a buffoon."[16] After Gray came M. Danny Wall, nicknamed "M. Danny Isuzu" after the prevaricating television pitchman.[17] Now, greet the staff: "In the 1980s . . . [the Bank Board often] hired CPAs and lawyers who weren't good enough to do anything else."[18] If there is a common theme to these condemnations, it is that the bureaucrats were the thrift industry's patsies.

Scholars writing about the thrift tragedy are loathe to focus on individual misdeeds.[19] Instead, the scholarly view points the finger at the political system itself. Academic analysis has emphasized that the tragedy's principal political causes lay in the government's structure, and especially, in officials' incentives regarding their self-interest. As one scholar summarized it: "The problem is the result of the structural flaws in the system. Because of these flaws, the industry and its regulators, which include the United States Congress, are faced with virtually irresistible incentives to ignore signals of pending insolvency, and to postpone the inevitable day of reckoning until 'someone else' takes over and becomes responsible."[20]

The academic case against Congress is that it was biased against considering the good of the nation as a whole when it made public policy for the thrift industry.[21] This conclusion is based on the following argument. Reelection is the primary motivation of legislators.

Congress is designed so that members of Congress are elected by local constituencies, and these local constituencies prefer to receive benefits and avoid costs. This interaction between incentives and institutional design implies that members of Congress will provide services to their individual constituents, promote policies that benefit important constituency groups, and block policies that these groups oppose.

Thomas Romer and Barry R. Weingast have argued that congressional incentives and structure produced two types of congressional activity concerning FSLIC that increased its losses. Individual legislators intervened on behalf of specific institutions seeking relief from the regulators. The whole Congress delayed giving FSLIC the resources it needed to minimize its losses. Together, these activities created the "essential component" of FSLIC's downfall.[22]

Scholarly criticism of the thrift bureaucracy has also focused on the incentives of its officials and the structure of the FHLBS. The critique goes like this. The organizational design of the FHLBB left it too susceptible to influence from Congress and the thrift industry. The incentives of its officials led them to defer to thrift industry preferences, as they were expressed either in congressional legislation and oversight or through the industry's lobbyists. The combination of incentive and structure thus led FHLBB officials to give the thrift industry the policies and policing it sought. By doing so, FHLBB officials greatly increased the size of the FCLIC's losses.[23]

The specific criticisms of these scholars are part of a broader intellectual approach known as "public choice," which applies economic theory to political life.[24] While public choice theory is a diverse and complex body of literature, it is distinguished by two main claims. The first is the assumption of self-interest. In Anthony Downs's model statement of this assumption, officials "act solely in order to attain the income, prestige, and power which come from being in office. . . . [They] never seek office as a means of carrying out particular policies; their only goal is to reap the rewards of holding office per se. They treat policies purely as a means to the attainment of their private ends."[25] From the public choice perspective, officials never ask what policies are best for the public, but only what policies are best for themselves. The second claim is that this pursuit of self-interest in the political domain leads inexorably to inferior public policies, as well-organized "special interests" seek to exploit government for their own purposes and as officials find such exploitation personally rewarding.

The public choice evaluations of the thrift tragedy have ranged from quiet resignation to deep disgust. Romer and Weingast find nothing unusual in the political activities that led to FSLIC's losses because these were simply the predictable outcomes of congressional incentives. As the authors conclude:

> Congressional behavior with respect to the thrift industry should be seen as fairly routine politics, rather than as an outrageous deviation. . . . The way Congress handled the emerging thrift crisis fits into a more general pattern of the way Congress responds to constituencies and to regulatory developments. . . . The political behavior surrounding the thrift debacle is absolutely ordinary. Through 1988, congressmen behaved as they do in ordinary circumstances: paying solicitous attention to active, well-organized interests, provided that the readily apparent costs to their other constituents are not noticeably high.[26]

Edward J. Kane, while also arguing that officials' incentives were a leading cause of FSLIC's losses, has drawn more cynical conclusions about politicians and bureaucrats. Calling officials' actions during the thrift tragedy "indefensible," Kane declares:

> The modern code of public service has three unspoken precepts. First, almost anything may be okay if one can keep from getting caught at it. Second, even if caught, one's behavior may still be okay if one can find a credible scapegoat on which to point the blame. Third, even when scapegoating fails, one may still be exonerated by claiming that there was nothing else one could reasonably do.[27]

Much academic commentary on the thrift tragedy is thus as scornful about the performance of the government as is the popular view. Indeed, the pessimism of the public choice view is conventional wisdom among scholars.[28]

Public Choice: A Critique

Individual self-interest obviously influences political decision making. Our nation's founders understood this clearly, and deliberately designed our government to moderate and balance self-interest. But the public choice assessment of interests is incomplete if not incorrect. Self-interest alone is a woefully inadequate explanation of official behavior and policy choice, for several reasons.

First, public officials have varying kinds of self-interest. Many politicians are motivated primarily by the desire for reelection, but others seek legislative influence or public stature.[29] There is also little agreement about what it is that bureaucrats seek to maximize. Job security? Permanent income? Political advancement? Professional reputation? Agency budgets? Each of these motivations has been assumed to be the dominant bureaucratic interest. And one official may favor certain interests, while another may favor others. This is important because officials who value security may behave differently from those who seek advancement; those who are motivated primarily by money may not act the same as those who aspire to professional respect. Most officials probably value some combination of all these things. This suggests that most officials are not single-minded, but human beings who try to balance competing personal goals.

Second, officials have various ways of pursuing their interests. The lawyers, economists, and accountants who are bureaucrats may attempt personal advancement (whether that means permanent income, political advancement, or professional reputation) by being overly solicitous to business concerns, but they may also seek these interests by challenging industry prerogatives. Government lawyers see vigorous prosecution of lawbreakers as a career-enhancing move, for example, and government economists frequently argue against protecting regulated industries.[30] Notably, these officials often disagree about what the government should do, and these disagreements are based on their diverse professional concerns. Successful politicians, for their part, do not just do the popular thing, but instead try to make their views the popular ones.[31]

Third, the best way to obtain these various aims is often uncertain. Even if officials have a single goal, it is not consistently clear what must be done to achieve it. Making important decisions, and in particular, making important policy decisions, is less a matter of calculus than of judgment. At best, officials make educated guesses about the consequences of their choices. (This should be obvious to anyone who has fallen in love, played the market, or chosen a career.) As a result, even officials with similar interests may make very different decisions. Many of these decisions prove harmful to the self-interest of the officials themselves. For example, some scholars have assumed that public officials' main incentive is to enhance their future political power.[32] As Fernand St. Germain, Tony Coelho, Jim Wright, the Keating Five, Ed Gray, and Danny Wall have all discovered to their dismay, involvement with the thrift industry has not exactly promoted political careers.[33] The fact that these decisions turned out badly for the officials who made them does not show that the individuals themselves felt uncertain about their choices; but it does show that the consequences of their choices were actually uncertain. This objective uncertainty is a key fact of political life.

Fourth, officials have conflicting interests. Conflicting interests arise from varied motivations, constituencies, and responsibilities, and can manifest themselves within individual officials or among officials. Any official who wanted to aid "the thrift industry" had to face the possibility that large or profitable S&Ls had different policy goals than small or unprofitable ones: helping some would harm others. Furthermore, the desire to help the thrift industry sometimes conflicted with the demands of other businesses or constituency groups. It was impossible to satisfy simultaneously all these interests; giving benefits to one often meant taking benefits from another. And even where one official's constituency was unified in its interests, these interests would clash with those of officials with different constituencies.

Public choice theory is most useful when officials have consistent, definite, and harmonious interests; it can best predict political behavior under these conditions. But public choice theory is less compelling when officials have interests that are diverse, uncertain, and conflicting. In these cases, concluding that outcomes are determined by self-interest is equivalent to inferring that *any* result can be explained in this way. This is not theory, but tautology.

But there is a more important reason why self-interest is inadequate as a guide to political behavior: officials often pursue the public interest. In doing so, officials act in an attempt to produce the best overall result for the public and not simply the best result for themselves. Steven Kelman suggests the general rule that "the more important a policy is, the less important is the role of self-interest in determining that policy."[34] The increase in transfers to the poor in the 1960s; the growth in health, safety, and environmental regulation in the 1970s; and the deregulation of protected industries such as trucking, airlines, and telecommunications in the 1980s, among other policies, could all be cited as examples of a larger purpose winning out over a narrower one. This result is difficult to explain in terms of self-interest. (Note also that in cases like these, where the policy issues are broader, officials' self-interests are most likely to be diverse, uncertain, and conflicting.) Especially in these episodes, "the skill at making a good argument, of having the facts on one's side, of being able to present an appealing public vision, or having a reputation for seriousness and commitment" can be the critical factors by which public purpose triumphs over the personal.[35]

Two objections might be raised: How do officials know what the public interest is? And, why would they pursue it? These are legitimate and difficult questions. Let us consider each of them in turn.

Attempts to prove the existence of an objective public interest seem doomed to failure; or at least, there has never been absolute proof it exists or unanimous agreement on what it might be. Political philosophers hardly attempt to define it any more.[36] But this metaphysical problem is not unique to public interest; after all, it is also impossible to demonstrate what self-interest really is. Public choice scholars get around this simply by assuming that individuals have self-interests, know what they are, and pursue them. But these are all just assumptions. As a theoretical matter, how is this different from stipulating that individuals grasp and seek the public interest? Fortunately, the public interest is not a purely theoretical notion, since there are at least three practical ways that officials can determine what is in the public interest.

First, officials come to learn the public interest through their legal obligations: the public interest is what an official's job description says it is. While these formal duties do not specify the entire public interest or typically define exactly what the official must do to obtain it, they do give officials a view of their own part in it. Especially for lower-ranking officials, job descriptions also link public and private interest by establishing public standards for private success.

Second, public officials can determine the public interest by participating in the life of their organization. Organizations have cultures, and these cultures can provide a distinct view of the public interest.[37] For example, the United States Forest Service has a culture championing "progressive conservation"—"the expert, nonpartisan, and professional management of the national forests for the benefit of many kinds of users."[38] The General Accounting Office holds that its purpose is to ferret out waste, fraud, and abuse in government spending, and its employees act on this belief.[39] The Social Security Administration developed a "client-serving ethic."[40] In Congress, Democrats and Republicans alike belong to partisan organizations espousing policy principles. Organizational culture can have a powerful effect in influencing officials' views of the public interest.

Third, public officials can determine the public interest through their own beliefs. Officials are not blank slates, but typically bring to their offices convictions about what is good public policy. This does not mean that officials necessarily have detailed and specific policy objectives, though it does suggest they at least have general beliefs about what the government should do and how it should do it. Moreover, officials are often attracted to organizations that embody these views.[41]

The public interests embedded in job descriptions, organizational cultures, or individual beliefs may of course also be diverse, ambiguous in their operation, or conflicting, just like individual interests. This means that the public interest, like self-interest, is elusive, but not that it is an illusion. It also suggests that political outcomes often cannot be deduced from either self-interest or public interest; instead, outcomes are highly contingent and often depend largely on the specifics of the particular political issue.

The matter remains: Even if individuals can ascertain the public interest, why would they pursue it? To answer this question, it may be helpful to consider the logical possibilities: public and private interests can be complementary, neutral, or contradictory. The happiest case is when private and public interests coincide; in that instance, by aspiring to serve the public interest, one also pursues self-interest.[42] This may be the case for the bulk of political activity. Furthermore, when self-interest and the public interest are neutral in relation to each other (that is, when pursuing the public good neither helps nor harms the official personally), there are still good reasons (obligations, cultures, and beliefs) for individuals to continue pursuing the public interest and no special reason for them to subvert it.

The toughest—and most newsworthy—calls are where self-interest and the public interest diverge. In the dramatic cases when officials choose society over self, heroes blossom; when officials sacrifice the public good for private gain, they decay to scoundrels. Although these situations pose the most difficult challenge for officials, the outcome cannot simply be taken for granted: there are both heroes and scoundrels. Before one concludes that public servants are more villanous than valiant, it is worth pausing to remember that millions of individuals (in armies and police departments, for example) have sacrificed their lives for their country in the ultimate choice between private and public interest. Perhaps the desire to do the right thing is less rare than we are often led to believe.

The three logical possibilities are all empirical realities. In the vast majority of instances, it is not easy to show whether officials are acting out of self-interest or in the public interest; indeed, when public and private interests coincide it is impossible. It is nonetheless worthwhile to scrutinize the actions of officials to identify instances where they have sacrificed the public good for personal gain. The actions of top officials are especially important, for several reasons. The constraints of legal obligations and organizational culture are relatively weak for government leadership: job descriptions are ambiguous and "culture" may be less than compelling. The leader's actions have a broader and deeper immediate impact than actions by the staff; a high-ranking official who writes policies to serve private ends has a greater effect than a staffer who merely interprets them for his or her own benefit. More important, when the leadership disregards the public interest, the staff may be encouraged to ignore legal obligations, thus weakening any public-spirited aspects of the organizational culture.

Political Causes of the Thrift Tragedy:
An Alternative View

In this book, I present an alternative interpretation to the public choice view of the thrift tragedy. The core idea is that most government officials acted—or at least attempted to act—primarily in the public interest. Officials, rather than being motivated solely by self-interest, were influenced in large part by "public spirit."

Public spirit, as Kelman has defined it, is "an inclination to make an honest effort to achieve good public policy."[43] The public spirit view of Congress thus begins with what Norman J. Ornstein has described as "a startling and—sadly—unconventional assumption: that politicians are neither driven by evil or weak motives, nor are they all, beneath the surface, conniving and dishonest . . . [and therefore] the decisions our policy makers have made have been neither irrational nor irresponsible." Instead, Congress is "an institution making reasonable and understandable decisions, as its members struggle in good faith to balance legitimate competing views."[44] American bureaucrats, for their part, are likely to see themselves as promoters of and advocates for policy ideas.[45] This advocacy cannot be arbitrary if it is to be authoritative, since official decisions must be backed by reason and evidence; they must be placed on the public record and opposition to the decisions must be addressed and rebutted in the same forum.

According to a public spirit view of politics, officials do not just have policy preferences; they also have policy commitments. Officials' positions on taxes, defense, abortion, social security, and numerous other policy issues are typically not matters of convenience, but rather of conviction.[46] The public spirit manifests itself in part through these policy commitments. When officials are committed to a policy, their support for it cannot be bought, sold, or traded (at least not easily, often, or without commensurate policy gains).[47] Most public officials have substantial policy commitments, and most major public policies have officials committed to them—and against them.

The public spirit view recognizes that officials have conflicts over policy commitments. Officials disagree among themselves and with those outside the government regarding which public purposes are worthwhile and which policies are likely to achieve those purposes. Like the commitments themselves, these disagreements are real, not just calculated efforts to enhance political position.

Public officials, then, live in a world of commitments and conflicts. To make policy, they must resolve conflicts. No single formula can be discovered for doing this. To the extent that conflicts are settled (and sometimes they are not) they are resolved through deliberation and compromise marked by analysis, bargaining, and discussion.[48] These resolutions are sure to be imperfect, since it is not possible to completely reconcile opposing beliefs or divergent interests.

A "public spirit" view of policy making is thus radically different from public choice theory. It assumes that officials are primarily motivated not by self-interest but by the public interest. It suggests that policy making is marked in large part by commitment and conflict, not just guile and collusion. It proposes that conflicts are usually resolved through deliberation and compromise, not just through the estimation of individual gains.

The public spirit view thus questions the public choice view that FSLIC's losses were caused primarily by the self-seeking actions of government officials. But if personal incentives did not cause the thrift tragedy, what did? How could public spirit lead to this dismal end? The answer is that public spirit did not cause it, but that it occurred in part due to public spirit, in part in spite of it, and in part in the absence of it. The political causes of the thrift tragedy, like the financial causes, may be divided into three main components. In political terms, FSLIC's losses can be attributed to policy commitments, policy conflict and uncertainty, and miscellaneous other factors, including policy "fraud and abuse."

Policy commitments made before 1982 were the major cause of the losses. In particular, the thrift industry was induced through legislation and regulation, first, to make long-term, fixed-rate home mortgage loans and, second, to accept short-term deposits backed by federal deposit insurance. These policies were conscious attempts to protect citizens and thrifts in their efforts to finance homes and enhance savings. These policy commitments left thrifts vulnerable to the increase in interest rates, which brought about the first wave of financial losses. In this sense, public spirit contributed to FSLIC's failure.

Between 1982 and 1989, policy conflict and uncertainty were the main political source of FSLIC's losses. This conflict and uncertainty permitted thrifts to make the investments that led to their second round of financial losses and prevented FSLIC from getting the resources that could have reduced its losses. Many of the policy "investments" made during this period, like many of the financial investments, were losers (both to the public and to the officials who made them). Policy uncertainty and conflict during this period allowed FSLIC's losses to grow larger than they would have been *if* policy knowledge and consensus had been greater. In these years the thrift tragedy unfolded despite public spirit.

Policy fraud and abuse have been the most publicized political causes for FSLIC's losses, but they were the least costly. Some officials were willing and able to sacrifice the public interest for their own interest, and these officials increased costs to the taxpaying public. Unfortunately, this part of the thrift tragedy can be linked to the absence of public spirit. Like Kathleen Day, we may hope that these individuals end up in S&L hell.[49] In wishing this, however, we must be clear about what policy fraud and abuse are and what they are not. They are not stupidity; they are not making decisions that turn out badly; they are not choosing policies with which one disagrees. They are, more narrowly, breaking the law and, more broadly, violating the public trust. When an official gets a direct or indirect payoff in his or her personal capacity in exchange for providing favored treatment to a constituent, or when an official withholds or falsifies official information, the public trust is violated.[50] Judged by these perhaps restricted standards, policy fraud and abuse have occurred fairly infrequently. Cases of official misconduct can account for only a small portion of FSLIC's losses.

FSLIC's downfall thus contained all the elements of tragedy. The thrift system was created for honorable purposes, to protect savings and to provide homes. This system was vulnerable to economic forces, however, that thrift regulators and members of Congress could not control. Once these forces struck, the demise of FSLIC and large portions of the thrift business was inevitable no matter what the officials did. Their efforts could only delay, but not prevent, this ending.

Comparing the "Public Choice" and "Public Spirit" Perspectives

The public choice and the public spirit views of the thrift tragedy can be contrasted empirically in numerous ways but not, unfortunately in the most important one. In neither case is it possible to directly test the assumption that officials are motivated primarily by self-interest, by public spirit, or by some combination of these incentives.[51] There are, however, other criteria that can be used to make an empirical comparison of the public choice view and the public spirit perspective.

First, there is the matter of institutional structure. Ideally, government organizations would be devised to work most effectively to accomplish their goals; defective structures hinder officials in their attempt to accomplish their purposes. The public choice perspective argues that government organizations are designed to be ineffective, and that they indeed perform as designed. Public officials have incentives to create incompetent organizations and lack motivations to run them effectively.[52] The public spirit view sees things differently. It suggests that government agencies are designed to do many valued tasks; it is primarily because these tasks are difficult and conflicting that they do not always do them well.[53] Officials within these organizations nonetheless make good faith efforts to fulfill their multiple responsibilities.

Second, there is the question of institutional resources. Again, both perspectives agree that resources are important. Resources play an especially critical role in public choice theory: officials are motivated largely by the desire for additional resources (staff, budgets, salaries). Officials do what is required to gain or retain these things. In the public spirit view, in contrast, more staff, larger budgets, and higher salaries are valuable to the extent that they help officials get their jobs done. Lack of resources, moreover, need not weaken public spirit.[54]

Third, there is the question of representation. Ideally, the widest variety of interests would be advocated in the policy process.[55] A seriously flawed process, in contrast, would systematically exclude some interests, give undue weight to others, and ignore the shared interests of the community. The public choice perspective suggests that a relatively small number of narrow interests will be favored in the policy process, and that, as a consequence, the public interest will be neglected. Although the public spirit view acknowledges that these results can occur, it does not assume they will occur automatically. Indeed, this perspective expects that a wide variety of interests will normally be represented in the policy process, even if some interests do not actively participate in the process.[56] Furthermore, the public spirit approach suggests that officials will also consider broader common interests.

Fourth, there is the standard of deliberation. In an ideal process, deliberation would consist of policy makers who rank their goals, examine evidence comprehensively, evaluate alternative policies, and choose policies based on these evaluations. We know, of course, that policy makers do not act with such "synoptic rationality." Instead, they commonly make incremental decisions based on multiple, flexible, and varying goals, and on a restricted analysis of limited data concerning a narrow range of potential policies. Furthermore, they gradually adjust their policies to the problems over time.[57] But if all deliberation is incremental, there are still more and less responsible kinds. More responsible deliberation involves honest attempts to weigh various public goals, to examine evidence, evaluate alternatives, and choose policies on the basis of these goals, evidence, and alternatives. The public choice perspective holds that real deliberation plays a minimal role in the policy process. What might look like deliberation is merely collusion, where policy makers cut deals to improve their personal position. The public spirit view finds deliberation a normal, perhaps defining, characteristic of the policy process because officials aspire to remedy public problems even as their aspirations are clouded by disagreements and uncertainties. Deliberation is an effort to resolve these disagreements and uncertainties.

Fifth, there is the question of oversight. The ideal oversight would ensure that the Congress has effectively and efficiently monitored the agency and that the regulatory agency has done the same for the regulated industry. Effective monitoring involves recognizing both individual infractions and systemic problems as they arise, gathering the necessary information to correct these difficulties, and imposing the sanctions necessary to ensure they are corrected. The monitoring is efficient to the extent that it is accomplished with the fewest possible resources.

The public choice perspective of the thrift tragedy sees government oversight as deficient because it is used primarily to accomplish the self-interested goals of officials and only incidentally to achieve a public goal.[58] Much oversight of regulatory agencies involves specific complaints of the regulated against the agency and not general considerations about the stability of the regulatory system. And, according to this view, much oversight of regulated firms is an "oversight" in the other sense: because regulators have limited personal incentives to find trouble among the regulated, they tend to overlook it. The public spirit view, in contrast, suggests that the quality of congressional and bureaucratic oversight depends on a large number of contextual factors, and that generalizations are difficult to make.[59] One generalization, however, might be offered. Government officials typically perform oversight duties as best they can not because they have incentives to do so, but because these duties are part of their job.[60]

Finally, there is the issue of timeliness. In an ideal process, policy makers would begin and conclude their deliberations within an appropriate time frame—that is, as quickly as possible. They would react rapidly to problems as they arise (or, better, would anticipate problems before they arise) and resolve them promptly. As desirable as timeliness is, however, it is often in conflict with the other criteria. Representation, deliberation, and oversight take time, and attempts to be timely can reduce the ability to satisfy the other goals.

The public choice perspective maintains that policy makers routinely fail to recognize and resolve policy problems in a timely fashion. On the one hand, policy makers have no public incentives for timely resolution; on the other, they have private reasons for delaying their resolution.[61] As a result, the public choice view maintains that the policy process as a rule moves too slowly. The public spirit view is more ambivalent about time. It accepts the fact that policy makers will sometimes act precipitously but, more often, act glacially. Prolonged deliberations are less a sign that private motives have encouraged delay than that there are significant disagreements about goals, evidence, and alternatives.

All these criteria (except structure) are examples of the "Goldilocks" rule. The policy process works best when there is not too much and not too little, but just the right amount of resources, representation, deliberation, speed, and oversight. It is not prudent to specify in advance how much "just the right amount" is, since it undoubtedly varies with the complexity, divisiveness, uncertainty, size, and urgency of any given issue. Absolute standards, however, need not be defined in assessing the two competing perspectives on politics: the two views diverge less on what is ideal than on where existing processes lie on the scale.

Public choice theorists tend to see the policy process as seriously flawed. They find too much representation of special interests and too little representation of the public interest, too little deliberation yet too little speed, and too little and too ineffective oversight. Public spirit scholars, in contrast, typically find the policy process more healthy (while recognizing specific defective cases). The process generally incorporates widespread representation, much of it directed toward the common good, and substantial deliberation. The process is frequently sluggish, but primarily because of the representation and deliberation it incorporates. The quantity and quality of oversight are less problematic than are the issues of how to use the results of the oversight.

Examining organizational structure, resources, representation, deliberation, timeliness, and oversight will help us assess the thrift tragedy and determine whether the public choice or public spirit view of politics best explains FSLIC's downfall. These criteria do not allow unequivocal hypothesis tests between the two approaches, but do help to assess their relative validity. Furthermore, the differences between the two approaches in relation to the criteria involve general tendencies, not absolute conditions. Nonetheless, these criteria are useful in assessing the validity of the scholarly perspectives as well as the responsibility of government officials. They will thus help us judge whether politicians and bureaucrats should be blamed for the thrift tragedy.

Many journalists and scholars have already written about the thrift tragedy. Both groups have wrestled with the question: Why did officials do what they did? In their answers, journalists have tended to focus on the "human element" (e.g., sexual and financial scandals) and the telling anecdote. They look behind closed doors. What really matters for investigative reporters is not what officials say in public but what they whisper in private. These private conversations must reveal the true beliefs, while public statements provide mere window dressing.[62] Correspondents have made particular efforts to determine who did what and why. In doing so, they rely heavily on the personal statements of insiders. Public choice theorists tend to avoid personal anecdotes, instead emphasizing the impersonal, general, and abstract. What counts is not confessions, but incentives; not what officials said, but what they did. Scholars have thus assumed the why, ignored the who, and made ingenious attempts to infer the what.

My research methods borrow substantially from each group, but also differ significantly from both. Like the journalists, I have tried to highlight the human elements of the thrift tragedy, in particular focusing on actual officials' policy decisions from their own perspectives. Like the scholars, I have attempted to identify general trends and consistent patterns. Rather than relying on private confessions or inferring outcomes, however, I stress the public record of officials as they attempt to make or justify decisions. To the journalists, I say, policy debates are at least as trustworthy as personal disclosures for explaining policy choice. Why would officials be more willing to lie, use subterfuge, or rationalize in public than in private? To the scholars, I say, policy debates are at least as significant as personal incentives in understanding political decisions. After all, why would officials be any less concerned about producing good policy than scholars are about doing good research?

The Plan of This Study

Chapter 2 contains a brief history of the savings and loan business and the Federal Home Loan Bank System from its inception through 1989. The main purpose of this chapter is to explain the policy commitments that induced thrifts to make long-term, fixed-rate home mortgage loans and to accept short-term, federally insured deposits. While most of the episodes described in this chapter occurred before the thrift tragedy commenced, they are central to its development. I also present the basic outline of the events of the 1980s in this chapter. (For those unfamiliar with the thrift business, appendix 1 outlines the basics of balance sheets and operating statements. Those who understand financial matters can safely skip this material.)

The next three chapters investigate the bureaucratic issues. Chapter 3 assesses the effect of the FHLBS's structure on FSLIC's losses, focusing on the role of the Bank Board. Chapter 4 evaluates the influence of other aspects of the FHLBS's structure and resources on FSLIC's losses. Chapter 5 examines the major issues the Bank Board faced between 1979 and 1989 and how these issues were resolved. In this chapter I emphasize the role of uncertainty and conflict in the Bank Board's deliberations.

Chapters 6 through 8 examine Congress's role in the thrift tragedy. Chapters 6 and 7 contain a qualitative assessment of congressional debates and action on the major thrift industry issues, considering in particular the role of representation, deliberation, oversight, and timeliness. Chapter 8 is a quantitative analysis of congressional voting patterns regarding thrift industry legislation. By identifying and estimating the influences on these roll call votes, I reveal the multiple and conflicting interests legislators faced. The final chapter reexamines the thrift tragedy in light of the public choice and public spirit interpretations, attempts to provide some perspective on the affair, and evaluates proposals for reform.

The thrift tragedy ought to be the toughest case for the public spirit perspective and the easiest for public choice theory. If public spirit can be demonstrated in this "history sadly lacking in heroes," then it may be worthwhile to consider whether public spirit plays a more extensive role in the American political system than is commonly accepted.[63]

2

A Brief History of the Federal Home Loan Bank System

"Savings and Loans": In the 1980s, these words became synonymous with greed and corruption. It was not always so. For most of its history, "savings" and "loans" were precisely the two primary concerns of the thrift industry. The historical purpose of the S&L business was to bring together the personal savings of individuals and distribute home mortgage loans to families.

Government policy deliberately encouraged this saving and lending. Since the Depression, government policy for the thrift industry had been built on two core principles. First, individuals should be encouraged to save, and their savings should be guaranteed. The main protection came through the federal deposit insurance provided by the Federal Savings and Loan Insurance Corporation; a variety of other policies encouraged individuals to deposit their savings at thrifts. Second, families should be encouraged to buy their own homes. Home ownership was promoted through a number of policies, primarily those inducing S&Ls to finance long-term mortgage loans with fixed interest rates.

Today, federal deposit insurance and long-term, fixed-rate mortgages are a conventional part of the financial scene. Since FSLIC's creation in 1934, millions of depositors have been covered by federal deposit insurance, and not a single one of them has ever lost money on an insured savings deposit. Millions of home purchases have been financed through what is by now the "traditional" thirty-year, fixed-rate mortgage. But until federal deposit insurance was established, individuals always risked losing their money when they put it in the bank, and much money indeed was lost. Until the federal government made the long-term, fixed-rate mortgages a tradition, homes were harder to buy and easier to lose. The federal policies that protected savings and promoted home ownership have indeed provided enormous financial and emotional benefits to the American public.

These same policies have also received scathing criticism as the root financial cause for the thrift tragedy. Requiring thrifts to offer traditional mortgage loans, it is commonly argued, placed them in a position where they would almost inevitably lose money. Federal deposit insurance, critics contend, provided S&Ls the opportunity to gamble with taxpayers' money in a "heads the S&L wins, tails FSLIC loses" game. By implication, the public officials responsible for these financial policies designed to protect savings and promote home ownership are in large part politically responsible for the thrift tragedy.

This chapter traces the evolution of government policy toward the thrift industry. We need to understand this evolution to see how the thrift tragedy began. Before we can discuss government policy, however, the development of the thrift business itself bears mention.

The American Thrift Business in Its First Hundred Years

The first known savings and loan in the United States was organized in 1831 in Frankford, Pennsylvania (now part of Philadelphia) by a group of local businessmen and wage earners.[1] Members made monthly contributions to the Oxford Provident Building Association, and whenever $500 was available for a loan the members submitted bids to use this money to buy or build a home. In February 1832, one misnamed Comly Rich made the high bid for the first loan of $375, which he used to buy a two-and-a-half-story frame building at 4276 Orchard Street, Philadelphia. Perversely, Mr. Rich fell hopelessly behind on his payments and, as a result, another member of Provident took over the loan and the house.

Over the next few decades the savings and loan idea gradually spread across the country. By the time of the Civil War S&Ls existed in several states, and by the 1880s every state seems to have had associations. These associations were all voluntary and unincorporated, though they gradually became more formal and complex. There was no public supervision of these institutions. Almost all S&Ls were entirely local in nature.

The Rise and Fall of the Nationals

Even then, however, "the savings and loan business . . . had fringe elements trading on its goodwill."[2] One such element was the "National" savings and loans that came on the scene in the 1880s. Rather than collecting deposits and distributing home loans locally, the Nationals sold shares through the mail and passed out loans across the country. They promised investors security and high profits. By the mid-1890s there were about 240 Nationals, and they operated in every part of the country. Within a decade the assets of the Nationals had grown to about one-quarter the size of the local S&Ls.[3]

These firms had little in common with the local thrifts from which they took their name, and many were actually "speculative schemes designed to benefit their promoters."[4] Nearly all of them went bankrupt in the years following the panic of 1893. The reasons for their failure may sound familiar to modern ears:

> Many were of a fraudulent or near fraudulent nature. Their stock was sold on misrepresentation, sometimes intentional and sometimes the result of over-optimism and lack of understanding of the true nature of compound interest, among other things. Even where the leaders were men of integrity they found it difficult to control their agents. When more and more associations were unable to carry out their promises . . . there was a general lack of confidence in the whole movement so that all were weakened. There was another inherent weakness in the whole system. In attempting to make loans

throughout the country they were assuming considerable risk which was accentuated by the fact that they did not make the best efforts to secure the ablest local supervision of loans. As a result, there was a tendency to pick up loans rejected by other investors.[5]

In the end, the Nationals were "victims of a depressed real estate market as well as of their own immoderate expenses, questionable loans, and widely scattered and poorly controlled operations."[6] Most investors lost their money.

The rise and fall of the Nationals had long-term consequences for the thrift business. In the first place, the experience with the Nationals soured that generation of investors, local thrifts, and politicians on the prospects of thrift institutions operating nationwide, engaging in speculative investments, and promising high profits.[7] On the other hand, the Nationals affair reinforced the view that thrifts should borrow and lend locally, invest mainly in "safe" home mortgages, and yield only modest returns to investors and owners.

Perhaps more important, traditional savings and loans responded to the development of the Nationals by forming the USL, the "United States League of *Local* Building and Loan Associations" in 1892.[8] The main business at the USL's initial meeting, at least rhetorically, was to adopt resolutions denouncing the Nationals. More pragmatically, the USL, together with its state affiliates, sought to enact legislation limiting the Nationals and to initiate state supervisory systems to enhance public confidence in the local S&L businesses. From its inception, the USL has attempted to influence public policy toward thrifts in ways that protect both its interests and what it perceives as the public's interest.

Home Ownership

At the end of the last century, home loans were much more difficult to obtain than they are today; thus, at least for nonfarm residents, home ownership was a more elusive goal.[9] In 1890, for example, fewer than 40 percent of the nonfarm homes were owned by their occupants. Of these owner-occupied homes, fewer than 30 percent were mortgaged, with the rest owned outright. Of these mortgaged homes, the median loan-to-value ratio was 40 percent; homeowner equity accounted for the remaining 60 percent of the value.[10] In other words, in 1890 a distinct minority of urban Americans owned their homes, a smaller minority of these homeowners had obtained mortgages, and these mortgages were for less than half of the home's value. Buyers had to make substantial down payments to obtain mortgages, so relatively few buyers were able to obtain mortgages. As a result, relatively few individuals were able to purchase homes.

Housing credit increased substantially over the next four decades, and especially during the boom years of the roaring twenties. Total mortgage debt increased more than tenfold, from $2.3 billion to almost $30 billion.[11] The S&L business contributed to this growth, with its home loans growing from less than $400 million to over $6 billion. By 1930 nearly half (46 percent) of nonfarm homes were owned by their occupants, and about 40 percent of these owners held mortgages.

The most common form of home mortgage during this period was a "straight" short-term loan (usually of one to three years), with only interest paid during the term and the principal due at the end. Borrowers normally expected that the loan would be automatically renewed at the end of the term. These expectations were typically met during the prosperous decades, that is, through the 1920s. Nonetheless, the short-term, unamortized loans "created problems of continuous refinancing and drove many home purchasers into expensive and risky borrowing upon secondary liens."[12] As long as the economy continued to grow, however, these risks usually paid off.

The Depression

Then came the Great Depression. The losses to the savings and loan business were large. During the 1930s, over seventeen hundred S&Ls failed, and industry assets fell by about 30 percent. The personal cost of these failures to management and employees was no doubt substantial. But rather than focusing on the costs to those in the business, let us devote our attention to the losses the Depression imposed on the individual depositors and borrowers.

These losses came in many forms. The most obvious is the money lost by savers at thrifts that failed. Because there was no deposit insurance, whenever a thrift failed individuals lost part of their deposits. Thrift failures cost depositors about $200 million, or about 3.5 percent of total thrift assets, when their associations failed.[13] These numbers do not by themselves reveal the full burden of these losses on the individual depositors. In the 1930s, thrift depositors tended to be of fairly modest means, with most of their savings located in their association. Those who lost these savings rarely had the luxury of being bailed out by a diversified investment portfolio. When they lost their deposits, they often lost a substantial portion of their total savings.

A second form of loss is harder to quantify, but was apparently substantial. Savings and loans that did not actually go bankrupt often went "on notice." This meant that they gave cash to individuals making withdrawals only as the cash came in; many depositors were kept waiting indefinitely. To obtain currency, individuals who could not wait often sold their deposits at cut-rate prices to those who could. No estimates exist of the prevalence of this practice. It was common enough, however, that some cities had well-organized markets for selling deposits, complete with published price quotes for various S&Ls. One source indicates that deposits were commonly sold at discounts of 20 to 30 percent (meaning that depositors were able to obtain only 70 to 80 percent of their savings).[14]

It is worth remembering that depositors' losses at thrifts were only a small portion of Depression-era financial losses. Banks were much harder hit than savings and loans. Between 1930 and 1933, almost nine thousand commercial banks failed. Bank failures imposed losses of about $2.5 billion on bank depositors, stockholders, and other creditors.[15] Depositors also took substantial losses on deposits they sold at banks that went "on notice." These losses, in turn, were dwarfed by those suffered by investors in the stock market.[16] These facts do not suggest that thrift misfortunes were trivial, but they remind us that such misfortunes were part of the massive losses suffered throughout the entire financial system.

The Depression hurt home buyers as well as depositors. As individuals lost their jobs or savings, they found it increasingly difficult to make their mortgage payments or to refinance their mortgage loans.

For example, before the Depression, about 75,000 urban homes were foreclosed upon each year. Foreclosures soared to over 270,000 in 1932 and 1933.[17] It has been estimated that as much as 40 percent of home mortgage debt was in default.[18]

The structure of the typical home mortgage loan contributed to difficulties facing both home buyers and mortgage lenders. At the time of the Depression the vast majority of home mortgages were in short-term (hence, variable rate) loans. The Depression put an end to the assumption that short mortgage loans would be automatically renewed. As lenders increasingly needed cash, they increasingly demanded that borrowers repay their loans when they came due. Given the difficulty of finding other sources of credit, borrowers often were unable either to refinance or to repay; foreclosure was the result. These short-term loans thus further aggravated the depression in the real estate markets.[19]

As a result of home foreclosures, savings and loans became major owners of residential real estate. By 1936, real estate accounted for more than 20 percent of the thrift business's assets. These assets were essentially frozen. Relatively few people could afford to buy these foreclosed homes at their original selling price, and thrifts were reluctant to sell them at their market values because real estate prices had dropped so sharply. Thrifts by and large chose to hold, maintain, and rent these properties until they could be sold at the least loss.

Depression-Era Federal Policy Toward Thrifts

The immediate goal of federal legislation was to provide credit to S&Ls in order to support financing of homes and residential construction.[20] Lending money to thrifts would accomplish this goal in several ways. It would make more funds available for thrifts to lend for home mortgages. It would also allow S&Ls to meet demands for withdrawals more promptly, reducing the pressure on them to foreclose on delinquent properties. Perhaps most important, it would help restore confidence in the thrift business. When confidence returned, the logic went, individuals would themselves be more willing to make deposits, and thrifts would thus be better able to make home loans.

Temporary support for these goals was first provided through the creation of the Reconstruction Finance Corporation (RFC) in 1931. The RFC lent $118 million to savings and loans over the next few years.[21] RFC loans provided the thrift business with valuable breathing room.

The Federal Home Loan Bank System was established in 1932 to provide a more permanent solution.[22] The FHLBS was designed largely in imitation of the Federal Reserve System for commercial banks. It was to be directed by a board of directors appointed by the president and called the "Bank Board."[23] Twelve regional Federal Home Loan Banks were created to lend money to thrifts within their region. These regional banks would sell stock to their members, use the proceeds to issue bonds, and then use the receipts of these sales for short- or long-term loans to their member thrifts.

The FHLBS was hardly an instant success, however. It had a difficult time getting organized and beginning operations. By June 1933, the FHLBS had lent less than $50 million to its members. As a result, Congress became concerned that the FHLBS was helping neither the nation's homeowners (through easier mortgage terms and fewer foreclosures) nor the S&Ls (through increased profitability).

To relieve homeowners and bring new finance to the housing markets, in 1933 Congress enacted the Home Owner's Loan Act (HOLA), which created the Home Owner's Loan Corporation (HOLC). The HOLC was authorized to purchase delinquent mortgages held by various lenders, providing them with fresh resources, and then to refinance these mortgages for longer terms and at lower interest rates. By doing this, the HOLC was able to help both borrowers and lenders.

Unlike the FHLBS, the HOLC did have an immediate impact. Between 1933 and 1936 HOLC purchased and refinanced over 1.8 million delinquent mortgages worth $6.2 billion—about one-sixth of the home mortgage debt.[24] At the peak of the Depression, an agency of the federal government thus owned about one out of six home mortgages. The HOLC provided enormous short-term benefits to both lenders and borrowers. It helped nearly 2 million families keep their homes. It also provided lenders with over $3 billion in new resources that could be used for additional lending.[25]

The HOLC also had tremendous long-term consequences through its institutionalization of the long-term, fixed-rate, self-amortizing home mortgage loan. When HOLC refinanced home mortgages, it typically offered fifteen-year loans, charged 5 percent interest, and required monthly payments to pay off the loan.[26] By stretching out maturities and lowering interest rates, HOLC was able to lower payments by individuals and reduce their risk of default. At the time, these loans had substantially longer terms and lower rates than those offered by private lenders.[27] While comparatively few private lenders offered long-term, fixed-rate, self-amortizing loans before the Depression, HOLC's experience helped make these loans standard after that time.

Two final features of the HOLC are worth mentioning. First, HOLC was designed to be a temporary agency, and it was. It sold the last of its loans and went out of business in 1951. Second, the HOLC returned a small profit to the Treasury.[28]

In addition to creating the HOLC, the HOLA also helped institutionalize the home ownership role of S&Ls and the FHLBS. The HOLA authorized the Bank Board to grant federal charters to savings and loan associations, to regulate them, and to promote their growth. Federal S&Ls, in return for the benefits of membership in the FHLBS, were restricted almost completely to financing home ownership. To ensure they would be dedicated to home finance, federal S&Ls were allowed to use their funds almost solely for making home loans and repaying depositors.[29] State-chartered S&Ls generally had to comply with similar rules.[30]

The National Housing Act of 1934 was the last major Depression-era piece of legislation affecting the thrift business. This legislation had two main components. It created federally guaranteed home mortgage insurance, to be administered by the new Federal Housing Administration (FHA). It also established the Federal Savings and Loan Insurance Corporation, a subsidiary of the Bank Board, to insure savings deposits at thrifts. Congress hoped that by creating federal mortgage insurance and insuring savings deposits, it would see funds flow back into residential real estate and housing construction as the confidence of both borrowers and lender increased.

The FHA would guarantee home mortgage loans that had long terms (twenty-year maturities), fixed, low interest rates (limited to 5 percent), and low down payments (20 percent of the home's price). Congress expected that, even during the Depression, individuals would be able to afford to obtain mortgages with these terms. Lending institutions (banks more so than thrifts), however, were reluctant to make home mortgage loans on such terms because they saw them as too risky. By providing federal insurance for home mortgages, Congress believed it would lead more lenders to make such loans. The FHA-insured loans further institutionalized long-term, fixed-rate mortgage loans with low down payments.

The creation of FSLIC was the capstone of Depression-era legislation. The FSLIC was modeled in large part on the Federal Deposit Insurance Corporation (FDIC), created the previous year to insure deposits at commercial banks. The FSLIC was to insure individual savings accounts (up to $5,000) at S&Ls that became members. Premiums were a flat ¼ of 1 percent (reduced the next year to ⅛ of 1 percent, the same as banks) of insured deposits. Federal thrifts were required to become members, and state-chartered associations could do so at their discretion. The Bank Board became FSLIC's board of trustees.

The Politics of Depression-Era Policy

One might imagine that the Depression produced a golden era of federal policy, as brilliant and dedicated public officials worked swiftly and in cooperation to devise bold programs that restored the nation's economic health. There is much truth in this, but much fiction also. In many ways, the politics of thrift policy during this era foreshadowed those of the 1980s.

The savings and loan business, even before the Depression, was already justifiably proud of its ability to influence legislation. As a history of the thrift business published in 1931 noted, due to the USL's efforts,

> [thrifts] had been exempted from the provisions of every income, excise, and stamp tax act which has been enacted by Congress during the existence of the [League]. Upon the appeals which have been made upon it, Congress has recognized the distinct value of the

[saving] and loan associations to the community and to the nation in developing a sounder citizenship and has consistently given them special consideration on account of their benevolent and helpful purposes.

This success was attributed to the "aggressive and persistent presentation" of the league and its member thrifts.[31]

The league was more successful in avoiding taxes than in achieving its other goals, however. Since 1918 the USL had sought without luck to have Congress establish a federal source of credit (such as the FHLBS) similar to the Federal Reserve System for commercial banks. By 1928, the USL had actually given up these efforts.[32] On other issues the league was split. In 1931 and 1932, for instance, it opposed the creation of federally chartered thrifts (even though a league committee had recommended their creation).[33] The league changed its mind only after it became clear that President Franklin D. Roosevelt and members of Congress were considering more dramatic measures, such as having the federal government make direct loans to home buyers, circumventing thrifts altogether.[34] On some issues the thrifts simply lost. The USL and the savings and loan business in general opposed federally insured mortgage loans.[35]

All the major programs—the creation of the FHLBS, FSLIC, and FHA—were highly controversial, and supporters and opponents of each had a combination of public and private concerns. The USL and its allies (such as the National Association of Real Estate Boards) supported the establishment of the FHLBS, arguing that home ownership was essential for a strong democracy, and that federal assistance was essential for home ownership. (The USL's motto, after all, was "The American Home: The Safeguard of American Liberties.") Thrifts, realtors, home builders, and home buyers, naturally, also stood to benefit financially from government support of home finance. The main opposition to the FHLBS came from the thrifts' competitors, such as the Mortgage Bankers Association, and those who opposed federal expansion into financial markets on principle. Its adversaries argued (not always consistently) that a federal system was not needed, that it was poorly designed and so would prove to be a failure, or that it would succeed to such an extent that it would create overbuilding of residential real estate. Like the advocates, the opponents had various economic interests and various conceptions of the public interest. Similarly, support for and opposition to federal deposit insurance and mortgage insurance involved individuals and groups with different views regarding their self-interest and the public interest.

Most of the programs adopted were not truly innovative, nor were they considered for the first time during the Depression. A central credit agency for commercial banks (the Federal Reserve System) had already existed since 1916. Congress, as it turns out, had also considered creating a central reserve (such as the FHLBS) for thrifts in 1919, 1920, and again in 1927, but the proposals had not been enacted. At least fourteen state governments had experimented with deposit insurance as early as 1829. Congress had also considered deposit insurance since the 1880s, and the Senate had adopted one such proposal in 1913.[36] Thus, the major federal programs to assist the thrift business had already been adopted for banks, or enacted by the states, or at least considered by the Congress years prior to their enactment.

Yet, prior to the Depression, political consensus was never reached on the principles underlying the FHLBS and the FSLIC. What distinguished the Congresses of the 1930s from those before them was the consensus that the victims of the Depression—especially those who lost their homes to foreclosure—needed to be helped. Supporters in Congress emphasized that the thrift programs would "alleviate human misery."[37] Given the severity of that misery, the opponents of federal intervention did not have a persuasive response.

Still, enactment of the programs was not a foregone conclusion. Republican President Herbert Hoover, in his State of the Union address in December 1931, strongly recommended that the FHLBS be created. Members of Congress, with the Democrats controlling the House and an election approaching in the fall of 1932, were not necessarily ready to cooperate with one another or with the president. Neither house got around to approving the legislation until after the legislature was scheduled for adjournment. An irrelevant amendment (to legalize 3.2 percent beer) was nearly added at the last minute;

booze probably would have killed the bill. Proponents in the Senate obtained funding for the FHLBS only by slipping it into a routine District of Columbia bill, a maneuver condemned by opponents. The Federal Home Loan Bank Act was not approved by Congress until the last hour of the last day of the session. Even then, its future was tenuous. The next year, some officials within the new Roosevelt administration considered the FHLBS a remnant of Hoover's policies not worth keeping, and sought to repeal it.[38]

Similarly, creating federal deposit insurance involved political struggle. House Banking Committee Chairman Henry Steagall sponsored a deposit insurance bill that passed the House in 1932, but Senate Banking Chairman Carter Glass killed the bill in the Senate. In 1933, newly elected President Roosevelt came out against deposit insurance, as did prominent individuals in the Federal Reserve System and leading bankers. Deposit insurance for banks (the FDIC) was ultimately enacted in 1933 through the persistent advocacy of Chairman Steagall and an unusual coalition of those who feared the alternatives.[39] The thrift business opposed federal deposit insurance on its merits, and came to favor it only after the thrifts perceived that the FDIC was giving the banks a competitive advantage. The thrift business thus sought and obtained the FSLIC one year after the FDIC was established.

President Roosevelt's famous first hundred days in office created the impression that he was responding decisively to the financial crises of the Depression. But the government on the whole did not move rapidly to handle the Depression. Mortgage foreclosures were dealt with in a serious way by the HOLC's creation in 1933, but this was only after foreclosures increased by an average of 25 percent each year between 1926 and 1932 (from fewer than 70,000 to almost 250,000 annually).[40] Deposit insurance was established for banks in 1933 only after bank failures rose steadily, from fewer than 500 in 1928 to more than 4000 in 1933.[41] Yes, the government did take swift action to address the Depression, but it took four years for the swift action to finally occur.

The Depression-era reforms did create important legacies for thrift policy and politics. First, they set the precedent for broad government intervention in specific financial markets to assist both individuals (depositors and home buyers) and institutions (the thrifts themselves). Second, the interventions were intended to protect both individuals and institutions: they were designed to keep individuals from losing their savings or their homes, and to keep thrifts open for business (even if they were in fact insolvent). Third, these interventions appeared to work. Although the improvement was slow, the new federal programs were seen as contributing to the financial recovery. Fourth, the programs did not impose great costs on the government (and taxpayers). Once all the bills were paid, the RFC, FHLBS, HOLC, FSLIC, and FHA assisted thrifts and individuals without draining the Treasury.

These legacies of broad, sympathetic, effective, and inexpensive intervention appear to be beneficial, and they were. But they also carried the seeds of the thrift tragedy. The federal policies created during the Depression and the lessons learned from them established a thrift system designed to protect individuals and associations by institutionalizing long-term, fixed-rate mortgages and federal deposit insurance. These policies demonstrated that the federal government could effectively and inexpensively intervene in troubled financial markets.

The Thrift Business Between the Depression and the Tragedy

The FHLBS, FSLIC, HOLC, and FHA did not end the thrifts' woes, but they did greatly relieve those of depositors and homeowners. Individuals with FSLIC-insured accounts no longer lost money—and no longer had to fear losing money—when their thrift failed (though even at the end of the 1930s only 50 percent of all S&Ls were insured). Home foreclosures declined in number every year after 1933, finally falling to pre-Depression levels by 1940. Yet the number of S&Ls that failed was even higher during the second half of the 1930s than the first, and not until 1940 did the business hold as many assets as it had held in 1930.

Easy Street: The Postwar Period

After World War II, the thrift business and the housing industry both flourished. Between 1946 and 1965, over 30 million new homes were built, and the vast majority of home sales were financed by mortgage loans. The S&L business grew by an average of 14 percent each year during this period (compared to an annual growth rate of about 9 percent for commercial banks). Total thrift assets rose from $10 billion to $130 billion, and the vast majority (85 percent) of these assets were in home mortgages. The thrift share of the mortgage loan market increased steadily.

The thrift business was comfortably profitable. S&Ls obtained most of their funds through passbook savings accounts, which were a stable and low cost source of funds. Unlike banks, thrifts were exempt from interest rate ceilings, so they could also obtain sufficient deposits by paying slightly higher rates than banks. They used most of their funds to make long-term, fixed-rate home mortgage loans. Thrifts' profits came primarily from the difference between what they paid for deposits and what they earned from mortgage loans; this difference was substantial. Profit margins of over 10 percent were the norm.

The thrift business was not only profitable, it was also popular. It was seen—correctly—as serving to fulfill the American dream of home ownership. The business helped create this image, of course: full page ads in *Life* magazine showed happy families posing by the white picket fences in front of their newly purchased homes (with the FSLIC logo prominently displayed). The S&L image was bolstered by the fact that most thrifts were small, local "mutuals" (owned by local depositors, not distant stockholders), apparently run for the good of the community and not only for the benefit of the wealthy. The classic Frank Capra movie *It's a Wonderful Life* further reinforced the portrait of S&Ls as good guys.

The FHLBS also prospered in the postwar interval. The number of federally chartered thrifts grew gradually to over two thousand in 1965; these associations held about half ($67 billion) of the business's total assets.[42] More significantly, by 1965 virtually all (about 97 percent) deposits at S&Ls were insured by the FSLIC.

The FHLBS's jobs were direct and, given the economic prosperity, fairly easy: to provide thrifts credit when they needed it, to administer the insurance fund, and to monitor thrifts to ensure that they complied with regulations. Credit needs were small; until the 1960s, the FHLBS generally had surplus funds because the demand for its loans was so low. The demands on the insurance fund were also minor. Even though its premiums were lowered and its coverage expanded, FSLIC never suffered a net loss in a single year, and its insurance fund consistently grew; its size relative to insured deposits also increased. At most, only a handful of S&Ls failed in any single year, and FSLIC was often able to merge them with other associations at little or no cost.

Monitoring thrift regulatory compliance was somewhat more time consuming. Over the years, the thrift business had gradually become more heavily regulated. These regulations specified in great detail not only what thrifts could and could not do, but precisely how they must do what they did (such as underwriting and documenting loans or conducting property appraisals). The central task of the FHLBS examiners was to ensure that thrifts followed these regulatory standards. Because the vast majority of thrift business involved savings deposits and home loans, the task of confirming that S&Ls complied with the regulations was tedious but routine. FHLBS examiners simply had to determine that the thrifts' financial books went by the regulatory books.

Throughout this period the thrift business was becoming more vulnerable to economic fluctuations. This weakness came about because associations financed long-term mortgage loans with short-term deposits.[43] The "maturity mismatch"—or "interest rate risk"—would be exposed if market interest rates increased suddenly. If this happened, thrifts would be in a predicament. If they attempted to retain their saving deposits by raising the interest rates paid, their profits would directly and immediately shrink; at some point, the profits would disappear entirely. If they did not raise the rates they offered, however, savers would be tempted to withdraw their deposits and place them where they could earn more interest. If this happened, thrifts could either attempt to maintain their size by borrowing funds elsewhere (which would raise costs) or they could shrink (which would lower profits).

The vulnerability of the thrift business could increase as a result of several conditions. First, thrifts would become less resilient if the average maturity of their loans increased. Second, they would become more susceptible if the effective maturity of their deposits decreased. Third, an increase in interest rates would make thrifts more vulnerable; and the more sudden and prolonged the increase, the more vulnerable the thrifts. During the postwar era the first two conditions pushed thrifts toward financial weakness. The trend toward thirty-year, fixed-rate mortgages elevated thrifts' average loan maturities. Meanwhile, effective deposit maturities became shorter, primarily due to the rise of attractive alternatives to savings deposits.[44] The danger to the thrift business due to changes in economic conditions seemed largely hypothetical, however. Since as early as 1890, short-term interest rates had not risen above an 8 percent annual rate, and had never been even 6 percent for more than two years in a row.[45] Since the Depression, thrift deposits had always grown. And never did it cost more to attract deposits than one could earn on mortgage loans.

Rocky Road: The 1960s and 1970s

During the 1960s and 1970s, the economic environment of the thrift business changed dramatically. Thrift policies changed only incrementally, however, as policy makers attempted to apply bandages to thrifts' wounds. During this period, economic change and policy stability set the stage for the thrift tragedy of the 1980s. If different policies had been chosen during these decades, FSLIC's failure in the 1980s probably could have been avoided, or at least minimized. The policies that might have saved FSLIC were real possibilities, since they had been debated at length over the years, yet they were not adopted. This should not be surprising. It is worth recalling that an essential element of tragedy is its inexorable unfolding.

Economics

The economic environment became increasingly hostile to thrifts in the 1960s and 1970s. After a generation of low and stable interest rates, market rates rose substantially; at times they rose swiftly, and always to record levels (figure 2.1). Interest rates increased most

FIGURE 2.1

Short-Term Interest Rates, 1960–1988

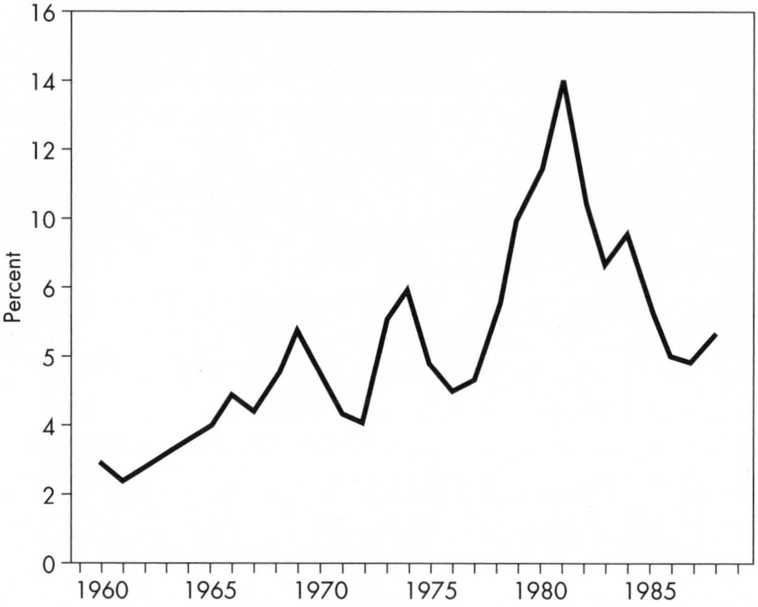

Source: Council of Economic Advisors, *Economic Report of the President* (Washington, D.C.: U.S. Government Printing Office 1991), table B-71, 368.

Note: Figure displays interest rate on new issues of three-month U.S. Treasury securities.

impressively during the "credit crunches" of 1966, 1969, 1974, and 1979. These interest rate swings had several important consequences for thrifts and thrift policy.

The first consequence involved thrift deposits. Thrifts typically offered to pay fairly low interest rates on savings deposits. As a result, whenever market interest rates rose, individuals became less willing to deposit their savings at thrifts and more eager to place them where they could earn higher returns. Some money that normally would have been deposited was not; some money that had been on deposit was withdrawn. (The decline in deposits is called "disintermediation.") Each credit crunch caused the amount of money deposited in thrifts to fall sharply (figure 2.2).[46] Each time, the disintermediation problem grew more severe.

FIGURE **2.2**

Net New Deposits at Thrifts and New Home Starts, 1960–1988

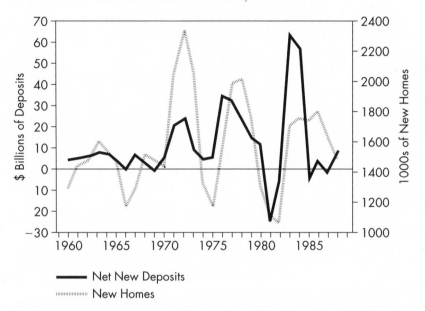

Source: Office of Thrift Supervision, *1989 Savings and Home Finance Source Book,* table A-10, a12–13; Council of Economic Advisors, *Economic Report of the President* (Washington, D.C.: U.S. Government Printing Office 1991), table B-53, 346; U.S. Bureau of the Census, *Historical Statistics of the United States: Colonial Times to 1970* (Washington, D.C.: Government Printing Office, 1975), Series N 156–169, 639.

The credit crunches also hurt the home finance markets. Rising interest rates and declining thrift deposits contributed jointly to tighter home finance. During each credit crunch, the number of houses being built and being sold dropped abruptly (figure 2.2).

Higher market interest rates, declining deposit flows, and fewer housing sales all bit deeply into thrifts' profitability. During credit crunches, thrifts found it more expensive to attract deposits and more difficult to make home mortgage loans. During the 1960s and 1970s thrift profitability was lower on average than the profitability of commercial banks, but the difference was especially pronounced around 1966, 1969, 1974, and 1979 (figure 2.3).

FIGURE 2.3

Profitability of Thrifts and Banks, 1960–1988

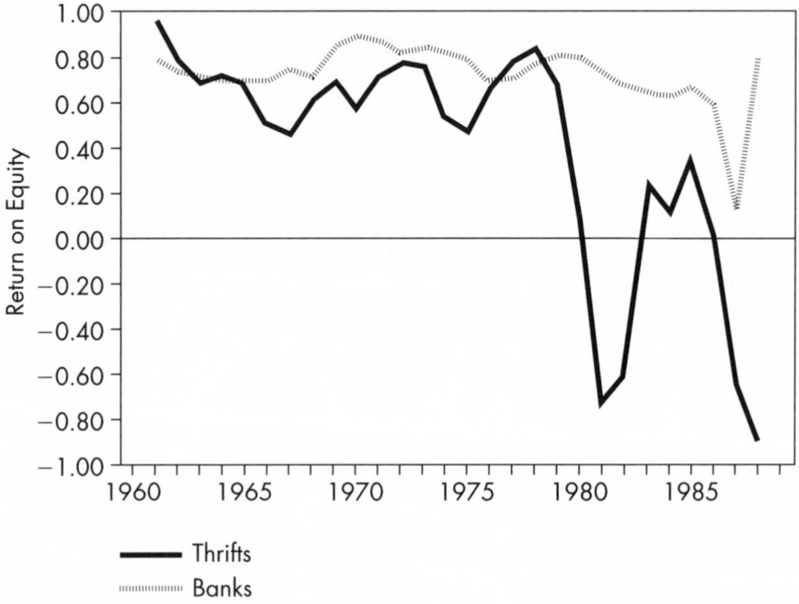

Source: National Association of Mutual Savings Banks, *National Fact Book of Savings Banking* (New York: NAMSB, 1982), 24; General Accounting Office, *Troubled Financial Institutions: Solutions to the Thrift Industry Problem*, GAO/GGD-89-47, February 1989, table II.1, 114; Congressional Budget Office, *Resolving the Thrift Crisis*, April 1993, table C-1, 86–87.

Note: Figure presents net after-tax income divided by total assets.

Politics and Policy

Policy makers struggled in these decades to cope with the increasingly inhospitable economic environment that threatened thrift deposits and profits as well as residential construction. The 1960s and 1970s were a crucial time for thrift policy, and a missed opportunity. Virtually all observers agree that "had fundamental reforms been implemented during this period, particularly during the early part of it, the S&L debacle could have been avoided."[47] Yet during this period incremental changes were adopted and fundamental reforms avoided.

"Fundamental reform" meant one thing in particular: reducing thrifts' maturity mismatch. There were two main proposals on how to do this. In the first, the mismatch would have been lowered for mortgage loans. The S&Ls would have been allowed to offer "adjustable rate" mortgage loans (ARMs). ARMs would improve thrifts' earnings during times of rising interest rates by increasing the rates paid on existing mortgages. Federal thrifts were prohibited by law from making ARMs, however, and with some exceptions (primarily in California) state thrifts were also forbidden to offer them. In the second case, the mismatch would have been reduced by allowing S&Ls to make more investments in assets other than home mortgages. It was argued that these other investments would have shorter maturities while providing additional protection to thrifts by allowing them to diversify into other business sectors.

Numerous scholars had argued during the 1960s that fundamental reform was essential for thrifts' long-term health. At least two prominent government reports during the 1970s advocated ARMs and asset diversification for thrifts, and reform proposals along these lines were introduced in legislation numerous times between 1965 and 1978. For example, the Presidential Commission on Financial Structure and Regulation (known as the "Hunt Commission") recommended in 1972 that S&Ls be given broader asset and liability powers, and in 1975 the Financial Institutions and the Nation's Economy (FINE) study, commissioned by the House Banking Committee did the same.[48] Yet over this period Congress refused to grant federal thrifts permission to offer ARMs and provided only limited opportunities for thrifts to diversify into other assets. In retrospect, it seems that Congress made a serious mistake in not adopting fundamental reforms before the thrift tragedy began with the abrupt rise in interest rates in 1979. Before condemning Congress for its apparent sins of omission, however, we need to consider why Congress did not approve ARMs and asset diversification.

The theoretical rationale for ARMs was clear and the empirical evidence concrete: ARMs would reduce thrifts' maturity mismatch and make them less susceptible to interest rate risk. Why, then, did Congress not authorize them? It was not, as one might surmise, because the USL and the thrift business opposed them. Hardly: S&Ls, as well as the Bank Board, actively sought the power to offer ARMs.[49] Congress refused these requests, instead siding with the realtors, home builders, and consumer groups who opposed variable rate mortgages. A head count, no doubt, would have shown that more vot-ers opposed ARMs than supported them. This stands to reason, since there are more home buyers than S&Ls, and home buyers have shown a clear preference for fixed-rate loans.[50]

Congressional refusal to authorize ARMs need not be seen as a simple balancing of interests, however, with legislators merely count-ing heads on both sides to determine who had the majority. There were also principled reasons to oppose ARMs as a matter of public policy.[51] Remember that, from the thrifts' perspective, the benefit of ARMs was that the interest rate on the loan increased when market interest rates rose, and that the higher loan rate increased thrift earn-ings. But view this from the loan holders' perspective: higher interest rates would mean higher monthly payments. This is not exactly a benefit to homeowners. ARMs, in other words, do not reduce interest rate risk, they simply transfer it from S&Ls to individuals. The policy question, then, is, "Who should be protected from interest rate risk, homeowners or thrifts?" We may disagree about the answer to this question: as an ethical matter, however, it is not obvious that mem-bers of Congress should have given preference to protecting institu-tions over protecting individuals.[52] By not approving ARMs, Congress undoubtedly contributed to the thrift tragedy. But by not authorizing them, Congress also saved homeowners many billions of dollars.

In the 1960s and 1970s, while Congress was rejecting calls for ARMs, it (as well as the Bank Board) did on several occasions autho-rize thrifts to modestly diversify their loan portfolios. The Housing and Urban Development Act of 1968, for example, allowed federal thrifts to make loans for mobile homes and home fixtures.[53] The Housing and Community Development Act of 1974 further liberal-ized the types and amounts of loans federal associations could make. Finally, the Financial Institutions Regulatory and Interest Rate Control Act of 1978 allowed S&Ls to invest up to a total of 15 per-cent of their assets in land development, construction, or education loans. These laws allowed S&Ls slightly—but only slightly—to diver-sify their portfolios during the 1970s.[54]

The political reasons for the congressional reluctance to allow thrifts to diversify their assets during the 1960s and 1970s are quite clear. On the one hand, many economic interests were against thrift diversification; on the other, few were for it. The firms (especially banks) that would have faced increased competition if thrifts had been allowed to enter new lines of business actively opposed efforts to expand thrifts' investment powers.[55] The businesses that stood to lose if home finance were more scarce actively sought to preserve the thrift business's concentration on mortgage lending. The thrift business, for its part, was split on the issue of whether S&Ls should diversify.[56] Some thrift executives—especially those in the larger thrifts—did advocate broader investment powers during the 1960s and 1970s.[57] Most of the thrift business, however, believed it should remain focused squarely on home finance. As USL President Norman Strunk testified before the House Banking Committee in 1975: S&Ls "do not want to become commercial banks."[58]

The Bank Board and the USL challenged the premise that asking thrifts to move into other lines of business was the correct way to approach the issue. They recognized, of course, that S&Ls were vulnerable to interest rate risk. But they argued that inflation—not home mortgages—was the culprit. The maturity problem (and many other economic difficulties) was best solved by stabilizing interest rates, not by making thrifts forgo home finance. According to this view, if the Federal Reserve Board did *its* job, then thrifts could keep on doing theirs.[59]

The major policy rationale for continuing to require that thrifts concentrate on home lending was the goal of promoting home ownership. There was little question that thrifts had made it easier for Americans to buy their homes.[60] There was a real question, however, whether it would be as easy to buy homes if thrifts were not required to make mortgage loans.[61] Of course, some argued that federal policy should not promote housing or that, if housing was to be promoted, more efficient alternatives than the thrift business could be developed. Nonetheless, it was difficult to ignore the historical contribution of thrifts to home ownership, and there was no consensus that thrifts should reduce their contribution.

Rather than providing thrifts with investment alternatives to reduce their maturity mismatches, Congress attempted to stabilize thrift deposits, thrift profits, and home construction by controlling interest rates, initially through the Interest Rate Control Act enacted in September 1966.[62] This law for the first time gave the Bank Board the power (through "Regulation Q") to set limits on the interest rates that thrifts could offer their customers.[63] The law also guaranteed that thrifts could offer slightly higher interest rates than banks (this was called the "thrift differential"). As interest rates fell in 1967 and 1968, profitability returned to the thrift business. The law seemed to work.

This episode established the pattern for the next decade. Interest rates rose and fell, but each time they rose to higher levels. Each time rates rose, thrift deposits dropped, thrift profits were squeezed, and housing starts fell. Yet each time, interest rates then dropped enough to restore thrift deposits, thrift profits, and home building.

Nevertheless, the thrift business and the Bank Board were on the horns of a dilemma every time rates rose. If Regulation Q ceilings were raised, thrifts would have to pay more for deposits, the business would be less profitable, and the price of mortgage loans would go up. But if ceilings were lowered, deposits would be lost, profits lost, and the supply of home mortgages decreased. In response to this dilemma, the Bank Board attempted the delicate balancing act of setting the rate ceilings not too high, not too low, but just right. This became ever more difficult each time the interest rates spiked. Interest rate ceilings did not eliminate the vulnerability of the thrift business. They simply masked it.

The Tragedy Unfolds:
The Thrift Business Between 1979 and 1988

By 1979 the elements of the tragedy were in place. The thrift business, relying on short-term savings deposits to finance long-term mortgages, had a dangerous maturity mismatch. Moreover, interest rate ceilings had been placed on savings deposits. A sharp increase in market interest rates would shrink deposits and erase profits.

And so it did. Between 1979 and 1981, rates rose like never before. In May 1981, short-term interest rates peaked at over 16 percent, triple the level of five years earlier (figure 2.1). These rising rates devastated the thrift business. Net new deposits fell sharply, so that by 1981 $25 billion more was withdrawn from S&Ls than was deposited in them (figure 2.2).[64] Profits plummeted (figure 2.3). The thrift business as a whole reported losses (after taxes) of $4.6 billion in 1980 and another $4.1 billion in 1982.[65] The number of thrift insolvencies handled by FSLIC exploded from 4 in 1978 and 1979 to 32 in 1980, 81 in 1981, and 252 in 1982. (In the thirty years between 1950 and 1980, a total of 114 S&Ls had been declared insolvent. In the three years at the beginning of the 1980s, 361 thrifts—or about 10 percent of all S&Ls—went out of business.) For the first time since its inception, the FSLIC spent more money handling insolvencies than it earned from insurance premiums. The thrift business and its federal insurer were on the edge of disaster.[66]

The Policy Response

Lawmakers acted swiftly once this initial crisis occurred.[67] In 1980 Congress passed (and President Carter approved) the Depository Institutions Deregulation and Monetary Control Act (DIDMCA). Although this law was hailed as "the most important financial legislation in 50 years," it was not enough to rescue the thrift business.[68] Subsequently, Congress again passed "the most important legislation for financial institutions in the last 50 years" in 1982, when it adopted (and President Reagan signed) the Garn–St. Germain Depository Institutions Act.[69] The Bank Board, for its part, took numerous regulatory initiatives to forestall the growing emergency.[70]

These policy responses had several means for reaching several goals. To expand thrifts' abilities to attract deposits, the interest rate ceilings on savings deposits were eliminated and deposit insurance limits were raised. To enhance S&Ls' prospects for making profits, firms were allowed to lend or invest in a wide variety of activities other than home mortgages. To assist thrifts weather the storm, several lifeboats were launched to keep foundering thrifts afloat until interest rates declined to "normal" levels.

These measures appeared to work. Deposits flooded into thrifts in 1983 and 1984, with net new deposits growing by over $110 billion in those two years (this was more new deposits than the business had accumulated in the entire previous decade). The business returned to modest profitability, though not to its previous levels, between 1983 and 1985. Interest rates, moreover, declined precipitously after 1981. FSLIC handled 101 insolvencies in 1983, and just 27 in 1984.[71] In 1983 FSLIC's insurance reserves stopped shrinking and began once more to grow. It appeared that, through new laws, regulations, and some good economic luck, a disaster had been averted.[72]

This appearance proved to be an illusion. Policy makers soon came to recognize that, despite falling interest rates, rapid deposit growth, and reported profits, the thrift business's problems were growing worse, not better. By 1984 the Bank Board had become worried that many thrifts were using their new powers to attract funds and make loans too aggressively. This aggressiveness, the Bank Board believed, would lead to further thrift insolvencies and losses to FSLIC. To prevent this from happening, the Bank Board began attempting to curb such rapid growth and reckless investment by thrifts by limiting their (new) powers to borrow and lend. It doubled FSLIC's insurance premiums. It doubled the size of its examination and supervisory staff between 1984 and 1986.

Despite these measures, the Bank Board found it was unable to handle the growing number of failing thrifts on its own. Thrift profits plunged in 1986 and 1987 and the number of insolvencies grew apace. Consequently, the board asked Congress in 1985 to provide FSLIC with $15 billion in additional capital. Congress did not approve this request for almost two years, and then, with the Competitive Equality Bank Act (CEBA) of 1987, it awarded FSLIC only two-thirds the amount it requested.

This was not enough.[73] In an effort to shut down insolvent thrifts before they lost still more money, FSLIC used creative financing techniques to stretch its new capital as it disposed of 205 failed S&Ls in 1988.

This was still not enough. Thrifts lost a record $12 billion (after taxes) in 1988, and over six hundred S&Ls were still insolvent but open for business at the end of the year. Shortly after his inauguration, President Bush proposed a sweeping program to end the thrift tragedy once and for all. This proposal called for an additional $50 billion to be spent to close down bankrupt thrifts. It imposed tighter regulations on S&Ls. In a final act of anger, Congress abolished the Bank Board and FSLIC, transferring their functions to other federal agencies. Congress approved the president's program in the Financial Institutions Reform, Recovery, and Enforcement Act (FIRREA) of 1989. Although additional funding to close bankrupt S&Ls would in fact be needed after FIRREA, since losses were even larger than estimated, the passage of this law effectively ended the thrift tragedy of the 1980s.

3

The Federal Home Loan
Bank Board

MUCH OF THE BLAME FOR the Federal Savings and Loan Insurance Corporation's huge losses has been heaped on the Federal Home Loan Bank Board, the regulatory agency responsible for the health of the thrift system.[1] The Bank Board has been blamed for choosing its regulatory policies unwisely and then implementing them poorly. The ill-advised structure and the inadequate resources of the FHLBB have in turn been held responsible for these inappropriate regulations and poor implementation. Officials' personal incentives have been said to have contributed to the FHLBB's structural and resource problems and, likewise, these difficulties are assumed to have reinforced the officials' selfish behavior.

The problems of the FHLBB have been linked to the design of the system's components—such as the size, composition, selection, tenure, and responsibilities of the board—and the relationships between these components. For example, the FHLBB is composed of a regulatory agency directed by the Bank Board and twelve Federal Home Loan Banks (FHLBs), each led by a board of directors. The FHLBB's components were generally characterized as weak in the face of political pressure and biased in favor of the thrift industry. Moreover, because authority was diffused throughout the structure, the different components of the board were allowed to pursue conflicting goals; this, it was believed, further added to the agency's weakness and bias.

The FHLBB's ability to do its job was determined not just by its structure but also by its resources, especially the size and quality of its staff and the size of FSLIC's insurance fund. In the first instance, the agency has been criticized for having too few staffers (particularly examiners) and for paying and training them inadequately. As a result, staff quality was low and turnover high. Because the FHLBB had insufficient staff resources, it was unable to minimize FSLIC's costs by properly monitoring thrift behavior, controlling thrifts that acted improperly, and taking over those that were going broke. In the second instance, FSLIC's lack of resources, especially insurance reserves, is alleged to have led it to adopt policies designed to minimize its short-term costs, even if doing so imposed much larger costs on the public in the longer term.

Inadequate resources and inappropriate structure are believed to have combined to reinforce improper incentives for regulators. Because the FHLBB's structure provided ample access to the thrift business, for instance, the regulators were motivated to maintain too friendly relations with the regulated. Division of authority between state and federal regulators provided inducements for a "competition in laxity" in establishing regulations and a willingness to leave them unenforced. Low salaries discouraged bureaucrats from vigorously enforcing regulations and increased their willingness to go easy on the regulated because regulators hoped to move to better-paying jobs within the industry. The too small insurance fund persuaded regulators to delay or hide losses rather than minimize them.

In the next two chapters we will examine the extent to which the structure and resources of the Bank Board and the FHLBS contributed to the thrift tragedy. In addition, we will consider whether structural and resource issues are best explained through public choice or public spirit perspectives. We will rely heavily, but not exclusively, on comparisons with other financial regulatory agencies such as the Federal Reserve Board, which are generally considered more effective than the FHLBB. In this chapter we will focus on the Bank Board itself; chapter 4 will consider the other components of the FHLBS.

The Structure of the Federal Home Loan Bank System

The core elements of the FHLBS were the Federal Home Loan Bank Board, the twelve Federal Home Loan Banks, and the thrifts receiving federal insurance.[2] The FHLBB was an independent agency of the executive branch of the federal government. Its governing body was the Bank Board, composed of three directors appointed by the president. The FHLBB was the regulatory agency for all federally chartered thrift institutions and shared with the states the regulatory authority over state-chartered but FSLIC-insured thrifts. The FHLBB oversaw and served the twelve FHLBs and their member S&L associations. The three members of the Bank Board also served as the directors for the FSLIC and the Federal Home Loan Mortgage Corporation.

The FHLBs served the country by geographical area. Although the banks operated within a framework established by the Bank Board, they were wholly owned by their member institutions and were supposed to be responsive to their members' needs. Each FHLB was controlled by a board of directors (some directors were elected by member thrifts while others were appointed by the Bank Board), and managed by a president appointed by the board. The two main functions of these district banks were to lend funds to member thrifts and to regulate them in accordance with Bank Board regulations.

The members (and owners) of the FHLBs were thrifts (i.e., savings and loan associations and mutual savings banks) that were insured by the FSLIC. In 1980 about half the thrifts were chartered by the federal government and half by the states. Federal thrifts were subject to all federal regulations while only some of these regulations applied to state-chartered thrifts.

Congress deliberately modeled the FHLBs after the Federal Reserve System (FRS). Like the FHLBS, the FRS is an independent agency headed by a board of directors (the Federal Reserve Board, or Fed) selected by the president. The Fed makes loans to commercial banks and regulates them. Unlike the Bank Board, it is primarily responsible for regulating state-chartered, not federally chartered, banks; it shares authority over state banks with state regulators.[3] The FRS also oversees and serves the twelve Federal Reserve Banks (FRBS) and the commercial banks that belong to the FRS. The FRBs are directed and managed along the same lines as the FHLBs and serve the same functions. Like the FHLBs, the FRBs are wholly owned by their member banks.

The major structural difference between the FHLBs and the FRS concerned deposit insurance for member institutions. The FSLIC was part of the FHLBB. In contrast, the Federal Deposit Insurance Corporation (FDIC) is not a component of the Fed, but a self-governing government corporation.

The Federal Home Loan Bank Board

Those who criticize the Bank Board (and there are few who publicly defend it) have generally argued that the board was too weak politically and too close to the S&Ls it was supposed to regulate. Many observers have shared the view that "traditionally, the Federal Home Loan Bank Board has been strongly influenced by the industry."[4] One writer argued that this influence was so great that in "the old days . . . the United States Saving and Loan League [actually] wrote many FHLBB regulations."[5]

The view that the Bank Board was too closely aligned with the thrift industry became widely accepted by the end of the 1980s. Congress took these criticisms to heart when it abolished the board as an independent agency in 1989 and moved its functions into the newly created Office of Thrift Supervision (OTS) within the treasury department. It was the clear intent of this reform to insulate the OTS from inappropriate industry influence or pressures from individual members of Congress.[6]

It is nonetheless difficult to identify particular regulatory decisions that were specifically influenced by an official's connections with the thrift industry.[7] In the following section, therefore, we will address two related, but indirect, questions that bear on business influence. Was the thrift industry able to place sympathetic individuals on these boards? Did board members evince undue sympathy for the thrift industry? To answer these questions, we will focus on the composition and actions of the Bank Board and those of the boards of directors of the FHLB.

The Bank Board's Structure

Formal statutory factors such as the board's composition, its method for selecting directors, the length of its members' terms, and its size may have played a role in biasing the FHLBB toward the thrift industry. Agencies headed by large boards with short-term memberships are often believed to be weaker politically than offices having a single executive with a long tenure, for example. Similarly, boards with members either selected by a certain constituency, or whose members come from that constituency, may be expected to be predisposed in favor of that constituency's interests.

These formal factors can be overridden, or supplemented, by the actual factors governing a board's "real" composition, selection, and size, however. Although there may be no statutory requirement that a certain percentage of directors come from a particular constituency, such an outcome may nonetheless occur as a normal event. Laws only provide the guidelines within which agencies exist, while practice determines how these guidelines are applied.

The statutory factors that affected the structure of the Bank Board are compared with those for the Fed in table 3.1. The two boards share a number of formal characteristics; in particular, the provisions are identical for the chairman of each agency. The Bank Board was half the size and its members' terms one-third as long as the Fed: the size of the board presumably strengthened it, while the length of terms may have weakened it. The Bank Board had to include at least one Republican and one Democrat, but had no other requirements concerning the constituency from which they were to come; the Fed has no partisan requirement and only a vague constituency condition. It would be difficult to conclude, on the basis of these formal criteria alone, that the Bank Board was likely to have been weaker or more susceptible to industry influence than the Fed (see table 3.1).[8]

If the Bank Board and the Fed differ little in their legal structure, perhaps their actual composition distinguishes them. Even though the selection criteria for the boards do not emphasize the directors' backgrounds, for example, the boards could differ in the professional or partisan backgrounds of their directors. In addition, even though

TABLE **3.1**

Structure of the Bank Board and the Federal Reserve Board

	Bank Board	Federal Reserve Board
Directors		
Number	3	7
Term	4 years	14 years
Selection by	President	President
Confirmation by	Senate	Senate
Selection Criteria		
Constituency	None	"Fair representation"
Partisan	Minimum 1 from each party	None
Chairman		
Term	4 years (renewable)	4 years (renewable)
Selection	President	President
Term concurrent with that of president?	No	No

Source: Federal Home Loan Bank Board; Federal Reserve Board.

the chair of each board is appointed for a four-year term, the boards could differ in the length of times that their chairs usually serve, or in the quality of the service they provide.[9]

Board Members' Professional Backgrounds

One common theme in American political lore is that government officials often come from regulated interests and thus serve those interests once in office.[10] It must seem only natural that businesses are able to place their representatives in positions of power and that these representatives will use this power to benefit the business from which they came.

This lore might appear true for thrifts and the FHLBB. After all, the original Bank Board in 1935 did indeed include the executive director (H. Morton Bodfish) and the president (William Best) of the

United States League of Savings Institutions, the major thrift interest group.[11] More recently, as Stephen Pizzo, Mary Fricker, and Paul
Muolo relate, Edwin Gray, a public relations man for Great American First Savings Bank, came to be selected Bank Board chairman.
According to these authors, USL Chairman Leonard Shane pulled
Gray aside at a USL meeting and said: "Ed, we want you to be the next
chairman." Bill O'Connell, president of the USL, concurred. Gray was
appointed shortly thereafter.[12]

The view that the thrift business was able to place its agents on
the Bank Board, and that these individuals consequently favored
thrifts rather than the taxpaying public, deserves closer scrutiny,
however.[13] First, we will want to learn the professional backgrounds
of Bank Board members to determine whether they usually came
from the thrift business. Then, we will describe some of the actions
of the board members to discover how their backgrounds may have
influenced their decisions.

I have analyzed the professional backgrounds of the fifteen individuals who served on the Bank Board between 1979 and its demise
in 1989 in the following manner. First, I collected data on virtually all
the post-college job experiences of the Bank Board's members.[14]
Second, I classified these jobs into five employment categories: thrift
business, housing industry, FHLBS, other government, and other employment.[15] Third, I assigned the members' professional careers to
the categories, based on their length of employment in each. The
Bank Board members' varied professional backgrounds are summarized in table 3.2.

Two chairmen (McKinney and Gray) did indeed have substantial experience within the thrift business, and three other members
(Marston, Jackson, and Grigsby) had spent most of their careers
working for and with thrifts.[16] It is noteworthy that the board's chairman never had a purely thrift background.

More commonly, board members had worked in and around the
housing industry. Four (Miller, DiPrete, Hovde, and Henkel) had
worked primarily in housing-related areas, while three others had
some experience in housing issues. These employment experiences,
moreover, differed substantially. DiPrete and Henkel, for example,
had represented housing interests (primarily developers) as attor-

TABLE **3.2**

Professional Background of Bank Board Members, 1979–1989 (in percent)

	Thrift Business	Housing Industry	FHLBS	Other Government	Other
Chairmen					
Robert McKinney	50	0	0	0	50
Jay Janis	0	40	0	53	7
Richard Pratt	7	0	0	0	93
Edwin Gray	50	0	0	50	0
M. Danny Wall	0	0	0	100	0
Members					
Garth Marston	74	26	0	0	0
Anita Miller	0	100	0	0	0
Andrew DiPrete	0	88	0	12	0
James Jackson	100	0	0	0	0
John Dalton	0	0	0	50	50
Donald Hovde	0	100	0	0	0
Mary Grigsby	100	0	0	0	0
Lee Henkel[a]	0	83	0	17	0
Lawrence White	0	0	0	0	100
Roger Martin	0	21	0	0	79

Source: U.S. Congress, Senate, Committee on Banking, Housing, and Urban Affairs, various confirmation hearings. For details, see Mark Rom, "Professional and Educational Background of FHLBB Members," unpublished manuscript, 1991.

Note: Figures represent the percentage of a member's career spent in each field. Members are listed in chronological order according to their tenure on the committee.

a. Interim appointment, not confirmed by the Senate.

neys, and Janis had been the coprincipal of a development company. Hovde was a realtor and served terms as president of the Wisconsin and the national realtors' associations. Martin was an executive for the Mortgage Guaranty Insurance Corporation for more than a decade. Miller was a program officer responsible for urban issues at the Ford Foundation.

Two chairmen (Pratt and Wall) and two members (Dalton and White) had spent only a small part or none of their professional careers working for thrifts or housing interests. Pratt and White were professors, though Pratt had worked briefly for the USL and had served as a financial consultant. Four directors (Dalton, Hovde, Henkel, and White) had worked in the federal government, but only Dalton and Hovde had worked on housing issues there, and for only a short time (two years each).[17]

Thus, only about a quarter of the Bank Board's members had professional backgrounds with S&Ls; another quarter worked in housing, government, or other sectors before coming to work for the Bank Board. The proportion of Bank Board members who had worked in the industry they regulated thus appears to be quite close to the proportion of Fed directors who had done the same.[18] Furthermore, Bank Board members were not more likely than officials in other federal agencies to have worked previously in the regulated industry.[19]

Not only did Bank Board members have varied professional backgrounds individually, but the composition of the board as a whole was also mixed. Members with thrift industry backgrounds never had a clear majority on the Bank Board during the thrift tragedy.[20]

The most amazing fact illustrated in table 3.2 is that *none* of these Bank Board directors had ever been employed by the FHLBS. Martin and Pratt each served on the board of a district bank and Miller served on the Federal Home Loan Board Advisory Council:[21] that was the sum total of FHLBS experience on the board. The Bank Board's inexperience stands in sharp contrast to the Fed's experience. Fully 60 percent of the Fed's board members had some official association with the board prior to their appointment, 40 percent started their careers at the Fed, and over 20 percent had their longest job there.[22]

In summary, most Bank Board members did not come from the thrift business. Neither did they come from the FHLBS. What distinguishes the Bank Board from the Federal Reserve is not how many members worked in the *regulated* financial firms, but how few worked at *regulating* financial firms. It is difficult to conclude that Bank Board members were predisposed to favor the thrift business due to their previous professional ties to it. Two alternatives suggest themselves. Perhaps Bank Board members favored the thrift business over the public interest *because* they lacked experience there: the seduction of the innocents. Or perhaps Bank Board members were precluded from fully protecting taxpayers because of their inexperience in government service. Expertise, not motives, may have been one of the Bank Board's central problems.[23]

Partisan Backgrounds

Because those nominated to the Bank Board had such varied professional backgrounds and such limited government (especially FHLBS) experience, it appears that a demonstrated financial expertise and government acumen regarding the thrift system were not prerequisites for appointment. Although the candidates were usually lauded by various thrift interests upon their nomination, there is little evidence that their prior connections with the industry were very important in their selection; indeed, few candidates appear to have had close professional affiliations with the thrift industry.

What does seem to have been critical—at least for those selected as board chairmen—was each candidate's personal connections with the president or with key members of Congress. Robert McKinney was President Carter's classmate at the United States Naval academy (class of 1946) and chaired Carter's presidential campaign in Indiana.[24] Ed Gray was a long-time aide to Ronald Reagan, first when Reagan was governor of California and later after Reagan was elected president. Jay Janis is said to have had an edge in receiving the nomination because of his friendship with Robert Strauss, who was a close adviser to President Carter and had been the chairman of the Democratic National Committee from 1972 to 1976.[25] Richard Pratt was a lifelong resident of Utah, and the champion for his nomination was Utah Senator Jake Garn, chairman of the Senate Banking Committee.[26] Senator Garn was also the backer of Danny Wall, who had served on Garn's banking committee staff for twelve years. Thus, all five chairmen serving between 1979 and 1989 had strong personal ties to either the president or the Senate Banking Committee's chairman before their appointment.

A number of other board members also had either significant experience in electoral politics or influential political patrons. John

Dalton, for example, served as the treasurer of the Carter-Mondale campaign during 1979, while Donald Hovde had been the chairman of Realtors for Reagan in 1989.[27] Still others appear to have been appointed for other partisan reasons. The professional background of Anita Miller, President Carter's second appointment to the Bank Board, suggests she was selected with an eye toward satisfying the liberal groups who had opposed Robert McKinney, Carter's first appointment.[28] Indeed, of the fifteen individuals who served on the Bank Board between 1979 and 1989, only one—Lawrence White— appears *not* to have been selected in large part for partisan reasons.[29]

Again, the Bank Board was quite different from the Fed regarding the effect of partisan connections on the selection of directors. Woolley concluded that "by all indications, in appointments to the Federal Reserve Board, partisan considerations have rarely been dominant" and, furthermore, that "there is little evidence of successful congressional influence on the presidential choice of board nominees. Rather, candidates have been judged by their experience, technical expertise, and acceptability to particular constituencies."[30]

Good political connections are not by themselves barriers to public service, of course. One need not assume that appointees are lacking in the ability or desire to serve general interests simply because they are well connected.[31] Given the vast number of potential applicants for a position on the Bank Board, it would indeed be surprising if many successful candidates did *not* have strong political connections. But it is one thing to be well connected *and* well qualified. It is another to have connections as one's main qualification.

Tenure of Chairmen

Just as the chairmen of the Fed had much more experience within their agencies prior to their appointments than did Bank Board directors, the Federal Reserve Board chairmen also had substantially longer reigns once there. Although by law the chairmen of both boards are appointed to four-year terms, in practice the tenures of the boards' chairmen are quite different (table 3.3). On average, the Bank Board's chairmen serve less than half as long (3.9 years) as the Federal Reserve's chairmen (9.7 years). The difference between

TABLE **3.3**

Tenure of Bank Board and Federal Reserve Board Chairmen

	From	To	Years
Bank Board			
Fahey	1935	1947	12
Divers	1947	1953	6
McAllister	1953	1958	5
Robertson	1956	1961	5
McMurray	1961	1965	4
Horne	1965	1968	3
Martin	1969	1972	3
Bomar	1973	1975	2
Marston	1975	1977	2
McKinney	1977	1979	2
Janis	1979	1980	1
Pratt	1981	1983	2
Gray	1983	1987	4
Wall	1987	1989	3
Mean			3.9
Median			3.0
Federal Reserve Board			
Eccles	1934	1948	14
McCabe	1948	1951	3
Martin	1951	1970	19
Burns	1970	1978	8
Volcker	1978	1986	8
Greenspan	1987	1995	8
Mean			9.7
Median			8.0

Source: Federal Home Loan Bank Board; Federal Reserve Board.

the average tenures would increase had I included acting chairmen, since the Bank Board has had four unconfirmed chairmen who served less than a year. The gap would grow still further if only more recent decades were counted because, after 1960, the average tenure of Bank Board chairmen fell to about two and one-half years. In the thirty years before the board's demise, only Chairman Gray served a complete term.

The Behavior of the Bank Board Chairmen

Donald F. Kettl's examination of the Federal Reserve Board noted that, for most purposes, "the Chairman *is* the Fed," serving as its spokesman, point man, manager, agenda setter, and coalition builder.[32] While no one would equate the power or prestige of the Bank Board's chairman with the chairman of the Federal Reserve Board, it does appear that the Bank Board's chairman had an equally dominant role within the agency. The Bank Board's chairman certainly dominates public accounts of the board's activities; members other than the chairman are almost never even mentioned. Conventional wisdom holds that the Bank Board chairmen were the mouthpiece of the savings and loan industry. A closer examination of these chairmen raises doubt about this view, however.

The members of the Bank Board came into office short on regulatory experience and long on political attachments. Their backgrounds did not necessarily predispose them to favor the thrift business, and their prior experiences did not indicate they could successfully manage a regulatory agency. So rather than inferring how Bank Board members behaved once in office, let us now examine what they actually did.

The effect of personal background on the behavior of public officials has been considered by a number of political scientists. The effect seems easiest to determine if the person studied regularly makes voting (yes or no) decisions. For example, those who have studied the Federal Reserve typically have focused on the formal votes of the Federal Open Market Committee to loosen or tighten monetary policy.[33] This line of investigation is not open here because the Bank Board made no such regular votes. I will thus present a brief qualitative look at the behavior of the Bank Board chairmen during their term in office.

When Robert McKinney was nominated chairman of the Bank Board in 1977, he faced tough confirmation hearings because of his ties to financial interests. McKinney had served as the chairman of a savings and loan association, as a senior partner in a law firm that provided counsel to that S&L, and as the chairman of a building supply company that was the parent company of a life insurance firm. During the hearings, Senator William Proxmire called McKinney "a textbook example of interlocking between banking and other professions."[34]

By the time he resigned in 1979, however, "the industry was calling for his head."[35] McKinney, as it turned out, implemented a number of consumer and financial regulations strongly opposed by various parts of the thrift industry. He introduced regulations to restrict "redlining" (discriminatory lending), and supported the Community Reinvestment Act, which imposed further controls against redlining. More significantly, McKinney began modestly deregulating the thrift industry, but in ways that much of the industry did not want. He implemented regulations allowing interstate branching between the District of Columbia, Virginia, and Maryland, even though the majority of small thrifts around the country opposed such market liberalization. He started deregulating interest rates by approving the creation of the first savings account (the $10,000 money market certificate, or MMC, in 1978) for which depositors could earn interest rates that were above the interest rate ceilings thrifts could pay. While the MMCs helped reduce the flow of funds out of the thrift industry during the credit crunch of the late 1970s, they also cost the thrifts a great deal of money in higher interest expenses, and S&L executives "roundly criticized" McKinney for approving them.[36]

Jay Janis, McKinney's successor, may be seen as more typical of a Bank Board chairman in thrall to the thrift industry. The USL had praised his nomination as board chairman, and in his one year (1980) as Bank Board chairman, Janis did little to alienate the industry. He opposed interstate branching of financial institutions and argued that interest rate deregulation should be implemented only slowly (he made no moves at all in that direction). Under Janis, the board used its administrative authority to implement regulations expanding the new lending powers that had been approved by Congress and reduced thrift capital requirements from 5 to 4 percent—both measures that had wide support within the thrift industry.[37] Janis resigned from the board when Reagan became president rather than face demotion from chairman to member.[38]

It is not clear, however, that Janis's apparent favor for the thrift industry should be attributed primarily to his professional experiences within it. Before coming to the Bank Board, Janis had worked for the most part in a variety of housing-related positions in government and business.[39] At the time of his appointment, those in the housing industry generally regarded it a matter of faith that the industry's health depended on the well-being of the thrift business. When Janis was nominated to the board, the National Association of Home Builders (NAHB) led the applause while the USL followed along.

Richard Pratt, board chairman in 1981–1982, was an academic and a consultant specializing in finance. If anything, he was more closely tied to the thrift industry than Janis.[40] Pratt's tenure as Bank Board chairman was driven by his economic conviction that deregulation is better than regulation; that markets, not governments, should determine the success or failure of financial institutions.[41] He believed that, for the industry to survive, the larger, stronger, and more efficient thrifts would have to swallow up the smaller, weaker, and inefficient ones and then raise their earnings through growth and diversification.

Pratt pursued this vision on two fronts. He sought to deregulate the thrift business through legislative proposals and regulatory practices. The most important deregulatory legislation, the Garn–St. Germain Act, was called the "Pratt bill" when it was first introduced in Congress because of his importance in drafting its key provisions.[42] Administratively, Pratt liberalized numerous regulations to provide thrifts greater flexibility in obtaining funds and making investments.[43]

At the same time, Pratt attempted to weed out the weakest thrifts by aggressively merging or closing them. During Pratt's tenure between 1980 and 1982, the Bank Board closed 434 failing thrifts; in its entire history until that time, the board had resolved only 165 failures.[44] Furthermore, Pratt rejected the idea that failing thrift institutions in general should be kept open, unless they had strong prospects of recovering when interest rates returned to normal levels. Testifying before Congress, Pratt argued that any federal assistance should encourage "market discipline" and "allow[ed] the weakest of the industry to go out of existence."[45]

Pratt's views on deregulation were hardly shared by all within the industry. Many thrifts, of course, praised the pleasant side of deregulation (i.e., giving thrifts additional powers to borrow and invest). Fewer celebrated the flip side (closing down failed thrifts). According to Pratt, his "strict approach" toward closures "alienated the Bank Board from the USL and engendered a hostile professional relationship between [him]self and the League's leadership, a friction which continued for years after [his] tenure."[46]

Yet many of Pratt's most significant policies were not "deregulatory" and cannot easily be attributed to theoretical convictions. These other policies consisted primarily of weakening accounting standards for thrifts by reducing the amount of capital (called "net worth") that an S&L needed and by changing how net worth was measured.[47] Each measure was designed to keep the thrift industry afloat until it was able to adjust to a deregulated environment. While some have argued that these measures provided unnecessary favors to the thrift business and harmed the taxpaying public, it is clear that their intent was to assist the thrift business through extraordinary economic circumstances with minimal social, political, and economic disruption.[48]

Both Janis and Pratt thus saw themselves as advocates for the thrift industry, yet they had markedly different attitudes about what to do in this role. Janis came into office without a clear ideology or an agenda, and he left with these words of warning to his successor: "I would urge that the new leadership not be beguiled by extremist ideology. . . . Now is the time for pragmatism."[49] Pratt, in contrast, was an "avowed deregulator who brought fierce determination [and] contempt for the industry he was about to supervise."[50] Whereas Janis wanted to slow down reforms such as interest rate deregulation, thrift conversions from mutual to stock forms of ownership, and interstate branching, Pratt worked to speed them up.

If any of the Bank Board chairmen had a background conducive to favoring the thrift industry, however, it was Edwin Gray. As Martin Mayer describes it, and as virtually all observers have agreed, Gray was made chairman of the Bank Board "because he was supposed to be a dope and a patsy who would go along with whatever the U.S. League and the Reagan administration wanted."[51] Yet by all accounts

Gray worked throughout his term to tighten regulations on the thrift industry, to increase supervision and enforcement, and to protect FSLIC from its impending insolvency.[52]

Gray became an increasingly vocal critic of the thrift business during his term. In fact, Gray blamed much of the thrift tragedy on S&L lobbyists who worked to thwart his efforts to regulate and supervise the business: "Each year of my tenure, I begged Congress for changes in the law that would help protect the deposit insurance system, and ultimately the taxpayers, from loss. The S&L lobby . . . and many others were always successful in blocking such efforts."[53] The thrift business, for its part, loudly opposed most of Gray's initiatives. Some of the opposition was direct and personal. According to Gray, the president of the USL told him that, if the Bank Board proposed certain regulations limiting thrifts' growth and investment powers, "it will ruin your career."[54] The Bank Board nonetheless proposed them.

Gray's attempts to tighten regulations also brought him into public disagreement with his predecessor, Pratt, on at least two occasions. At one conference in California in 1985, Gray warned about the "distortions and dangers" caused by thrift deregulation and Pratt "rose to denounce Gray for his lack of faith in the free market as the proper correction."[55] Later, when Gray proposed new regulations to limit the use of brokered deposits (which Pratt had approved), Pratt held press conferences to denounce the proposals.

The next Bank Board chairman, M. Danny Wall, had never worked for the thrift industry.[56] More than any other Bank Board chairman, Wall has been the scapegoat for FSLIC's huge losses.[57] His mistakes had more to do with underestimating FSLIC's problems than with increasing their severity, though some of that also occurred under his watch. He consistently understated FSLIC's losses before Congress (as had *everyone* else), and therefore consistently had to revise these estimates upward. He did not take vigorous action against Lincoln and Silverado as soon as he might have. He helped design the "Southwest Plan" (to handle 109 insolvencies in Texas), which provided large, but not fully understood, benefits to those who purchased these S&Ls.[58]

Yet these actions do not seem to have been caused by any affinity Wall had for the thrift industry. Several other factors probably had a greater impact on Wall's behavior as chairman. By all accounts, Wall was an optimist, not an analyst: it seems he did not understand the numbers and simply could not believe that FSLIC's losses could grow so large. In addition, Wall's experience as a Senate staffer apparently made him more willing to compromise than to crack down. His treatment of Lincoln and Silverado reflects these tendencies. Finally, FSLIC lacked the money to liquidate the Texas failures. Wall, to his credit, negotiated the Southwest Plan under extreme time pressures (the tax deals the Bank Board offered were expiring at the end of 1988), and he had to sell the S&Ls in a buyer's market. As Martin Lowy put it, "It looks like they [the buyers] all got good deals. The position FSLIC was in guaranteed it. But the deals did create viable and vigorously competitive institutions for the future."[59]

Ironically, among the five chairmen who served during the ten years between 1979 and 1989, it appears that the Bank Board chairmen with the closest professional ties to the thrift business (McKinney, Gray, and perhaps Pratt) were least "sympathetic" to its concerns. In contrast, the chairmen with the least professional experience with S&Ls (Janis, Wall) seem to have treated the business most favorably. Amazingly, in testimony before Congress in 1988, Janis, Pratt, and Gray could not even agree about the central purposes of the thrift system.[60]

Board Members' Professional Foregrounds

If Bank Board members were not inclined to oblige thrift interests because they came from the business, perhaps members favored these interests because they were going into it or because they hoped to profit in some other way from aiding the business. Perhaps board members were more influenced by where they hoped to go than where they had been.

Kane argues this is the case. He contends that individuals are willing to accept (relatively low-paying) official positions in part because of the "resume-enhancement" effect of government service. According to Kane, resume enhancement "promises to permit an undisgraced official to command a higher wage in postgovernment employment than would have been available in the absence of his or her period of government."[61] He then suggests that the resume-enhancement aspect of government service creates "serious conflicts of interest . . . between his or her career interests and responsibility to the general taxpayer."[62] These conflicts include the temptation to make decisions that are favorable to those being regulated and to cover up information that is adverse to the industry or the agency.

Kane does not offer a shred of evidence to support this argument. Testing it, admittedly, is difficult. What jobs should we expect Bank Board members to take upon leaving office, and how much should we anticipate they will be paid? Individuals who accept new jobs typically command higher wages than would have been available in the absence of their previous jobs. In that sense, the new job is a "promotion." These promotions might come exclusively from resume enhancement; they might come from real skills, experiences, or accomplishments; more likely, they come from both resumes and skills. Since Bank Board members have positions equivalent in importance to directors of Fortune 500 companies, it seems reasonable to expect that after leaving the board they would accept jobs with substantial responsibilities and salaries.[63] Without specific data to the contrary, it seems unwarranted (and given the private sector's assumed preference for competence, unnecessarily cynical) to assume that resumes are more important than abilities.

How did Bank Board members fare professionally after leaving the government? For the chairmen, the record is mixed: in the decade examined here, two received substantial promotions, one returned to his previous position, and two accepted positions of lesser status.[64] McKinney returned to Indianapolis and his previous position as chairman of a thrift and insurance company and senior partner in a law firm. The next two chairmen moved up: Janis was named president of California Federal Savings and Loan Association, the third largest federally chartered thrift in the country, and Pratt became chairman of Merrill Lynch Mortgage Capital, Inc.[65] The final two chairs were less fortunate. Gray became chairman of a modest thrift in Florida and Wall initially worked out of his home as a consultant and speech writer.[66] The other members of the Bank Board also had varied postgovernment careers. Some returned to their previous positions, while other moved up, retired, or died.[67] Based on this record, I find it difficult to conclude that Bank Board members exploited their positions primarily to enhance their employment prospects. Unless one expects public service to contribute toward downward mobility, the postgovernment careers of the directors appear perfectly ordinary.

Conclusions

Several conclusions and implications can be drawn from this analysis. It is difficult to conclude that the design of the Bank Board made it politically weak or biased in favor of the thrift industry. Although the Bank Board and the Federal Reserve Board differed somewhat in size, selection, and term of office, these differences do not appear to have made one board systematically stronger or more independent than the other. Neither do these differences make it likely that the Bank Board was any more (or less) motivated by self-interest or public spirit than the Federal Reserve Board.

The professional experiences of Bank Board members, furthermore, do not suggest they were more closely tied or more sympathetic to the thrift industry than Fed members were to the banking industry. The behavior of the Bank Board chairmen while in office also indicates they did not merely follow the thrift industry's wishes. Even though Bank Board chairmen saw themselves as industry advocates, different chairmen advocated different policies. In addition, each chairman angered portions of the thrift business while in office. While the chairmen's behavior undoubtedly contained elements of self-interest, it is equally clear that each chairman attempted in his own way to promote the public interest.

The Bank Board did differ from the Fed in a couple of key respects that probably influenced its agency's effectiveness. Bank Board members had much less prior experience within the agency they directed than did members of the Fed; indeed, Bank Board members had virtually no prior FHLBB experience at all. Bank Board members also generally had weaker and more varied educational experiences and professional reputations, and were selected to the board in large part because of their close personal relationships with the president or a key senator. Bank Board chairmen, furthermore, typically had much shorter tenures than Fed chairmen. Given the scanty experience members had in running a regulatory agency, and the high turnover among the chairmen, it would have been a re- markable accomplishment if the Bank Board had been a strong and effective governing body. Might expertise, not incentives, have played a large role in the Fed's good reputation and the Bank Board's bad one?

4

The Federal Home Loan Bank System

THE FEDERAL HOME LOAN BANK SYSTEM was led by an inexperienced Bank Board during the thrift tragedy. But what kind of system did it lead? Critics of the Bank Board's performance have alleged that the system was fatally flawed in numerous ways, in both its structure and its resources. In this chapter I will assess these allegations. I begin by examining the Federal Home Loan Banks, then the Federal Savings and Loan Insurance Corporation, and finally the staff resources of the Federal Home Loan Bank System as a whole.

The Federal Home Loan Banks

The FHLBS had two major responsibilities: first, to serve as a source of credit to their member thrifts, and second, to assure that these member thrifts complied with all applicable Bank Board regulations and laws. Active management of each FHLB was in the hands of the bank's president, who in turn was responsible to the bank's board of directors and the Bank Board. The Bank Board had final authority over the district banks' boards of directors. Yet as the FHLBS's guidebook itself noted, "In theory, nearly every action by district banks technically comes under Bank Board review, although in practice the Bank

Board delegates substantial operating authority to the banks."[1] It is the conventional wisdom that the thrift business had too much access to and influence over the FHLBs through their boards of directors, and that this access and influence translated into policies that were beneficial to the business to the detriment of the public.[2] As with the Bank Board itself, this view deserves closer scrutiny; again, comparisons to the Federal Reserve System prove useful.

The FHLBs' Composition

The composition of the board of directors for the FHLBs and the Federal Reserve Banks was defined by law. These legal requirements for directors do appear to have given thrift interests greater representation on their boards than commercial banks had on theirs, as table 4.1 indicates. While thrifts and banks each elected industry representatives to serve on the boards of their respective district banks, only a minority (three of nine) of the directors of an FRB come from the commercial banking industry, while a solid majority (at least eight of fourteen) of FHLB directors had to be selected from the thrift industry.[3] Furthermore, as long as they are members of an FRB board,

TABLE 4.1

Financial Industry Influence on Boards of Directors
(in percent)

	Federal Home Loan Banks	Federal Reserve Banks
Representation[a]		
De jure	57	33
De facto	—	64
Selection (elective)[b]	57	66

Source: A Guide to the Federal Home Loan Bank System (Washington, D.C.: FHLB System Publication Corporation, 1987); U.S. Congress, House, *A Racial, Gender, and Background Profile of the Directors of the Federal Reserve Banks and Branches*, Staff Report of the Committee on Banking, Finance and Urban Affairs, 101st Cong., 2nd sess. (Washington, D.C.: U.S. Government Printing Office, 1990).

a. Percentage of board members serving in management or on a board of directors at a thrift or bank immediately prior to selection to FHLB or FRB board.

b. Percentage of FHLB or FRB board members elected by member thrifts or banks.

three of the other (Class B) directors are not allowed to be officers, directors, or employees of a commercial bank while the final three (Class C directors) are not even allowed to own any bank stock. If this were the entire story, these differences between boards could have been decisive in giving thrifts greater control over the FHLBs than commercial banks had over the FRBs.

But this was not the entire story. Three factors made the difference between boards less significant than it first appears. First, although bankers comprised a smaller portion of the boards than did thrift representatives, commercial banks elected fully two-thirds of FRB boards (six of nine); FHLB member thrifts, in contrast, did not elect any directors other than the (eight of fourteen) thrift industry representatives.[4] The Bank Board appointed the other six of the fourteen directors of each FHLB; the Federal Reserve Board appointed the final three directors to the FRB boards. Overall, banks had the power to elect—and presumably influence—a higher percentage of directors than did thrifts.

Second, the prohibitions on bank employment or ownership by FRB directors can be, and are, easily circumvented. As a House Banking Committee staff report concluded: "The Federal Reserve and the member banks have subverted the intent of this limitation by having incoming Class B directors give up their bank directorships just before beginning service as a Federal Reserve Bank director."[5] Similarly, the committee found that one-half of Class C directors were employed by banks prior to becoming directors, and "over half of the candidates submitted by the Reserve Banks for consideration as a Class C director currently hold commercial bank or bank holding company directorships."[6] As a result, almost two-thirds of FRB directors are, or were, directly connected to the banking industry. Likewise, those appointed directors of FHLB who do not come directly from thrifts "are frequently involved in businesses closely related to the thrift industry," so the de facto thrift representation on these boards is undoubtedly higher than the de jure representation.[7] But as a political matter, does it really matter whether the interested industry provides three-fourths rather than two-thirds of the directors? Either way, if a majority is needed, industry-based directors should be able to provide it.

Boards are not always run by majorities, however. A skilled and determined chairman can dominate board decisions.[8] In neither the FHLBS nor the FRBS was the chairman chosen from among the ranks of directors elected by member thrifts or banks. The Bank Board and the Federal Reserve Board both selected the district bank chairman from among those it appointed. In neither case was control of the board necessarily in the hands of the interested industry.

Fourth, the board of directors was not responsible for the day-to-day operations of the bank: the bank's president was. In both the FHLBS and the FRS, one became a district bank president by being nominated by the district bank board of directors and approved by the Bank Board or the Fed Board of Governors. It is not clear how much influence the Bank Board exercised in the selection of FHLB presidents, but it seems plausible that the FHLBS was not unlike the FRS on this point. Within the Federal Reserve, "it seems clear that district bank boards of directors have often played a substantial role in selecting presidents." However, at least when Arthur Burns was chairman of the Fed, he on occasion "made sure that particular individuals were not appointed as presidents."[9] It is clear the Bank Board could remove an FHLB president who was not to its liking and install one it preferred, as Chairman Gray did at the Dallas FHLB in 1984. The Bank Board was reluctant to play this card very often, however.[10]

The FHLBs' Behavior

Were the FHLBS biased in favor of the thrift industry? Did they enforce Bank Board regulations less rigorously than another group (say, the Bank Board) would have? Was bias, if it existed, produced by the close connections between the FHLBS' leadership and the thrift industry? The anecdotes are mixed, but these questions do not seem open to a more systematic analysis. The Dallas and Topeka FHLBS appear to have been more lax in their supervision and enforcement than the Bank Board would have liked under Chairman Gray. In contrast, the FHLBS in San Francisco and Atlanta, the two largest FHLBS, recommended that actions be taken to control Keating's Lincoln S&L and Paul's CenTrust S&L, and the Bank Board delayed or overrode these recommendations.[11]

As credit providers to thrifts, the FHLBs have been quite prudent, that is, biased on the side of strictness. For example, *each* FHLB has been profitable *every* year of its existence, including the years when large portions of the thrift industry were losing money, in part because *no* FHLB has *ever* lost money on a loan to a member thrift.[12] This record has been built through the FHLBs' insistence that thrifts post collateral for all but short-term loans, and that this collateral be the thrifts' best mortgages and other marketable paper. No FHLB appears to have violated these rules by lending funds to thrifts without adequate collateral. The FHLBs are required by law to be conservative and to follow these lending policies, of course. But, then again, the FHLBs are required by law to enforce the regulations of the Bank Board. It is not clear why they would be so faithful to the law in the one case but not the other.

The Federal Savings and Loan Insurance Corporation

The Bank Board served as FSLIC's board of directors. It was commonly argued that, because the Bank Board had the incompatible purposes of promoting and of regulating the industry, it chose to emphasize inappropriately the former over the latter.[13] As a result of this conflict, FSLIC was believed to be incapable of properly controlling risk taking within the thrift business. It was noted that, in contrast, the FDIC is an independent agency responsible to no other financial regulator. FSLIC's alleged conflict of interest between insurance and advocacy was one of the rationales used in FIRREA for separating the FSLIC from the FHLBs and merging it with the FDIC, and for creating the OTS within the Treasury to regulate the thrift industry.

Other observers have disputed the notion that FSLIC's location within the FHLBB hindered its ability to effectively insure the thrift industry. Former Bank Board member White, for example, writes that "the notion of conflict of interest is fundamentally incorrect. The regulatory function establishes the set of rules that, if done properly, protects the insurance fund through limitations on risk-taking by the insured institution. The combining of the two roles within one agency meant that the regulator and insurer were automatically in consonance, not in conflict."[14] Indeed, White notes that FIRREA did not actually separate regulatory and insurance functions because FDIC itself combines them.

These differences of opinion regarding FSLIC's conflicts can be indirectly tested by comparing the experiences of federal and state thrifts. The United States has a long tradition of "dual banking," in which thrifts (and banks) can gain their business charters through either federal or state governments.[15] The laws and regulations a thrift had to follow were determined by its charter: state-chartered thrifts were subject to state policies and federal thrifts had to comply with federal mandates. FSLIC, however, was responsible for ensuring that both state and federal thrifts were run in a prudent manner. The Bank Board thus regulated and insured (through FSLIC) federal thrifts, but state banking agencies regulated state thrifts, while FSLIC insured them. Regulator and insurer were thus united for federal thrifts but not for state thrifts. If there was a conflict between the FHLBB's roles as regulator and insurer, then it might be expected that FSLIC would have been better able to insure (that is, to limit the losses) of the state thrifts, which the Bank Board did not regulate and had no real reason to promote.

Exactly the opposite happened. FSLIC's losses were disproportionately concentrated in state-regulated thrifts. The failure of state-chartered thrifts accounts for perhaps two-thirds of FSLIC's losses, even though there were more federal thrifts, federal thrifts held more assets, and more federal thrifts failed.[16] FSLIC was less—much less— able to limit losses in the thrifts the Bank Board did not directly regulate than in those it did. We can reject the idea that the Bank Board's joint tasks as regulator and insurer made it less willing and able to control the thrifts directly under its control than those chartered by the states.

FSLIC and the "Dual Banking" System

The dual banking system has been heavily criticized for increasing FSLIC's losses. The public choice argument is that the dual banking system creates a "competition in laxity" in which the various public officials are encouraged to weaken the rules to avoid losing regulated firms to other regulators. This perverse competition ostensibly affects both politicians and bureaucrats. National and state regulators supposedly fear that unless their rules are weakest thrifts will switch charters, thus diminishing the budgets and personnel of their regulatory agency. Politicians, for their part, are assumed to be eager to keep thrifts in "their" charter so that the politicians are better able to collect campaign contributions from them.

Neither logic nor history supports this interpretation. Even from a purely selfish point of view, public officials are not certain to weaken rules in order to attract firms into their regulatory system.[17] Self-interested bureaucrats may wish to maximize power or to minimize problems: in either case, tougher, not weaker, regulations are implied. In addition, a politician need not be the primary regulator of a firm to obtain campaign contributions from it. Indeed, not being the primary regulator allows the politician to collect funds without assuming responsibility for the firm's actions.[18] Most important, if public officials prefer only to weaken regulations to attract customers, then how did the regulations come into being in the first place?

Federal and state thrift regulation, moreover, has varied over time and across space. In general, federal and state governments have moved in concert during episodes of regulatory tightening and loosening. During the 1960s and 1970s, for example, federal and state governments tended to expand thrifts' asset and liability powers modestly while at the same time imposing new regulations to protect consumers.[19] Both levels of government then dramatically relaxed financial regulations during the 1980s.[20]

Thrift policies also differ from state to state. The charters in most states essentially copied the federal charter.[21] Other states traditionally have given state-chartered thrifts powers that federal ones did not have. For example, since the 1960s thrifts in Texas have been allowed to make a variety of loans and investments prohibited to the federal thrifts.[22] After Congress greatly expanded thrift powers in the Garn–St. Germain Act of 1982, other states—most notably California and Florida—followed suit in increasing the powers of their state thrifts. Most states, however, did not move to outdo the congressional deregulation. The causes and consequences of these state policies toward thrifts are worth noting. The regulatory experiences of Texas and California, the two states where FSLIC suffered its greatest losses, bear particular mention.

At the beginning of the 1950s, there were about an equal number of state and federal thrifts in Texas.[23] Over the next two decades, and especially in the mid-1960s, a series of laws was enacted granting Texas thrifts greater flexibility in making loans and investments. Texas was thus the first state to allow S&Ls to make commercial and consumer loans and direct investments in real estate. Virtually all new S&Ls in Texas chose the state charter (and a few thrifts switched from federal charters), so that by the end of the 1970s more than three-fourths of Texas thrifts were locally chartered.[24]

The Texas laws, rather than being seen as giveaways to the thrift business, were considered at that time to be a model for the nation. Both the Hunt Commission and the FINE study recommended that federal thrifts be awarded powers similar to those Texas S&Ls enjoyed. Texas's thrift policies strongly influenced the design of the Garn–St. Germain Act.[25] This influence seems well deserved. In the decades prior to the thrift tragedy, Texas thrifts had experienced stronger growth and profits than their federal counterparts. Even during the years 1979–1982, when the thrift business around the country was in dire straits, state-chartered thrifts in Texas expanded and prospered.[26] Texas, proud of its successes, continued its traditional pattern of giving its thrifts ever greater capacities to make loans and investments.

While Texas was consistent in its devotion to commerce, California was more capricious. During Jerry Brown's term as Governor (1975–1983), California thrifts found the state increasingly inhospitable to the business. Governor Brown's S&L commissioner, Linda Yang, was an aggressive regulator who vigorously sought to attach "fair lending" requirements to thrifts to force them to lend more to minorities.[27] After Congress enacted the DIDMCA in 1980, the federal charter became more attractive; twenty-four California S&Ls converted in the next two years. These conversions helped shrink the assets of California thrifts from $80 billion to $26 billion. Responding to this decline, the state legislature cut the S&L department staff from 178 persons (in 1978) to a low of 44 (in 1983), who were still responsible for supervising 109 California thrifts.[28]

At the end of his term, while he was preparing to run for the United States Senate, Brown sought to mend fences with the thrift business. Seeing an opportunity, Pat Nolan, an ambitious Republican member of the state assembly who was familiar and friendly with the S&L business, introduced legislation that provided for almost completely deregulated California thrifts. The bill passed with only one opposing vote in each house, even though the California S&L league "didn't know anything about the bill [and] wasn't interested in it."[29] The Nolan law, in fact, helped convince only a small handful of thrifts to reconvert to California charters. But under the next S&L commissioner (Larry Taggart), appointed by newly elected governor George Deukmejian, it did bring many new thrifts into the business.

The overall impact of state regulations on FSLIC's losses can be roughly measured by comparing the magnitude of each state's failures, that is, its "loss ratio." A state with a loss ratio of 1.0 imposed the same cost on FSLIC, relative to the size of the thrift business in that state, as the national average.[30] States with higher loss ratios might be thought to have had worse regulations (at least in terms of their ultimate effect on FSLIC) than states with smaller loss ratios.

If every state were competing to create a regulatory environment that was favorable (that is, permissive) toward its thrifts, as the public choice view implies, one might expect state loss ratios to be similar in size but random across the country. In other words, no state would differ very much from its peers and any difference in losses would be the result of chance. In contrast, if states chose distinctly different regulatory policies, as the public spirit approach would allow, the loss ratios should vary more between states with differing policies and yet be more consistent among states with similar policies.

The results are striking. Losses varied dramatically across the country, and FSLIC's losses were concentrated in the states with perhaps the greatest antipathy toward government and the greatest support for business: Texas, and its surrounding states, had average loss ratios three times the national average.[31] Regions less enamored with speculation, and more disposed towards circumspection, did much better: the upper Midwest and most of New England had loss ratios approaching zero.[32] California, even though it had large thrift losses in absolute terms (because its thrift business was so large), had a loss ratio that was less than half the national average. To be sure, much of the variation does seem to be random, and factors other than regulation undoubtedly account for some of the patterns that do exist.[33] But it is clear from the loss ratios that some parts of the country had regulations that reduced thrift losses, while the rules (or lack thereof) in other areas increased them.

One inference that may be drawn from this is that, in general, the states most hostile to regulation created more losses for FSLIC than states that were less hostile. The conclusion I want to emphasize, however, is that the states did not all choose the same policies. Instead, state politicians acted on their political ideas and chose distinctly different policies. These ideas and choices, not incidentally, typically accord with longstanding patterns in political culture among the states.

FSLIC's losses were thus concentrated in state-chartered thrifts, and thrift failures were clustered in certain states. But what is it about these state-chartered thrift failures that made them so expensive? Three possibilities suggest themselves. First, the Bank Board may not have had the legal authority to restrain state-chartered thrifts from engaging in risky behavior. Second, although the Bank Board may have had this authority, it may not have actually supervised state-chartered thrifts as extensively as federal ones. Third, the Bank Board may have had the legal authority to regulate state thrifts and it may not have differentiated between state and federal thrifts in supervision, yet it may still have failed to control improper risk taking by state thrifts.

Lack of authority should not have been a major problem. The FHLBB—not state banking agencies—was the primary supervisor even for state-chartered thrifts.[34] It is the Bank Board that declares thrifts, whether federal or state, insolvent and places them into FSLIC receivership.[35] The GAO has also argued that the Bank Board did not lack "the necessary legal authority under the National Housing Act to promulgate regulations needed to ensure that all thrifts, regardless of their charter, operated in a safe and sound manner."[36] When the Bank Board imposed its first regulation to restrain the use of the direct investment authority given to many state-chartered thrifts, it noted its "longstanding position, supported by legislative history and prior administrative practices, that the National Housing Act authorizes the Board to regulate state-chartered institutions."[37]

Differences in Bank Board supervision of federal and state thrifts do not seem to have been a major failing either. Federal examiners had the sole responsibility for examining federally chartered thrifts, and in more than half the states, federal and state examiners conducted joint examinations of state-chartered thrifts. In a few states, federal and state examiners examined institutions at the same times and shared their work (though they issued separate reports). In the other states, federal and state examiners took turns conducting examinations but shared the results.[38] It is difficult to determine from published data whether the Bank Board actually devoted equal resources to examining federal and state thrifts, however. Table 4.2 provides one estimate of its devotion.[39] If the assumptions underlying these results are reasonably accurate, it would appear that about the same percentage of federal and state thrifts were examined each year.

The fact that the Bank Board possessed the legal authority to control state thrifts and examined them regularly does not mean that the board was always willing to use this authority to act on what it

TABLE **4.2**

FHLBB Examinations of Thrifts
(in percent)

	Federally Chartered Thrifts	State-Chartered Thrifts
1979	88	82
1980	83	77
1981	84	84
1982	83	84
1983	63	71
1984	80	69
1985	63	52

Source: Author's estimations from data in Federal Home Loan Bank Board, *Annual Report*, various years.

found. During much of the 1980s, the Bank Board was reluctant to assert itself.[40] As the GAO noted, "Bank Board officials have indicated that they thought their authority to issue regulations to restrain state-chartered thrifts from engaging in high-risk activities was 'question-able.'"[41] Some state thrifts in some states exploited the Bank Board's reluctance to act by loading up their portfolios with high risk assets. The state thrifts that imposed the greatest costs on FSLIC typically had high concentrations of such assets in their portfolios.[42] The Bank Board did not prevent these state thrifts from exploiting FSLIC. Yet the Bank Board's reluctance to use its legal powers forcefully was not a *structural* problem inherent to dual banking. The main problem was that the Bank Board was unwilling to use the powers it had.

FSLIC's Resources

FSLIC's insurance fund was much too small to cover its losses during the 1980s. As we will see in the coming chapters, there were good reasons for FSLIC's fund not being larger at the beginning of the decade and for the difficulty in increasing it after that. The question that needs to be considered here, however, is whether FSLIC's ulti-mate losses would have been significantly reduced if FSLIC had had a much larger fund throughout the 1980s.

To many observers, the answer is obvious. If FSLIC had had more money up front, it would have needed less later. But such observers fail to appreciate properly money's changing value. Misperceptions about two truisms—that it costs more to put off until tomorrow what can be done today and that it costs less to pay cash than to buy on credit—are worth noting. Both of these statements are true, in nom-inal terms, given inflation and interest. But because real costs de-pend on inflation and interest rates, it may cost less in real terms to put some expenses off or to buy on credit. It is impossible to know in advance when real costs will be lowest.

Rather than discuss FSLIC's resources in the abstract, we may find it helpful to consider two concrete examples. The first concerns the effort to provide FSLIC with additional funds in 1986 and 1987.

The second involves the "Southwest Plan" of 1988, in which FSLIC arranged a low cost (for it) way to have a large number of S&Ls (primarily in Texas) taken over. Both examples suggest that it takes money to save money, but that FSLIC's savings would probably not have been enormous even if it had been adequately funded.

FSLIC Recapitalization

Beginning in 1986, Congress debated whether to provide FSLIC with an additional $15 billion to handle insolvent S&Ls. In August 1987 Congress finally authorized $10.8 billion for FSLIC.[43] What would have happened if Congress had given FSLIC every penny the administration had requested when it was requested? White, in the only published estimates, states that this would have saved FSLIC about $0.5 billion. As White describes it,

> If earlier action by FSLIC would have meant forestalling further risk-taking (and eventually costly) actions by these thrifts, the cost savings could have been higher. But by 1986 these insolvents were under supervisory control. . . . Though a few insolvent thrift managements might have slipped additional costly actions past their regulator managers, the major source of the FSLIC's costs were the bad loans and investments that these insolvent thrifts—and the additional hundreds of thrifts that would slide into insolvency in the following three years—had already made in earlier years; by 1986 it was too late for the FSLIC to cut its losses by much.[44]

The 1988 Deals

During 1988 FSLIC liquidated 26 insolvent thrifts and arranged for 179 others to be bought. The total cost to the federal government of these transactions was estimated to be about $36 billion (in 1988 dollars). FSLIC did not have nearly that much money. It was able to pay the almost $3 billion necessary to liquidate the 26 thrifts, but had to rely on a combination of notes, guarantees, and tax breaks worth nearly $33 billion to finance the sale of the other 179 thrifts.[45]

Most observers believe that FSLIC got taken to the cleaners on these deals.[46] This view is based largely on two facts. A number of wealthy individuals (Carolyn Hunt of the Hunt family, Robert Bass of the Bass family, Ronald Perelman of Revlon cosmetics) who purchased the failed thrifts did grow wealthier from the transactions.[47] In addition, numerous transactions required FSLIC to provide continued assistance (for example, by guaranteeing that interest payments on loans in the failed thrifts' portfolio would exceed market interest rates) to the purchasers over a number of years. It is almost irresistible to conclude that giving continued assistance to the rich purchasers of failed S&Ls is wasteful.

Such a conclusion, however, draws an unwarranted link between the beneficiaries, methods, and costs of FSLIC's transactions, and implies that the costs are greater than they should be because the beneficiaries are rich and the methods opaque. To understand why these links are unfounded, we need to review FSLIC's situation in identifying an insolvent S&L.

A thrift is insolvent when its assets (such as loans) are smaller than its liabilities (such as insured deposits). Consider a thrift that has a total of $100 in insured deposits, but only $75 in loans: it is insolvent, with a net worth "hole" of $25. FSLIC has two methods to handle this insolvency.[48] It can shut down the thrift, paying the depositors their $100, then liquidate the thrift's assets. Or FSLIC can find someone to buy the S&L, though in this case FSLIC will have to provide $25 to bring the level of assets up to that of liabilities. Either way, it will cost FSLIC about $25 to fill the net worth hole.

Selling a failed thrift requires FSLIC to use much less cash than does liquidation, however. For FSLIC to liquidate the thrift, it must first come up with the entire $100 to repay the depositors, since it will only gradually market the $75 in assets. To sell the thrift, however, FSLIC need only convince the buyer that it will receive the equivalent of $25 in assets (which could take the form of cash, notes, guarantees, or tax breaks, for example). As a result, although the total cost to FSLIC is the same in both cases, if FSLIC is short on cash it will favor sale over liquidation. Yet even if FSLIC had enough funds to pursue either option, there are two economic reasons for preferring to sell a thrift rather than close it.

First, the thrift itself may be worth something as an institution: it has established business relationships or customer loyalty, for example. If the thrift is liquidated, this worth vanishes. If the thrift is sold, on the other hand, FSLIC can charge the buyer for this value and hence reduce the total cost to FSLIC. Second, the assets of the thrift may be worth more as a whole than they would be if sold separately. When FSLIC sells a thrift it immediately transfers all the thrift's assets to the purchaser, who can then decide how to maximize their value. In contrast, when FSLIC liquidates a thrift it disposes of the assets piece by piece. It was generally believed that FSLIC could get a higher price for the assets if thrifts were sold whole rather than piecemeal.[49]

Both factors have led FSLIC (and also FDIC) to favor sales over liquidations. Between 1980 and 1987, when it was becoming increasingly strapped for funds, FSLIC sold 232 S&Ls while liquidating only 52. From 1934 to 1980, however, FSLIC liquidated only 13 of the 130 thrifts that became insolvent.[50] In other words, FSLIC favored sales to liquidations even when it had ample resources for either course of action. A shortage of resources did not necessarily bias FSLIC toward selling insolvent thrifts. They already were so inclined.

An additional problem facing FSLIC concerned the value of the assets at the failed thrifts. The above example assumed that the thrift had assets worth $75 and a net worth hole of $25. Unfortunately, estimating the value of the assets and thus the size of the hole is usually difficult and unpredictable.[51] Any buyer would want to put the lowest possible price on these assets; however, the lower the price, the larger the hole that FSLIC would have to fill.

This placed FSLIC in a dilemma. If FSLIC allowed the buyer to set low prices on the assets, FSLIC would have to spend more money up front to fill the larger hole and run the risk of underpricing the assets.[52] Yet if FSLIC set the prices higher than buyers were willing to accept, FSLIC would still have to pay off the depositors, run the risk that the assets would continue to decline in value, and face the costs of managing and ultimately selling them.

There was no straightforward way for FSLIC to minimize its total real cost for disposing of these insolvent S&Ls with large quantities of dubious assets. Here is what FSLIC generally did: it wrote contracts with the purchasing thrifts providing "capital loss coverage" on the failed thrift's "covered assets."[53] This meant that FSLIC transferred the assets to the purchaser at their book value (e.g., $100) while promising that the purchaser would receive at least this amount if the assets were eventually sold.[54] In addition, "FSLIC provided 'yield maintenance' payments on the assets (many of which yielded little or no current income) so that the acquirer could cover its deposit interest and other operating costs until the time when the asset was sold."[55]

Several other features of these transactions are worth noting. First, although FSLIC did bear most of the "downside" risk (that is, FSLIC stood to lose if the covered assets were sold for less than their book value), it was entitled to share in any appreciation if the purchaser was able to sell the assets for a profit. Because the purchaser would also profit from asset appreciation, the purchaser had some incentives to maximize the sales price of its covered assets.[56] Second, the transactions generally allowed FSLIC to repurchase the covered assets (or pay off the notes it had issued to the purchaser) if FSLIC judged that it could manage and sell them at less cost to the insurance fund. Finally, FSLIC shared in any appreciation of the stock of the purchasing thrift.[57]

These arrangements allowed FSLIC to minimize its immediate cash payments and—FSLIC hoped—its long-term costs as well. Despite the criticism these deals have received, no one has demonstrated, nor is it possible to demonstrate, that the long-term cost of FSLIC's 1988 deals was greater than the cost for alternative arrangements. For example, the GAO concludes merely that "we cannot say if FSLIC used its limited resources most efficiently in resolving the problem thrifts."[58] Lowy writes that these deals "can't be evaluated today. [They] may never be evaluated very well, because evaluation would entail an examination of what eventually is realized from the assets of the failed S&Ls compared with what might be realized if they had been dealt with by a different mechanism. As a consequence, any evaluation of the 1988 deals will be strictly hypothetical."[59] Even Mayer, one of the harshest critics of the 1988 deals, concedes that "admittedly, the denunciation of what the Bank Board did in 1988 is a lot easier than the construction of an alternative."[60]

The FHLBB's Staff Resources

Many observers have suggested that FSLIC's losses were huge not just because the agency had too little money but also because the Bank Board had too few staffers to monitor behavior and enforce its rules.[61] Civil service personnel limitations—and especially, low salaries—are blamed for making it difficult for the Bank Board to attract and retain high quality staff. The inexperienced and incompetent bureaucrats were thus overwhelmed by the problems in the thrift industry—or chose to look the other way.

Why would a regulatory agency have an inadequate staff? One possibility is that elected officials find little political benefit in funding regulators and thus systematically underfund regulatory agencies. Agency officials, for their part, may have weak personal incentives to vigorously enforce the laws and therefore have no creditable reason to seek larger and better staffs.[62] A contrasting possibility is that politicians and bureaucrats seek the "right" level of regulatory personnel, in keeping with their view of the public interest and of the best way to obtain it. Accordingly, public officials would prefer to hire enough staff, and pay them enough, to fulfill their policy goals. These goals—and thus views about staff size and salaries—will be different for different officials.

Before we can evaluate whether public officials acted responsibly in determining the FHLBB's staff resources, we might find it helpful to consider the following questions: How many staff members did the Bank Board need, how much did it need to pay them, and how much turnover should it have expected? None of the answers are obvious. There is no conclusive theoretical or empirical guidance concerning the size, salaries, or turnover of federal agencies.[63] Regarding agency performance, this much is clear: agencies can be either too large or too small; salaries can be too high as well as too low; and turnover can be too sluggish as well as too rapid.

Focusing on the FHLBB's resources in isolation will do little to answer these questions, moreover, since staff size, salaries, or turnover can grow (or decline) in absolute terms while shrinking (or increasing) relative to the agency's tasks. To determine whether staff size, salaries, and turnover were truly adequate, several kinds of comparisons need to be made.

Staff Salaries

Because federal agencies must compete with the private sector (as well as other bureaus) for employees, it is tempting to think that federal salaries need to match private sector salaries for similar positions. But because salaries are only one aspect of the attractiveness of a job, there is no reason to conclude that government and private sector salaries must be equivalent. Implicit compensation includes other forms of monetary compensation not included in salaries (such as job security, health benefits, retirement programs, or deferred compensation through resume enhancement). In addition, nonmonetary compensation (such as prestige, power, or "interesting and challenging work") can influence the desirability of a job.

Comparing the salaries of the FHLBB and its competitors at any given time provides only limited insight into whether the FHLBB salaries were too low: any gap between the salaries may be completely filled by other monetary and nonmonetary compensation, to make the jobs equally attractive.[64] Comparing salaries over time can give a better, though still imperfect, picture of the relative attractiveness of jobs in the FHLBB and its competitors. If the gap between the explicit salaries for the FHLBB and its competitors remains stable over time, then it seems reasonable that Bank Board salaries are competitive. If the gap between explicit salaries grows wider, it is probable that the FHLBB is becoming less competitive unless there is good reason to believe that its implicit compensation has increased.[65]

A snapshot of the salaries for examiners in the federal financial regulatory agencies (FHLBB, OCC, FDIC, and FRS) in 1984 are presented in table 4.3. FHLBB salaries were substantially lower than those of the other agencies at that time; the reason for this is that the other agencies were exempt from the civil service pay scale. Given their higher salaries and the likelihood that their implicit compensation was at least as high, the other agencies undoubtedly were able to hire better-qualified examiners.

The data on the starting salaries for college graduates entering the federal civil service (which included examiners in the Bank Board until 1985) and for accountants in the private sector for the years 1977 through 1985 are presented in table 4.4.[66] Throughout

TABLE 4.3

Examiner Salaries in Financial Regulatory Agencies, 1984

	FHLBB	OCC	FDIC	FRB
Entry Level	$14,390	$17,000	$17,750	$17,690
Average	24,775	30,764	32,505	37,900
Senior Analyst	37,599	48,876	48,876	48,876

Source: Norman Strunk and Fred Case, *Where Deregulation Went Wrong: A Look at the Causes Behind Savings and Loan Failures in the 1980s* (Chicago: United States League of Savings Institutions, 1988), 141; Paul Zane Pilzer with Robert Deitz, *Other People's Money: The Inside Story of the S&L Mess* (New York: Simon and Schuster, 1989), 162.

this period, there was also a fairly large gap—about 20 percent—between the explicit compensation of the Bank Board and the private sector. The gap was also fairly consistent: between 1977 and 1982 starting salaries at the FHLBB varied between 79 and 83 percent of starting salaries in the private sector for accountants. In 1983 and

TABLE 4.4

Starting Salary for FHLBB Examiners and Private Sector Accountants (in current dollars)

	Accountant[a]	GS-5 Examiner[b]	%[c]	G-7 Examiner[b]	%[c]
1980	$14,784	$12,265	83	$15,193	103
1981	15,720	12,854	83	15,922	101
1982	16,980	13,368	79	16,559	98
1983	18,648	13,903	75	17,221	93
1984	19,476	14,390	74	17,834	92
1985	20,628	21,000	101	—	—

Source: U.S. Office of Personnel Management, *Federal Civilian Workforce Statistics: Pay Structure of the Federal Civil Service* (Washington, D.C.: Office of Workforce Information, 1985), 51; U.S. Department of Commerce, *Statistical Abstract of the United States, 1988*, (Washington, D.C.: Government Printing Office, 1989), 130, 308.

a. Accountant salaries represent what corporations plan to offer graduates graduating in the year shown with bachelors' degrees. Based on a survey of approximately 200 companies.

b. Examiner salaries for 1980–1984 are governmentwide civil service starting salaries for GS-5 and GS-7.

c. Percentages indicate examiners' salaries in relation to accountants' salaries.

1984 the salary gap did widen: starting Bank Board salaries fell to 75 percent of accountants' job offers.[67] The starting salaries of federal government did continue to increase each year, however, so that the gap between federal and private salaries increased only because private salaries grew slightly faster. Given the prestige accorded to the private sector during the 1980s and the disdain extended to bureaucrats, however, it seems likely that the gap in implicit compensation became even larger in the mid-1980s than the gap in explicit compensation.

In short, at the beginning of the 1980s staff salaries at the Bank Board were lower than at the other financial agencies and lower than in the private sector. The gap between the FHLBS and private sector salaries grew slightly wider during the early years of the thrift tragedy.

Staff Turnover

The Bank Board believed that its low salaries in the mid-1980s produced high turnover rates within the agency. The board claimed that the turnover rate in the system's field examination staff, for example, "substantially exceeded" that in the other financial regulatory agencies.[68] Attrition was also quite high in some major policy offices. For example, it is reputed that in 1985 the general counsel's office lost 52 percent of its staff, the Office of Examinations and Supervision 39 percent, and FSLIC 33 percent.[69]

A broader examination of employee turnover among FHLBB field examiners, the federal government, the private sector, and the banking and finance sectors between 1980 and 1984 does not necessarily support the board's claims, however (table 4.5).[70] The employee turnover rates among FHLBB examiners were lower than those in the federal government as a whole, the private sector, and even the banking and finance sector. If turnover of the FHLBB's staff was too high, it was also too high among other employers.

Of course, these averages may conceal important differences in turnover rates among particular categories of workers. Turnover rates may have been much higher, for example, among senior examiners or new recruits. Table 4.6 contains a more detailed view of the turnover rates within the FHLBB and the federal government. Turnover rates

TABLE 4.5

Annual Employee Turnover Rates
(in percent)

	1980	1981	1982	1983	1984
FHLBB examiners	12	10	12	14	14
Federal government employees	34	22	19	18	19
Private sector employees	17	—	15	—	16
Banking and finance employees	—	—	16	—	19

Source: Norman Strunk and Fred Case, *Where Deregulation Went Wrong: A Look at the Causes Behind Savings and Loan Failures in the 1980s* (Chicago: United States League of Savings Institutions, 1988), 142; U.S. Department of Commerce, *Statistical Abstract of the United States, 1988* (Washington, D.C.: Government Printing Office, 1989), 307; Edward G. Thomas, "Turnover Reflects Improved Economy," *Management World*, October 1985, 8–11.

TABLE 4.6

Turnover Rates Among Field Examiners in the FHLBB, 1980–1984

	Employed		Left Employment	
	N	**%ᵃ**	**N**	**%ᵇ**
GS-5	52	7	11	21
GS-7	58	8	10	17
GS-9	88	13	9	10
GS-11	137	20	18	13
GS-12	227	32	26	11
GS-13	137	20	12	9
Subtotal GS-5–GS-9	198	28	30	15
Subtotal GS-11–GS-13	501	72	56	12
Total	699	100	86	100

Source: Federal Home Loan Bank Board data, cited in Norman Strunk and Fred Case, *Where Deregulation Went Wrong* (Chicago: United States League of Savings Institutions, 1989), 142–43; Federal Home Loan Bank Board, *Annual Report, 1984*, 69; U.S. Office of Personnel Management, *Federal Civilian Workforce Statistics: Pay Structure of the Federal Civil Service*, 9.

Note: During this period 52 percent of federal employees were GS-5 through GS-9; 48 percent were GS-11 through GS-13.

a. Percentage of total employed.

b. Average turnover rate.

were indeed higher among lower GS-level employees of the FHLBB than among higher GS-levels; on a percentage basis, turnover was almost twice as high among GS-5 examiners as among GS-13s. Lower level (GS 5–9) examiners, however, made up only a small proportion of all examiners, since over 70 percent of the examiners were ranked GS-11 or above. In addition, average turnover rates were little different from those for the federal government as a whole. Relatively few examiners had rankings below the GS-11 level, and turnover rate among these lower level examiners was only modestly higher than that among the other examiners: these findings suggest that low starting salaries did not contribute very much to problems in turnover for the Bank Board.

It is certainly a stretch of the imagination to conclude that hiring a few more low level examiners, and paying them somewhat higher salaries, would have had much effect on FSLIC's resolution costs. These data also suggest that the turnover rate among examiners was not a special problem, or at least, that it was not much different from that of the entire federal government.

Did the low salaries and high turnover create problems for the Bank Board? Probably. It is easy to imagine that higher salaries and lower turnover would have made the FHLBS more effective. But one must be skeptical about how much impact these changes could have made on FSLIC's losses. Is it possible to believe that the thrift tragedy could have been averted if a wave of the wand had brought 1980 staff salaries to private sector levels and stopped turnover altogether?

Staff Size

A primary job of the FHLBS staff was to examine savings and loan associations by visiting them and scrutinizing their assets. The number of individual thrifts and the size and complexity of their assets influences the numbers of examiners needed. The ratio of Bank Board examiners to insured thrift institutions and the ratio of examiners to thrift assets are two indicators that take these things into account.[71] But while these ratios are useful in measuring the relative size of the regulatory staff over time, they alone cannot determine how many examiners were needed. For example, if institutions or assets grew in size but not in complexity, or if examination techniques improved, a declining examiner-to-asset ratio could still have left institutions properly monitored.[72]

Two measures that may help take into account changes in size and complexity are the ratio of thrift industry employees to institutions and of employees to assets. Since thrifts have economic incentives to hire the "correct" number of people to do their work, these ratios should reflect any change in the relative number of employees needed to handle the thrifts' business. Because thrifts have no civil service restrictions on their ability to hire the number of employees they need (and can pay for), these ratios may also adjust more smoothly and automatically to changes within the industry than do the examiner ratios. If the Bank Board examiner ratios fall below the thrift industry employee ratios, then there is good evidence that the Bank Board was understaffed.

Such evidence is good, but not conclusive. Thrifts can fail at least in part because they have "excessive operating costs" or "inadequate underwriting," that is, because they also had too many or too few employees. If this is the case, the examiner ratios will fall below the employee ratios not because there are too few examiners but because there were too many employees. In addition, examiner and employee ratios can diverge for reasons that have little to do with the adequacy of either staff. It is therefore also helpful to compare examiner, employee, asset, and institution ratios for the FHLBS to the same ratios in the commercial banking industry. Examiner-to-asset and employee-to-asset indices for both thrifts and banks are detailed in figure 4.1, and examiner-to-institution and employee-to-institution indices appear in figure 4.2.[73]

Several features of figure 4.1 are noteworthy. First, although the thrift examiner-to-asset ratio did fall between 1979 and 1984, so did all three other indices. Although the number of thrift examiners per dollar of assets shrank during those years, so did the number of thrift employees, bank examiners, and bank employees. Second, before 1985 the examiner-to-asset index dropped even farther for banks than for thrifts, though both fell faster then the employee-to-asset ratios. Furthermore, the gap between the examiner and employee indices was wider for banks than for thrift in every year except 1984,

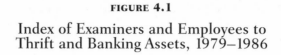

FIGURE 4.1

Index of Examiners and Employees to Thrift and Banking Assets, 1979–1986

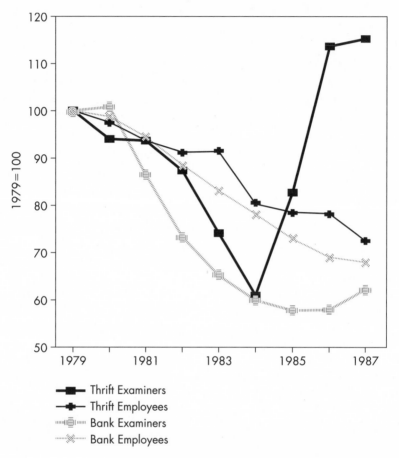

- ━■━ Thrift Examiners
- ━✚━ Thrift Employees
- ⸱⸱⸱▤⸱⸱⸱ Bank Examiners
- ⸱⸱⸱◈⸱⸱⸱ Bank Employees

Source: Author's calculations from unpublished data and various annual reports of the FHLBB, FRB, OCC, FDIC.

when both were about the same. Third, the thrift examiner index grew dramatically from 1985 to 1987, even as the bank examiner index stayed essentially the same.

The examiner- and employee-to-institution indices for banks and thrifts are illustrated in figure 4.2. Several points should again be clarified. It was the thrift examiner-to-institution index that grew every year except 1984; in 1985–1987, the growth was enormous. In con-

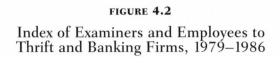

FIGURE **4.2**

Index of Examiners and Employees to
Thrift and Banking Firms, 1979–1986

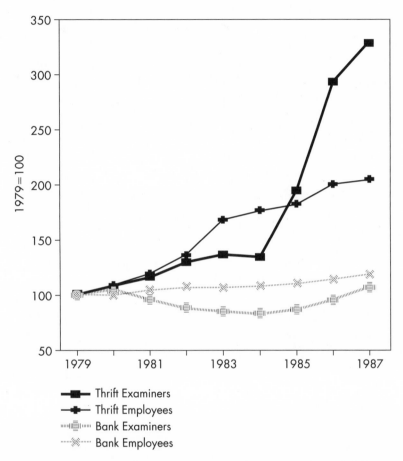

Source: Author's calculations from unpublished data and various annual reports of the FHLBB,
FRB, OCC, FDIC.

trast, the bank examiner-to-institution index actually fell from 1981 to
1984 and rose modestly after that. Because the thrift employee-to-
institution also grew rapidly after 1980, the thrift examiner-to-
institution index did not keep pace. Only in 1984, however, was the
gap between examiner and employee indices larger for thrifts than for
banks.

Another perspective on the staffing of the financial agencies is displayed in figures 4.3 and 4.4. These figures compare the numbers of staff for the financial regulators per asset and institution during these years. From 1979 to 1984, both bank and thrift examiners had falling examiner-to-asset ratios, and the differences between examination work forces also declined. After 1984 the Bank Board increased the size of its examination force much more than did the bank regulators, so that by 1985 it had more examiners-per-asset dollars than did the bank regulators. The examiner-to-institution ratios in figure 4.4 show that, by 1982, there were more examiners per institution within the thrift industry than in the banking industry.

Personnel changes in the thrift industry were clearly more turbulent—to judge by these figures—than were those in the bank industry.[74] It is nonetheless difficult to conclude that the trends for thrift

FIGURE 4.3

Number of Examiners per Thrift or Bank Assets, 1979–1986

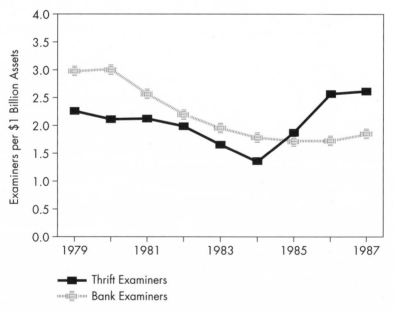

Source: Author's calculations from unpublished data and various annual reports of the FHLBB, FRB, OCC, FDIC.

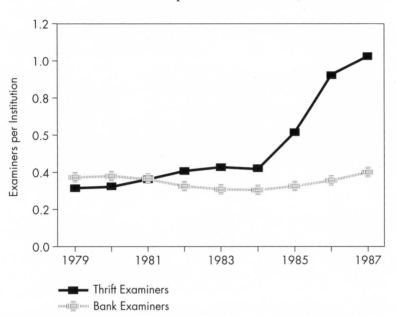

FIGURE **4.4**

Number of Examiners per Thrift or Bank, 1979–1986

Source: Author's calculations from unpublished data and various annual reports of the FHLBB, FRB, OCC, FDIC.

examiners from 1979 to 1984 were much different from trends in the thrift and banking industry. Furthermore, the aggressiveness with which the "weak" Bank Board expanded its examination force after 1984 stands in sharp contrast to the moderate increase in examiners in the "strong" banking agencies.

These figures do not conclusively answer the question whether the Bank Board had too few examiners after deregulation, or whether more examiners would have made a major difference. They do show that, before 1984, trends for the FHLBS's examination staff did not diverge markedly from those for bank examiners or for the thrift and banking industries. They also demonstrate that, since 1984, the FHLBS's examination staff grew much faster than the examination staff of the banking agencies or the numbers of thrift industry employees. During 1984 the Bank Board acted vigorously to increase its staff of field examiners by transferring them out of the civil service and into the Federal Home Loan Banks, which allowed the Bank Board to increase salaries by about one-third and to almost double the size of the examination force; this action was completed by July 1985.

Would more examiners have reduced FSLIC's ultimate costs? While there can be no doubt that deregulating thrift assets increased the need for examiners, it also seems likely that increasing the examination force would have had only a modest impact before 1984 and did have only a moderate effect after that time. For examiners to be effective, they must be able to identify objectively illegal, or at least unsafe, activities. It is not clear that examiners—or outside accountants or academics—could do this very well in the first several years after the 1982 Garn–St. Germain Act deregulations. As Texas S&L commissioner Lin Bowman noted, the financial transactions (and especially the shady transactions) of deregulated thrifts were often so complex that "an examination force of hundreds could not possibly get to the bottom of these things because of the nature of the very transactions themselves."[75] Another perceptive observer of the thrift mess explains that "despite much mumbling about supervision replacing regulation, the fact is that without preexisting written rules government insurers cannot effectively police what insured depositories do with these dollars."[76] As the following chapters will demonstrate, between 1983 and 1985 the examiners did not have the "preexisting written rules" necessary to limit thrifts' losses.

Bank Board Chairman Gray, responsible for doubling the number of FHLBB examiners, himself recognized that adding examiners alone could not contain thrift industry problems. As he testified before Congress in 1985,

> Short of an examiner listening in on every phone call and monitoring every wire transfer, it is impossible for our agents in the field to fulfill their routine responsibilities with regard to institutions that are exploding in size and dramatically shifting the composition of their assets. Additionally, with many new loans, especially in real estate construction and development, it usually takes several years or more for the underlying problems to become so apparent that we have legal justification for supervisory action. Although examination and supervision can presumably detect these problems over time, it will

usually be beyond the point at which corrective actions can reverse what have become substantial losses.[77]

Gray's comments were prescient. After 1985 the large increase in examiners did little to stop FSLIC's costs from growing. By then, most of FSLIC's losses had already been incurred.

FHLBB Staff Salaries and Size in Political Context

Despite the particular problems the Bank Board's salaries may have caused in attracting and retaining staff, the FHLBB in the 1980s was nonetheless a part of a federal government that was widely seen as overstaffed and overpaid. Many prominent politicians—including President Reagan—certainly held this opinion, and the public agreed. As part of his campaign against big government, Reagan had appointed a blue-ribbon panel, the Private Sector Survey on Cost Control (better known as the "Grace Commission"), to find ways to reduce federal spending. The commission focused in part on the federal work force.

The Grace Commission released its report in 1984.[78] It concluded that pay inflation had created a federal "grade bulge." In 1984, almost 40 percent of the federal work force earned salaries in the grade 11 to 15 range, compared to one-third in 1969 and one-fifth in 1959, for example. Furthermore, only about a quarter of the private sector work force earned salaries at comparable levels. The Grace Commission recommended shrinking the grade bulge, so that federal pay scales would more closely approximate those in the private sector and in the federal government in earlier years.

To this end, the Office of Personnel Management (OPM) began examining the grade bulge in individual agencies, identifying those agencies, and recommending that the Office of Management and Budget (OMB) cut their compensation budgets to force them to trim back. Despite the inadequate salaries it seemed to have, the Bank Board bulged: over 60 percent of its staff were in grades 11 to 15. Although this proportion was comparable to that of other financial regulators, it was considerably higher than the governmentwide average. As a result, in fiscal 1985 OMB imposed a 2 percent cut in the

Bank Board's compensation budget for grades 11 to 15. In the face of further cuts, the Bank Board attempted to fill job openings at lower grade levels.[79]

In hindsight, these staff cuts may appear incomprehensible. But consider the Bank Board's situation from the perspective of OPM and OMB, which were trying to make payroll decisions for the entire government. They had clear directions from the president to reduce (or at least maintain) the size and cost of the government. The FHLBS already had a far greater percentage of higher level positions than did the federal government as a whole. Bank Board requests for additional senior staff would, appropriately, be met skeptically because most federal agencies could (honestly) make the same claim. How were OMB and OPM expected to know that, of all the other agencies, the Bank Board's claims were most urgent? On what basis could OMB justify allowing the Bank Board to hire more senior examiners, especially when it claimed to need not just a few more, but *twice* as many as it currently had?

This problem is illustrated in a revealing anecdote concerning Bank Board Chairman Ed Gray and OMB Assistant Director Constance Horner. In 1984 Gray pleaded with Horner for more examiners, asking to double his staff to fourteen hundred while raising its base pay. Horner insisted that "deregulation . . . meant *fewer* regulators, not more." Horner, however, agreed to get Gray thirty more examiners if Gray "would be more cooperative and get back into step with the administration." At this point, Gray threatened to transfer the examiners out of the civil service (and the control of OMB) and into the district banks. "You mean you're going to have *nongovernment* employees regulating?" Horner asked. "They're already doing it. I don't see a problem with it," Gray replied.[80] A week later, Horner increased her offer to thirty-nine new examiners. Gray rejected it, and proceeded immediately to transfer the examiners to the district banks.[81]

By July 1985, Bank Board examiners had been transferred out of the civil service and into the district banks. This transfer removed the examiners from the oversight of the OMB, meaning that it could no longer determine the number of examiners or their salary.[82] As a result, the board told the district banks to hire at least seven hundred new examiners immediately and to raise starting salaries from

$14,000 to $21,000. By 1986, the FHLBS had doubled the size of its examination force.

For those who believed that civil service personnel restrictions made it difficult if not impossible for the Bank Board to hire enough examiners or to pay them enough, the necessary reform was clear: the Bank Board needed to be removed from the civil service so that it could hire as many examiners as possible and pay them as much as necessary. Such a proposal raises important questions, however. Should each agency be able to withdraw from the civil service and set its staff size and pay scales (and by extension, all other personnel matters)? If not, why should the Bank Board but not others be allowed this privilege? If each agency does set its own pay system, what forms of oversight would elected politicians—that is, representatives of the public—maintain? If each agency were able to conduct its own pay system, how would a unified federal budget be developed?[83] Would it merely be the sum of the individual components, without any control exercised from the top? Answers to such questions are not easy to come by, and reasonable people are likely to disagree. Believing that personnel decisions for the federal government should be unified and controlled by a single agency does not make one irresponsible, however.

Was transferring the examiners to the district banks a good thing? Yes, to the extent that the transfer gave the Bank Board the ability to increase its examination force greatly and to pay them salaries that were closer to market salaries. But it also removed them from direct political oversight. As one report notes, by transferring examiners to the district banks, it "strengthened the district banks and got Washington bureaucracy out of their lives—two things the industry liked."[84]

Conclusions

Did the structure and resources of the FHLBS make the thrift tragedy inevitable? No. Did they make it worse? Yes, but only modestly. FSLIC was bound to lose many billions of dollars in the 1980s even if the FHLBS had had a different structure or additional resources.

The relationship between the FHLBS structure and FSLIC's losses is obscure. The structure of the Federal Home Loan Banks did not distinguish them from the Federal Reserve Banks. The Bank Board's roles as regulator and insurer need not, and did not, create conflicts of interest that reduced its ability to limit FSLIC's losses. That the failure of state-chartered thrifts was so costly to FSLIC does raise serious concerns about the operations of the dual banking system. But the questions have more to do with the willingness of the Bank Board to exert control than its authority to do so.

The Bank Board's lack of resources did increase FSLIC's ultimate losses. Of course, almost any agency could save the government money in the future if it spent more today. We are all familiar with this idea, yet none of us pay cash for our homes. There is good reason to conclude, however, that even if the Bank Board had had additional resources earlier, such resources would have barely reduced the board's expenses later. The reason is this: a dollar spent is a dollar saved only if it is spent well. Better-trained, better-paid, better-qualified examiners and additional insurance reserves would have reduced FSLIC's losses if the Bank Board could have quickly identified and eliminated unnecessarily risky and illegal activities. But it could not do so when it most needed to. Additional resources at that time would have saved FSLIC relatively little.

5

The Bank Board
and the Thrift Business

THE FHLBS'S STRUCTURE AND RESOURCES were not the major causes of the losses FSLIC suffered. Thus, changing the FHLBB's structure, or giving it additional resources, would probably have reduced FSLIC's losses only modestly. Why, then, were the losses so large? Why did the FHLBB not work more effectively to limit them? In the next two chapters I will examine these questions by considering the situation the Bank Board and its staff faced during the thrift tragedy and what they did about it.

The Thrift Business Between 1978 and 1982

The year 1978 was considered a very good year for the thrift business. Net income after taxes was reported to be at an all-time high of almost $4 billion. The return on assets was higher than it had been since 1960.[1] The next year, though not quite as lucrative, was still solidly profitable. Reflecting the health of the thrift business, the thrift business's worth ratio grew slightly from a reported 5.5 to 5.6 percent, or from over $28 billion to nearly $32 billion.

Or did it? Table 5.1 gives four different estimates of the net worth of the thrift business between 1978 and 1984.[2] These include

TABLE 5.1

Estimated Net Worth of FSLIC-Insured Thrifts, 1978–1984
(in $ billions)

	Assets	Book Value				Market Value			
		GAAP		RAP		Kane		Brumbaugh	
	GAAP		%		%		%		%
1978	$511	$28	5.5	$28	5.5	$ −35	−6.9	—	—
1979	567	32	5.6	32	5.6	−53	−9.3	—	—
1980	615	32	5.3	32	5.3	−79	−12.8	$ −77	−12.5
1981	651	27	4.2	28	4.3	−100	−15.4	−113	−17.3
1982	686	20	3.0	25	3.7	−73	−10.6	−83	−12.0
1983	814	26	3.1	33	4.0	−49	−6.0	−46	−5.6
1984	978	28	2.9	37	3.8	—	—	−27	−2.7

Sources: Author's calculations based on data in FHLBB, *Combined Financial Statements, FSLIC-Insured Institutions,* 1987, iii; Kane, *The S&L Insurance Mess,* 75; Brumbaugh, *Thrifts Under Siege,* 50.

two estimates of book value and two of market value net worth. The values determined by "generally accepted accounting principles" (GAAP) and "regulatory accounting principles" (RAP) values show the net worth actually reported on thrift business balance sheets.[3] The net worth estimates by Kane and R. Dan Brumbaugh Jr., in contrast, represent the market value of thrift business assets and liabilities had they been sold at auction that year.

This table vividly illustrates several key points. It shows that book and market values already differed dramatically by 1979 and so yielded sharply differing views of thrift business health. For example, GAAP indicates that the thrift business had a relatively healthy net worth of 5.6 percent, or over $30 billion, in 1979, while Kane estimated that the business as a whole was already deeply insolvent with a market net worth of minus 9.3 percent, a deficit of nearly $53 billion. According to GAAP, the thrift business was thriving in 1979; in market terms, it was already dead.

The Importance of Accounting

Both assessments are accurate, though regrettably, neither provides a prognosis. The book net worth reported by GAAP accurately describes the condition of the thrift business based on its previous transactions. The market net worth estimated by Kane gives a snapshot of the value of the business were it to be sold at auction. Neither net worth figure tells much about the future value of the business, however. But remember that GAAP was the accounting system used by thrifts (and virtually every other business), accounting firms, and regulators in making decisions about financial health. At the end of the 1970s, GAAP indicated that the thrift business was solid.

Table 5.1 also shows how slowly book values change and how quickly market values can diverge from them. GAAP net worth for the business changed only slowly between 1978 and 1984; average changes in market value net worth were almost three times as large. The changes in dollar value are especially striking. Business net worth fell by $1 billion between 1978 and 1982 according to GAAP but by $65 billion judged by estimated market values.

In 1978, the gap between book and market net worth was about twelve percentage points; by 1982, this gap had grown to almost twenty percentage points. This implies that, on average, a thrift with zero net worth according to GAAP would have a market net worth of approximately minus 20 percent. In other words, unless a thrift had a GAAP net worth of 20 percent—and no thrift had such a high net worth—it was probably insolvent in market terms. When a thrift with $1 billion in assets reached zero GAAP net worth, it would have a market net worth of minus $200 million. And unless the thrift reported $200 million in GAAP net worth, it was probably insolvent.

The divergence between book and market net worth is important for two reasons. Regulators "go by the book" in at least two senses. First, regulators are guided, and often bound, by regulations (their "book") in dealing with S&Ls.[4] Regulatory requirements for thrifts were based on formal accounting reports, and these reports were based on book values specified by RAP. Regulators often could not take actions against thrifts unless these requirements were violated. In particular, FSLIC could not declare a thrift insolvent and take control from its managers until the S&L was insolvent by RAP standards. Second, RAP was based on book values. If book values diverged from market values—as they increasingly did after 1978—by the time a thrift was insolvent by book value, it was usually seriously insolvent by market value. Seriously insolvent thrifts are very expensive to liquidate.

If thrift regulators lived by the book, they died by the market. Regulators were limited in their ability to take actions against thrifts, and especially, to take control of them by declaring them insolvent, until book values showed they had zero net worth.[5] Once this determination was made, however, the FHLBB had to dispose of the thrift, most often by selling it whole to another thrift and less frequently by liquidating its assets. Potential buyers were understandably less impressed by the book value of the insolvent thrift than by its current and future market value to them. The FHLBB thus had to sell insolvent thrifts at market prices. Because these market prices were almost certainly below book values, FSLIC was almost guaranteed to suffer large losses on each thrift it declared insolvent.[6]

Thrift Capital

One conclusion that might be drawn from table 5.1 is that by 1978, when it was booking record profits, the thrift business was already grossly insolvent at market values. Between 1978 and 1981, moreover, the market value of the thrift business declined substantially. The magnitude of this market insolvency is worth exploring. If FSLIC had shut down the entire thrift business in 1978—before the business was considered to be in serious trouble—and sold it off, it would have cost the federal government an estimated $35 billion (or approximately $75 billion in 1991 dollars). This table suggests that the estimated cost (in 1991 dollars) for liquidating the business would have been $106 billion in 1979, $149 billion in 1980, and $180 billion in 1981.[7]

This bears repeating. If FSLIC had taken over the thrift business ten years ago and sold it off, it would have cost about $180 billion.[8] These costs are not trivial, even by the jaded standards of 1995. Although it is difficult to make direct comparisons between the different estimates of the total costs of thrift insolvencies to the deposit insurance system, these estimates are not much out of line with recent claims that the thrift business cleanup will cost $150–220 billion.

Some have rejected this approach of estimating the probable costs of resolving all FSLIC's obligations at different points in time. In

1982, for instance, Carron flatly stated that "it is not appropriate to use the (negative) market-value net worth as an estimate of the amount payable to depositors by FSLIC . . . [because] liquidation of the entire industry is a purely theoretical exercise. Thus, while the potential for serious difficulties exists, these estimates do not serve as a guide to the cost of recovery."[9] Bank Board Chairman Pratt, however, commenting on the rapid deterioration of the thrift business in 1982, wrote that "at [this] rate of decline, the virtual elimination of the S&L industry . . . became more than a theoretical possibility."[10] Indeed, much of the business was liquidated over the course of the decade, with the number of thrifts declining by about 30 percent (from 4,000 to 2,880) during this period.

In addition, market value estimations do provide an estimate of the real contingent liabilities of the deposit insurer. Most analysts have recommended that the thrift business be forced to adopt market value accounting instead of relying on book value methods. But it is inconsistent to make this recommendation without recognizing what its implications would have been for the deposit insurer throughout the 1980s.

Should FSLIC have acted sooner to remove the insolvent thrifts from the system? Most observers have answered "yes" and have castigated the regulators for waiting so long to shut bankrupt S&Ls.[11] The evidence presented above does not unequivocally support this view. Although the market value insolvency of the thrift business grew dramatically between 1978 and 1981, from about $35 billion to $100 billion, it fell just as abruptly between 1981 and 1984, from about $100 billion to perhaps $30 billion. Waiting from 1978 to 1981 would have increased expenses enormously, but waiting from 1981 to 1984 would have reduced probable costs by about the same amount.

What can we learn from this analysis? First, although preserving the insurance fund by resolving thrift market insolvencies as they happen may have been a viable option at some point, its viability eroded quickly after 1978. Because the net worth of the thrift business deteriorated so rapidly after that, FSLIC would have had to take control quickly of virtually every S&L in the country. Nationalizing such a large and dispersed business would have been far beyond

American regulatory experience. Doing so would have been a revolutionary act.

Second, it was going to be extremely expensive for the deposit insurer (FSLIC and the federal government) to settle all the thrift business's insolvencies. A large share of the thrift business's ultimate losses was already incurred by the early 1980s. At a conservative estimate, it would have cost between $75 and $170 billion (in 1991 dollars) to remove all the insolvent thrifts from the market between 1978 and 1982. The regulators could have done almost nothing to avert these losses except wait for general economic conditions to improve and allow thrifts new ways to seek to increase their profits and net worth.

Policy decisions made during the 1960s and 1970s, together with the changed economic environment of the 1970s and 1980s, were together largely responsible for the pre-1984 thrift losses. The history of these earlier policies was discussed briefly in chapter 2. If the congressional decision making studied in that chapter (and in chapters 6–8) is any guide, however, one might infer that these earlier decisions were made in good faith as Congress grappled with difficult policy issues. But by the 1980s, these policies could not be changed in such a way as to save FSLIC. Virtually every savings and loan was insolvent at market values between 1981 and 1982.

Bank Board Options

What options, then, were open to the Bank Board in the early 1980s? It could "resolve" the thrift insolvencies by liquidating them, merging them, providing them with financial assistance, or placing them in a receivership. Patience—that is, forbearance—was another option: the Bank Board could allow thrifts to continue operating until economic conditions improved. Deregulation was a third option: thrifts could be permitted to invest in assets other than home mortgages to boost their earnings.

The Bank Board aggressively pursued the first option. Between 1980 and 1982, the Bank Board sold, merged, liquidated, or provided financial assistance to 361 S&Ls in return for close supervision— that was more than three times as many thrifts as had failed in the previous forty years.[12] In 1982 alone, the Bank Board handled 247 thrift insolvencies, or about the same number of thrifts that appeared insolvent according to GAAP.

The Bank Board also chose the second option by taking several steps to give marginal thrifts breathing space until economic conditions improved. It exchanged "net worth" certificates with thrifts, it altered RAP standards to allow thrifts to report higher asset values, and it lowered the amount of net worth that thrifts were required to hold. The first two steps served to increase the amount of book value net worth that thrifts could report, and the third reduced the amount of book value net worth they were required to have. The net worth certificate program provided the thrift business with a relatively small increase in net worth (less than $3 billion at its peak); it need not be discussed further.[13] Changing the RAP and lowering net worth requirements have been much more controversial steps.

RAP (or, as it is sometimes called, "creative regulatory accounting principles") has been vilified by most commentators. Paul Zane Pilzer, for instance, writes that "the regulators instituted an array of gimmicky accounting rules that completely ignored traditional notions of profitability, safety, and soundness. The new accounting procedures . . . represented the most cynical kind of misuse of official power."[14] Pizzo, Fricker, and Muolo call RAP "voodoo accounting."[15] Mayer argues that RAP creates "deceptions," "legitimates fraud," and gives "a direct invitation to cheating."[16] The kindest thing said about RAP was that it was "perverse."[17] Yet some changes in RAP were clearly sensible.[18] Other modifications of RAP—such as those involving "appraised equity capital" and "deferred loan losses," designed to increase the reported net worth of the thrift business— deserve discussion both because they have been the object of such scorn and because they help illustrate the dilemmas regulators faced.

Under GAAP, thrifts carried any property they actually owned on their books at its purchase price. In November 1982, RAP was changed to allow thrifts to revalue this property at its currently appraised market price and to count this "appraised equity capital" as part of its net worth. In other words, RAP moved away from book value accounting and toward market value accounting, at least regarding the property the thrifts owned. While many experts have lauded market value accounting in principle, they have been appalled at the way it worked in the appraisal of equity capital. Although most thrifts could and did properly credit their accounts for the appreciation of their own offices, a number of thrifts abused this provision horribly.

> In "daisy-chain" situations, where a number of S&Ls worked to-gether, . . . it was child's play to trade land parcels and securities back and forth . . . at prices that apparently grew and grew. Such trades generated their own fake profits and gave appraisers whose main tool was the recent sales prices of comparable property an excuse to rocket up appraised values of all land in that neighborhood. . . . Given the low professional and moral state of the real estate appraisal, this [ap-praised equity capital] rule was a direct invitation to cheating.[19]

Thrifts and appraisers, by this account, manipulated market prices to their immediate advantage and to FSLIC's ultimate loss.[20]

Whereas the appraised equity capital provision was an attempt to move toward market value accounting, the Bank Board's deferred loan loss regulation moved in the opposite direction. Before this reg-ulation, when a thrift sold an asset for less than its purchase price, the thrift had to record this loss on its books immediately. In May 1982 the Bank Board ruled that thrifts could report these losses over a ten-year period (hence the term "deferred loan loss"). Thrifts could continue to carry the unamortized portion of the loss as an asset, even though the asset "had absolutely no market value whatsoever."[21] Thrifts, by carrying these "assets," were able to report higher net worths than they otherwise could have. This deferred loan loss provi-sion may look like an especially blatant attempt by regulators to cook the books. Let us review the situation that existed when the regula-tion was implemented, however.

At the end of 1981, thrifts had most of their assets in long-term, low interest home mortgage loans. Most of these loans were earning interest below the current market.[22] As long as market interest rates remained high, the net worth of the business would continue to erode. Most S&Ls were already insolvent at market prices, and virtu-ally every S&L was predicted to be insolvent according to GAAP within two years. Yet thrifts were reluctant to sell these assets be-cause GAAP allowed them to be carried at book value but required they be written down to market value if they were sold. However, unless thrifts could sell these low-yielding assets, they would not be able to invest in assets that would earn market rates.

Consider the implications. Under GAAP, the ultimate loss to the thrift would be the same whether the thrift sold low-yielding assets now or later; GAAP affected only the timing, not the size, of the loss. But GAAP encouraged S&Ls to hold on to their money-losing assets so that they could delay recognition of losses that had already occurred. RAP reversed this. Like GAAP, only the timing, not the size, of the loss was affected. Unlike GAAP, however, RAP encouraged S&Ls to restructure their portfolios by selling the low yield loans and purchase higher-yielding ones. In this way, RAP encouraged the thrift business to take action to improve its earnings.

Whatever one concludes about the merit of these changes to RAP, it is important to note they had only a modest effect, compared to GAAP, on the net worth of the thrift business. Between 1981 and 1984, thrift business RAP net worth grew from 0.12 percent to 0.94 percent above GAAP (see table 5.1).[23] Yet thrift business GAAP net worth was between 5.6 percent and 20.5 percent above market value net worth during this period. Between 85 and 99 percent of the discrepancy between market value and book value net worth was thus produced by GAAP; RAP provided the remaining 1–15 percent. Put another way, compared to GAAP, RAP overvalued thrift net worth by $9 billion in 1984; GAAP overvalued thrift net worth by $55 billion compared to market net worth. And this was the year GAAP overvalued market net worth least and RAP overvalued it most. Although accounting standards are to blame for overstating the thrift business's net worth, GAAP—the standard in the business world—is much more blameworthy than RAP.

In addition to setting RAP standards, the Bank Board also had the power to establish minimum net worth requirements. If a thrift's book net worth fell below this minimum, the Bank Board had substantially increased authority over the firm's operations. Prior to 1980 thrifts had to maintain a net worth of 5 percent of liabilities. When Congress passed DIDMCA, it gave the Bank Board the authority to set net worth requirements between 3 and 6 percent. The Bank Board took advantage of this power by reducing its RAP net worth requirement from

5 percent to 4 percent in 1980; in 1982 it further lowered the minimum to 3 percent.[24]

Two major criticisms may be addressed to the policy of reducing net worth standards. First, because net worth is the buffer that protects the deposit insurer, reductions in net worth increase the exposure of the insurer to losses. This is true. But the Bank Board reduced the *standards*, not the *amount* of net worth actually available to the business. Reducing net worth standards merely recognized that the real net worth of the thrift business had already vanished. If the Bank Board had maintained the 5 percent net worth standard, the vast majority of thrift assets would have been in S&Ls that were not in compliance.[25] Few have suggested that government can work effectively if it maintains standards with which few can comply (though such standards may highlight the severity of a problem).

The more important claim, however, is that reducing net worth standards reduced the ability of the Bank Board "to restrain thrifts whose incentives for risk-taking were increasing." In principle, thrifts that were solvent by RAP standards, but did not meet the Bank Board's net worth standards, were subject to "tighter regulatory scrutiny and control."[26] According to this line of argument, if the Bank Board had maintained higher net worth standards it would have been better able to keep thrifts from embarking on high risk, and ultimately costly, ventures.

There are problems with this claim, however. In 1982, 415 thrifts, with $220 billion in assets, had below 3 percent RAP net worth. The same year, another 1,100 thrifts, with $377 billion in assets (almost 50 percent of the business total), had between 3 and 5 percent RAP net worth.[27] In chapter 4 I discussed the human resources of the Bank Board and challenged the notion that the lack of staff was a major cause of FSLIC's losses. This does not imply, however, that the Bank Board did or could have obtained the personnel to oversee in depth more than twice the number of S&Ls it was already obligated to monitor.

More significantly, what exactly was the Bank Board to scrutinize, and on what basis would it exercise control? A regulatory agency operates best when its standards are clear and when violations of its principles can be clearly determined. The Bank Board's third option for bringing the thrift business back to health—deregulation—made it harder to do this.[28] The Bank Board entered 1983 having altered its RAP to provide the thrift business some breathing room until economic conditions became more favorable. The thrift business began that year with the new asset powers granted it through the DIDMCA and Garn–St. Germain Acts. And after mid-1982, economic conditions did improve rapidly as interest rates receded from their historical peak.

During the next two years the thrift business grew rapidly and made major changes in the assets and liabilities it held. In 1983 and 1984 the thrift business grew almost 10 percent faster than the economy as a whole—and even faster compared to the banking industry (figure 5.1). Hundreds of individual thrifts grew much faster than the

FIGURE 5.1

Thrift and Bank Growth, 1978–1988

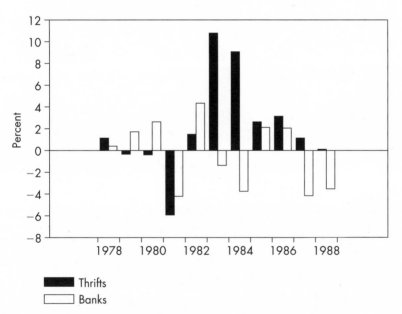

Thrifts
Banks

Source: Author's calculations from data in Office of Thrift Supervision, *Combined Financial Statements, FSLIC-Insured Institutions, 1988*, November 1989, iii; Federal Deposit Insurance Corporation, *Statistics on Banking, 1993*, April 1994, A-3; *Annual Report*, Council of Economic Advisors, *Economic Report of the President* (Washington, D.C.: U.S. Government Printing Office 1995), 274.

Note: Figure presents percent growth in total assets minus percent growth in gross domestic product. Positive numbers indicate that thrifts or banks were growing faster than the economy as a whole.

business average. "Nontraditional" liabilities (primarily brokered deposits and jumbo certificates of deposit), grew rapidly in size and importance (figure 5.2). Nontraditional assets (such as commercial mortgage loans, land loans, consumer loans, and commercial loans) tripled from $70 billion to $210 billion, or from 11 to 18 percent of all assets (figure 5.3). Rapidly growing thrifts, moreover, tended to rely most heavily on their new asset and liability powers. As figures 5.4 and 5.5 show, there was a direct correlation between thrift growth rates and the use of nontraditional liabilities and assets.

As it turned out, many of the most rapidly growing S&Ls failed. The 637 thrifts that FSLIC liquidated or sold between 1986 and 1989

FIGURE 5.2

Nontraditional Liabilities at FSLIC-Insured Thrifts, 1980–1988

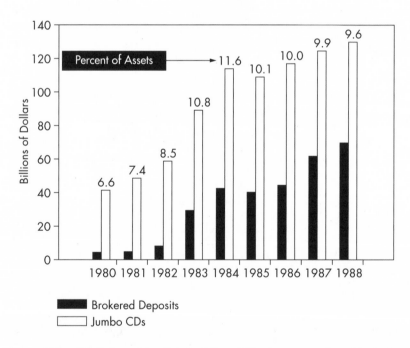

Source: Office of Thrift Supervision, *Combined Financial Statements, FSLIC-Insured Institutions, 1988*, November 1989, iii, viii; James R. Barth, Philip F. Bartholomew, and Carol J. Labich, "Moral Hazard and the Thrift Crisis: An Analysis of the 1988 Resolutions," Federal Home Loan Bank Board, Research Paper no. 160, 1989, 14.

Note: Brokered deposits and jumbo certificates of deposit are overlapping categories.

FIGURE 5.3

Nontraditional Assets at FSLIC-Insured Thrifts, 1980–1988

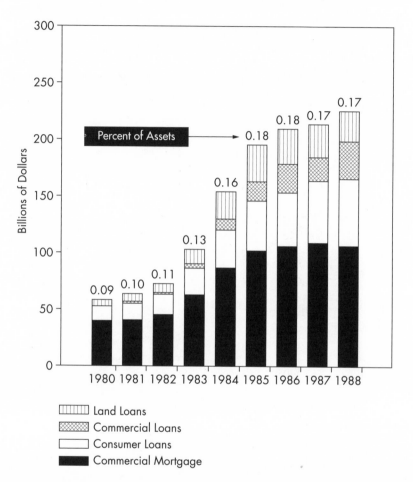

Source: Office of Thrift Supervision, *Combined Financial Statements, FSLIC-Insured Institutions, 1988*, November 1989, viii.

had doubled their assets between 1982 and 1985, while the rest of the business was only growing at about half that rate.[29] Furthermore, "a growing number of studies . . . indicate that the nontraditional investments (and methods) of the rapidly growing thrifts of the 1983–1985 period were disproportionately responsible for the wave of insolvencies and their huge costs to the FSLIC."[30] Most of the *increase*

FIGURE 5.4

Asset Growth and Liability Composition, 1984

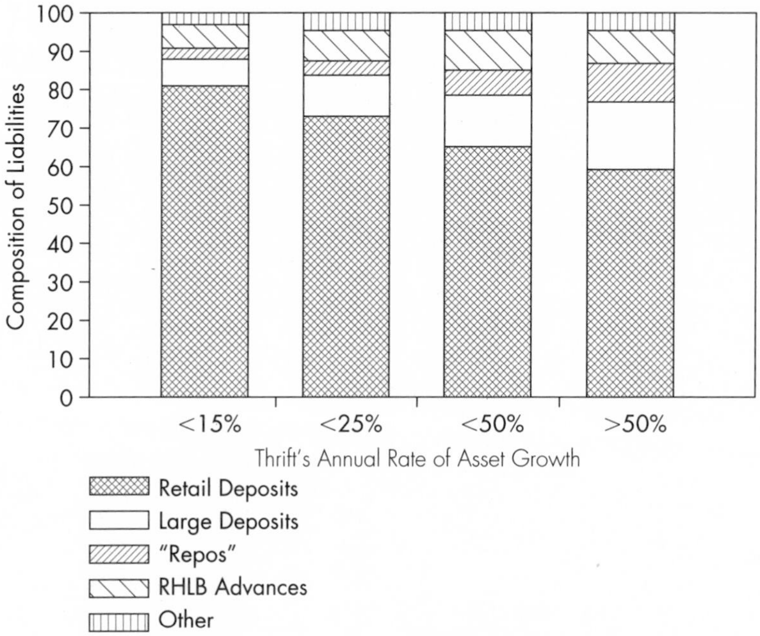

Thrift's Annual Rate of Asset Growth

Retail Deposits
Large Deposits
"Repos"
RHLB Advances
Other

Source: Patrick I. Mahoney and Alice P. White, "The Thrift Industry in Transition," *Federal Reserve Bulletin* 71 (March 1985), 137–56; data on 150.

in FSLIC's losses after 1982 came from assets that went bad at these rapidly growing thrifts.[31]

If the FHLBB had stopped these thrifts from growing so quickly and from making such bad investments, it would undoubtedly have reduced FSLIC's losses. Why did the FHLBB not do so? There are several possibilities. Perhaps the FHLBB allowed thrifts to grow quickly and to make large amounts of nontraditional investments because it thought such a strategy was good (or at least not bad) for the thrift business and FSLIC. Or perhaps the FHLBB saw this strategy as dangerous to FSLIC, yet lacked the legal tools to put a stop to it. Or finally, perhaps the FHLBB saw the strategy as unsafe and possessed the authority to stop it, but failed to do so anyway. For the FHLBB to prevent thrifts from growing rapidly and making high risk investments, in other words, the FHLBB needed to recognize the problem, develop policies to stop it, and

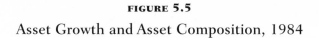

FIGURE **5.5**

Asset Growth and Asset Composition, 1984

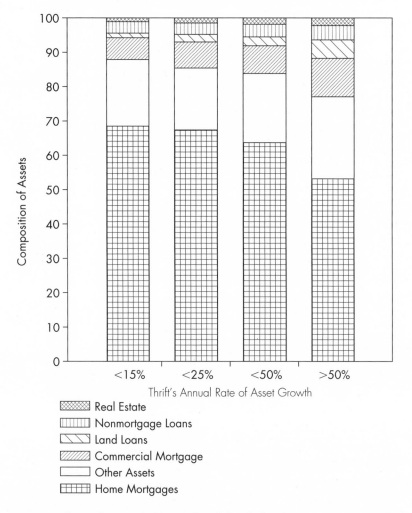

Source: Patrick I. Mahoney and Alice P. White, "The Thrift Industry in Transition," *Federal Reserve Bulletin* 71 (March 1985), 137–56; data on 150.

then effectively implement these policies. It took the FHLBB three long years to take these three steps (and, in some cases, full implementation took considerably longer). The next section will explain the reason. Appendix 2 offers some classic cases in which the Bank Board was unable to restrain excessive risk taking by individual S&Ls.

Recognizing the Problem

In the third quarter of 1982, deposits were still flowing out of the thrift business, as they had been for almost two years. This outflow was seen as a great threat to the business. The thrift business finally reported a net increase in new deposits during the final quarter, however, and beginning in 1983, money poured into the thrift business. In the next nine months, thrifts gained over $54 billion in new deposits, more than it had obtained in the previous six years combined. Although the pace moderated after that, another $68 billion in new deposits found their way onto the thrift business books in the next year and a half (before there was again a net outflow).[32]

The Bank Board did nothing to slow the flow during the first nine months of 1983. White, who served on the Bank Board between November 1986 and August 1989, argues that "through all of 1983 and early 1984 the FHLBB was largely unaware of the extent of the destructive processes that the unbalanced economic deregulation had encouraged. . . . Thrifts did seem to be growing their way out of their difficulties."[33] There are some good reasons why the Bank Board did not take action to stop the growth, and why the thrift business *did* seem to be growing out of its distress.

First, there was a solid consensus at the time that thrifts needed to expand to survive. As Mayer put it, in 1982 "very rapid growth to raise the average yield on mortgages seemed one of the few plausible ways for the industry to stay afloat."[34] It seems that regulators, economists, and thrift managers all agreed on this point.[35] I find virtually no *contemporaneous* disagreement with the idea that growth would help thrifts recover from their problems.

The reasoning behind the "progrowth" strategy is obvious. A key indicator of thrift business health is its net-worth-to-assets ratio. For the thrift business to regain its vitality in the early 1980s, it needed to increase this ratio. Logically, there are two ways to increase this ratio: increase the numerator (net worth) or reduce the denominator (assets). An S&L can boost its net worth from external sources (e.g., selling stock) or internal ones (e.g., making profits on investments), or it can sell some of its assets. Although net worth and assets are analytically distinct (and separate items on the balance sheet), they are empirically related: changing the value of assets usually changes the value of net worth. Since profits are generated from assets, for example, raising profits requires either growth or the exchange of lower-yielding assets for higher-yielding ones. Selling assets also affects net worth, however. If the assets can be sold at a profit, net worth may increase (if part of the profit is kept), but if the assets are sold at a loss, net worth must decrease.

After 1982, and especially in 1983 and 1984, the thrift business as a whole did attempt to grow out of its problems. During these years thrifts generally tried to increase net worth by increasing assets. Many of these assets, it turned out, were not profitable. Even though thrift GAAP net worth increased from $20 billion in 1982 to $39 billion in 1986, thrift assets increased even more, so the business's net worth ratio fell.

It is now fashionable to argue that the thrift business should not have been allowed to attempt to grow out of its problems, but instead should have had its assets reduced.[36] The reasoning behind this argument is that it is much harder to increase the net worth ratio by making profitable investments than by simply selling assets. This reasoning seems sensible, especially when the economy is in a recession and the real estate markets in particular are depressed. It seemed less sensible before the end of 1982. The net worth ratio can be increased by selling assets only if the assets are not sold at a loss.[37] Because most assets at most thrifts were earning below market rates of return, they could only have been sold at a loss.[38] This loss could only have been made up from net worth. Selling the worst assets would have reduced the net worth ratio most. To minimize these losses, thrifts would have had to sell their best assets first. This is hardly a sound long-term strategy. Yet studies about the effect of rapid growth were unfortunately not available at the time they were most needed.[39] The analyses that were finished—more misfortune— did not provide clear policy guidance to the Bank Board. Let us look at growth first, and nontraditional assets second.[40]

The Bank Board had already become sufficiently worried about the dangers that rapidly growing thrifts posed to the deposit insurance fund by the end of 1983, when they first proposed the rule to limit brokered deposits. This proposal, as we shall see in chapter 7, was eventually ruled illegal by a federal district court, and the Bank Board turned to other measures to limit growth.

The puzzle was that, although there were many specific examples of thrifts that had grown rapidly and were in financial trouble, there was no clear relationship between growth and problems.[41] Systematic studies could not demonstrate that rapid growth caused thrift net worth to decline.[42] Members of Congress made the plausible suggestion that the Bank Board should focus on identifying and controlling specific instances of abuse rather than imposing unnecessary, ineffective, and harmful regulations on both sound and unsound thrifts.[43] The problem, from an agency perspective, is that it is much simpler to work with businesses by monitoring and enforcing rules than by using regulatory discretion.

It is fair to wonder why the Bank Board did not better restrain the growth of these thrifts and better monitor their investments to prevent these huge costs from occurring. To determine why these regulatory failures occurred, it is important to examine the factors that were affecting thrift solvency. These factors presented the regulators with a conundrum. Although the evidence is not definitive, it appeared that the thrifts that were taking advantage of the new thrift powers and growing rapidly during the period of change in 1983 and 1984 were prospering, while those that were not were failing.

Studies examining the thrifts that failed between 1981 and 1984, for example, commonly drew two conclusions. Thrifts that failed tended to have "spread" problems: they had relatively high interest expenses compared to interest income. This should come as no surprise, since high interest rates were primarily responsible for eroding the net worth of the entire business. On the other hand, there was little evidence that risky investments—loans that turned sour—had contributed very much to these failures.

Loan Fees

In addition, growth seemed to work, at least at first. Although the fastest-growing thrifts would eventually fail in large numbers and at great expense to FSLIC, *Savings Institutions* magazine reported that through 1984 the fastest-growing S&Ls had the highest returns on assets and the highest reported net worth.[44] The main reason for this temporary profitability, and for the eventual losses, was the treatment of loan fees. In the most thorough published discussion of this issue, Lowy concludes that "permissive accounting for loan fees was the linchpin of the boom-and-bust process. Among the fastest growers, loan fees accounted for substantially all net income in the crucial years of 1983 and 1984. . . . Up-front fees were the drug—the crack, the heroin—on which S&Ls binged in the mid-1980s."[45]

The simple part of the loan fee issue is this.[46] When an S&L made a loan, it was allowed to collect an up-front fee and immediately report this fee as income. The size of the fee the S&L could charge depended on the size and riskiness of the loan: the bigger and riskier the loan, the bigger the fee. Borrowers, for their part, would be more inclined to pay high loan fees if they did not risk very much of their own money in doing so. Borrowers could avoid such risk if the loan they received included the fee as part of the loan, or if the interest rate on the loan was reduced by the amount necessary to offset a higher up-front fee. As a result, thrifts had incentives to make large and risky loans in order to charge high fees and boost their current income, and they could assess such fees by lending borrowers the fee itself or by reducing the interest rate they would pay. Stated in this simple fashion, the arrangement looks grotesque: "Obviously, an S&L shouldn't be able to record income just by making a speculative loan and paying itself fees by making more."[47]

It is, however, neither bizarre nor even controversial that thrifts (or any lender) should charge up-front fees for loans and should report these fees as income. The lender, after all, is providing a service to the borrower and charges a fee for this service just like any other business. These fees are income in the usual sense of the word. The accounting profession has certainly never questioned the appropriateness of treating loan fees as income. Between these obvious and commonsensical observations, and the puzzling and bizarre outcomes that actually occurred within the thrift business, lay three tough questions that lacked clear answers during the mid-1980s. These questions were: What is a loan? How much income does a fee on a loan create? How much loan fee income can be reported, and when can the S&L report it?

What Is a Loan?

The definition of *loan* may appear obvious, until one tries to distinguish between a loan and an investment. One difference concerns risks and returns. In general, investments are considered a higher risk, with a potentially higher return, than loans.[48] Therefore, the accounting profession treats the income derived from real estate loans and real estate investments differently. In particular, lenders are not allowed to count fees from investments as income until after the investment has begun to turn a profit, whereas fees from loans can be counted immediately.[49]

Although the accounting profession treated real estate loans and investments differently, it had not clearly defined the difference between them in the early 1980s. When S&Ls began making real estate "loans" in earnest in 1982, accountants were typically inclined to treat them as such under GAAP. As a result, "in audited financial statements for 1982, it is [now] clear that a great many transactions made by S&Ls which should have been accounted for as investments in real estate, and therefore should *not* have resulted in any income, were treated as loans and *did* result in immediate income."[50]

In November 1983, the major groups that set accounting standards (the Financial Accounting Standards Board, FASB, and the American Institute of Certified Public Accountants, AICPA) tried to devise better standards for distinguishing real estate loans and investments.[51] In doing so, the AICPA established a new category called "acquisition, development, and construction" (or ADC) loans which "in *some* instances" "*may* not" be treated as loans for auditing purposes.[52] Additional guidance provided by the AICPA did little to clarify exactly what "some instances" and "may not" meant.[53] The accounting profession, as well as the Bank Board, remained uncertain about how to differentiate between real estate loans and investments through 1983. Thrifts, in contrast, were certain that treating ADC loans as loans allowed them to claim higher profits; and they were certain they needed these profits. Thrifts therefore classified their ADC loans as loans, and recorded the income from the fees.

Accounting firms are in a tenuous position. They recognize that their credibility (and hence long-term success) depends on their ability to provide honest audits that fairly represent their clients' financial condition. Yet they gain work by satisfying their clients, who presumably are almost always interested in generously stating their true financial condition. Accounting firms can probably best balance these conflicts when GAAP is unambiguous. But when GAAP is ambiguous, an accounting firm may be inclined to accept the client's report in order to preserve the accountants' business. Since the 1983 AICPA did not provide plain guidance on the treatment of ADC loans, accountants continued to accept S&L decisions through 1983.

Little changed in 1984, even though the dangers of ADC loans to FSLIC were becoming increasingly apparent.[54] The AICPA issued further guidance that year, in essence reiterating the cryptic standards it developed in 1983. The FASB, for its part, concluded that the AICPA's guidance was "adequate." The Bank Board proposed that ADC loans be treated by GAAP standards, even though these standards were based on the confusing AICPA instructions. Thrifts, meanwhile, continued to make ADC loans and to record the fees from these loans as income. Accountants, applying unclear standards, continued to give thrifts the benefit of the doubt. Accounting groups and the Bank Board continued to study the issue.

Not until February 1986—three years after the issue first became significant—did AICPA and FASB clarify the issue and provide firm guidance on the treatment of ADC "loans" as investments. "Thus, the accounting profession permitted perverse incentives to persist for three years after they had been discovered."[55] By then, most of the growth generated by loan fees was over.

How Much Income Does a Fee Create?

When an S&L makes a loan, it receives income through fees. It also incurs expenses. One such expense is the creation of a "loan loss reserve" fund to help cover loans that are not repaid. Additions to the loan loss reserve are paid out of the fees and thus reduce fee income. In theory, the loan loss reserve should provide an accurate estimate of the likely cost of the expected defaults, and enough fee income would be transferred to reserves to cover these expected losses.

The problem is that no one knew—or knows—how large loan loss reserves should be.[56] Potential losses depend on the characteristics of the borrowers, the condition of the markets, and the judgment of the lenders. Because it is extremely difficult to predict the future performance of borrowers, markets, or even management judgment, thrifts typically looked to their past experience in assessing their likely losses. But past losses are of limited use in estimating future ones, especially if there were few losses in the past or if the thrift is moving into new lines of business.

This is exactly what happened. Thrifts had always made single-family home loans for the most part, and since World War II, defaults had often been close to zero and perpetually well below 1 percent. Therefore, "most S&Ls established *no* loan loss reserves. This was reflected in, and basically blessed by, the AICPA *Savings and Loan Accounting Guide*."[57] When thrifts began making many commercial real estate loans after 1982, they argued that such loans were little different from residential home loans and loan loss reserves should be set accordingly (that is, close to zero). Accountants, lacking both historical justification and GAAP guidance, allowed thrifts to avoid setting up what might have been sufficient reserves. When loan loss reserves were needed in a big way after 1986, there were no reserves to call upon.

How Much Loan Fee Income Can Be Reported, and When Can the S&L Report It?

Once it is determined that a loan *is* a loan so that fees can be considered income, and what actual income (fees minus loan loss reserves) is involved, questions still arise about the timing and reporting of this income. Once again, the answers were obscure. The AICPA's *Savings and Loan Accounting Guide* had "six confusing pages on the subject."[58] In this case, however, the Bank Board did provide clear guidance. Thrifts could declare fees of 2 percent of the loan's value (2.5 percent for construction loans) immediately, but had to defer any additional fee income until later. Thrifts took the Bank Board rule to heart and typically claimed the maximum fee possible. Because it was difficult to figure out what the GAAP standards were, accountants also typically went along with the Bank Board standard.

The Bank Board had itself raised the limit on fee income from 1 percent to 2 percent of loan value in 1979. It did so explicitly to increase reported earnings for the thrift business at a time when it was suffering from high interest rates. As fee income became an increasingly important source of earnings—remember, fee income equalled all reported earnings for the entire business between 1983 and 1987—it became increasingly difficult to remove it as a source of income. FASB did not approve a final rule on the deferral of loan fees until December 1986 (effective in 1988), when it declared that no fees could be reported as income at the time of the loan but instead had to be spread over the loan's life.[59] The Bank Board followed FASB's decision in its accounting standards.

The ability of thrifts to treat real estate investments as loans, to avoid setting up adequate loan loss reserves, and to declare fees of up to 2.5 percent as immediate income had two negative consequences. It encouraged thrifts to make loans because they wanted fees, not because the projects themselves were sound. Senseless individual projects and needless overbuilding resulted. It also allowed thrifts to boost their net worth, and thus to grow rapidly, even after the Bank Board had put rules in place to limit growth for S&Ls with little net worth. Both outcomes increased FSLIC's losses substantially.

The essential point, however, is not so much that loan fees were bad but that they were *legal* and *permissible*. Thrifts' use of them broke no law and violated no standard. It thus seems unlikely that the Bank Board could have prevented much of the growth in nontraditional assets unless it had changed its rules. The problem was not so much in the enforcement as in the rules themselves.

Well, one might respond, if loan fees had such negative consequences, then there should have been a law against them. The accounting profession and the Bank Board undoubtedly agreed. But it is a big step from agreeing that there should be a standard to actually devising one that both does what it is intended to do and does not make the problems worse. It took three years for the AICPA, FASB, and the Bank Board to develop a satisfactory distinction between loans and investments so that fees could be handled appropriately. It took a good number of unfortunate lessons in loan losses to determine that larger loss reserves should have been created and required. The

Bank Board did have a clear standard for allowing thrifts to declare fees as income, however, and this standard was too lenient. But tightening the standard would have wiped out the net income of the thrift business for about five years, a fairly serious consequence.

Members of the Bank Board, moreover, were not the only ones slow to come to terms with the growing problems within the thrift business. In particular, private sector accountants were equally slow. The one study conducted on the treatment of the thrift business by accounting firms during the post-deregulation period supports this view.[60] The General Accounting Office (GAO) examined the most recent audits performed by independent certified public accountants (CPAS) at eleven of the twenty-nine S&Ls that failed in the Dallas FHLB district between January 1, 1985, and September 30, 1987. This sample of thrifts had two things in common: they had grown rapidly in the three to four years before failing, and their financial reports did not show large loan losses.[61] The CPAs' final audit reports of these thrifts before their failure showed a total book value net worth of $44 million, yet at the time of their failure (five to seventeen months after their last audit) the thrifts had a combined market value net worth of approximately minus $1.5 *billion*.[62]

While a variety of factors (sloppy work, inadequate reporting, etc.) contributed to the inaccurate audits, the GAO also argued that "CPA firms did not always have sufficient knowledge of the risks associated with land and ADC [real estate acquisition, development and construction] loans, and . . . the CPA firms did not always respond quickly to the dramatic changes in the financial operations of their individual clients or the S&L industry."[63] That is, the accounting firms that GAO audited did not know how to appraise the collateral behind land and ADC loans; they did not know how to assess the likelihood that the borrower would repay the note or that the thrift would successfully collect; and they did not become overly concerned about the swift growth in thrift assets. But these weaknesses were not unique to the audited auditors. GAO also found that

> the American Institute of Certified Public Accountants has not responded quickly to all the major changes in the S&L industry. . . .
> The AICPA's auditing guide and procedures for S&Ls . . . was last

substantively revised in 1979. It contains little discussion of the risks associated with land and ADC loans; the effect of increases in restructured and past-due loans on collectibility; coordinating audit work with the results of regulatory examinations; the importance of disclosing regulatory actions and violations to depositors, shareholders, regulators, and other users of audit reports; nor does it include the requirement to report all material internal control weaknesses.[64]

In short, the accounting profession was scarcely prepared to audit the S&L business reliably as it made the transition to deregulation.

Other evidence also raises strong questions about whether accounting firms were able to judge thrifts' conditions accurately during this period. By 1994, four of the six biggest accounting firms had agreed to pay the FDIC (as the successor to the FSLIC) over $1 billion to settle claims regarding their handing of S&Ls.[65]

Summary: The Bank Board Between 1983 and 1985

Most observers have rebuked the Bank Board for acting too slowly during the critical years between 1983 and 1985, when so much of the thrift industry's ultimately costly growth occurred.[66] According to this view, the Bank Board should have recognized problems sooner, developed policies to remedy these problems more quickly, and implemented these policies more effectively. True enough, FSLIC's losses would have been reduced if the Bank Board had taken these steps. Nevertheless, two comments about this perspective are worth mentioning in conclusion.

Identifying Problems Does Not Equal Devising Solutions

The Bank Board did not recognize some incipient problems at the beginning of 1983. At the end of 1982, the Bank Board had indeed encouraged some of the activities—especially higher than normal asset growth and greater use of nontraditional investments—that would later create additional losses for FSLIC. The Bank Board, to be fair, was

not alone in making these mistakes. It is difficult to find anyone recommending in 1982 that thrifts would regain health by sticking with
their traditional home mortgage assets and forgoing growth. Remember, for the previous three years the big concerns for the thrift business
were disintermediation ("negative growth") and asset concentration in
fixed-rate home mortgage loans. At that time, growth and nontraditional investments were seen as the solution, not the problem.

Toward the end of 1983, however, the Bank Board became increasingly persuaded that rapid growth and nontraditional assets
were going to become big problems for FSLIC. The evidence supporting this view was, alas, slim. Primarily because of the way GAAP
treated up-front loan fees, rapid growth and heavy use of real estate
(especially ADC) loans actually looked like the most profitable strategy. It must have seemed perverse (if not vindictive) for the Bank
Board to try to stop these "healthy" S&Ls when so many others that
were not expanding as aggressively appeared to be in worse shape.

One could argue that the regulators were in the best position to
know what needed to be done, and that they should have been given
the power to do it even though little generalizable evidence existed to
support their views. Activists may be sympathetic with this argument,
both in this specific case and more generally. Yet this view is not widely
accepted; there is a strong presumption in the United States that the
federal government should be distinctly limited in its ability to take action against businesses unless it can convincingly demonstrate that action is needed and that it can be applied consistently across firms.

Unfortunately, deciding to take action to address the problems of
loan fees, risky real estate investments, and rapid growth is not the
same as determining the correct course of action. The Bank Board
spent a lot of time and energy trying to slow down rapidly growing
thrifts by limiting their use of brokered funds, for example, even
though most analysts argue that such regulations were both ineffective and counterproductive.[67]

Acting Quickly Does Not Equal Acting Effectively

It did take a long time to impose regulations to restrain excessive risk
taking by thrifts. For example, the Bank Board first proposed to limit

growth (by restricting brokered deposits) in January 1984, but did not have a growth-limiting regulation in place for more than a year, when net worth requirements were imposed (January 1985). Regulations limiting direct investments were first proposed in May 1984, yet final regulations were not imposed until May 1985. It took at least five years to create rules that treated loan fee income in such a way as to reduce the perverse incentives that existed for making loans to boost immediate income rather than not long-term stability. Given the possibility that FSLIC's losses might have been substantially reduced if these regulations had been imposed earlier, it would be easy to conclude that the Bank Board delayed too long in adopting these rules. Before accepting this conclusion, however, we need to examine what happened in three cases where the Bank Board did act swiftly to change its regulations.

Two of these regulations—concerning appraised equity capital and loan loss deferrals—have already been described. Both were approved rapidly. The appraised equity capital regulation was proposed and adopted in just over two months. The loan loss deferral rule was approved in September 1981 without even receiving public comment. Both regulations, as we have seen, were ruthlessly criticized as increasing FSLIC's losses.

The third regulation concerned ownership of joint-stock thrifts. (Thrifts could be chartered as either joint-stock firms, owned by the stockholders, or mutual firms, owned by the depositors.) Before 1981, a joint-stock thrift had to have at least 400 stockholders, with at least 125 from the community the S&L served, before it could qualify for deposit insurance. No individual could own more than 10 percent of the stock, and no "control group" could hold more 25 percent. (Commercial banks, in contrast, could be owned by a single stockholder, usually a holding company.) To create a "level playing field" and bring new investors into the business, Richard Pratt dropped the 400 owner requirement almost immediately after becoming Bank Board chairman in early 1981.

This rapid policy shift, like those described earlier, appears to have increased FSLIC's losses. The GAO, in a study of twenty-six large thrift failures, found that nineteen thrifts had the "presence of a dominant figure": "The dominant individual . . . initiate[s] a large number of poor-quality loans . . . before the board is aware of risks assumed, may commit the institution to unsound courses of action, or may take abusive practices."[68] Mayer has argued that "Pratt's decision to approve insurance charters for individually owned S&Ls was hugely expensive to the insurance fund."[69]

To review: the Bank Board has been chastised for moving too slowly to implement "good" regulations and castigated for choosing "bad" regulations (which it adopted too quickly). It is conceivable that there is something about the Bank Board decision-making process that leads to bad rules being approved quickly and good ones slowly. More plausible, perhaps, is that rules approved quickly are likely to prove unwise *because* they were adopted without due consideration, and that effective rules are helpful in part because they have been more carefully scrutinized.

Of course, it would be ideal if regulatory agencies made correct decisions quickly. But it is not easy for them to do so. Speed and quality often conflict. Speeding up the rule-making process does not guarantee that better rules are made.

The Bank Board and the Thrift Business Between 1985 and 1987

Between 1985 and 1987 the Bank Board implemented a number of regulations to reduce FSLIC's exposure to losses. For example, in early 1985 it limited the ability of thrifts with low net worths to grow rapidly.[70] In March 1985 it restricted the ability of state-chartered thrifts to make direct investments.[71] In September 1986, the Bank Board started phasing in higher net worth requirements that depended in part on the riskiness of the thrifts' assets. In addition, as noted in chapter 4, the Bank Board greatly increased its examination and supervisory staff in July 1985, and increased the salaries for this staff. Better regulations, and more staff to enforce them, helped the Bank Board get a better grip on the business.

This shows up in the numbers. Thrift business growth, which had averaged almost 20 percent in 1983 and 1984, fell to about 8 percent in 1985 and 1986—still somewhat faster than commercial banks, but not much (figure 5.1). In addition, the Bank Board appears to have been able, by and large, to restrain growth at shaky thrifts.[72] Nontraditional assets and liabilities both played a smaller role on thrift balance sheets in 1986 than they did in 1985 (figures 5.2 and 5.3). The relative importance of these assets and liabilities declined still further in 1987. The new regulations and the enlarged supervisory staff gave the Bank Board the rules and resources it needed to keep thrifts from increasing FSLIC's losses by very much after 1986 or so.

Most of FSLIC's eventual losses thus had already been incurred—if not actually paid—before 1986. The major sources of these losses were caused by the high interest rates between 1979 and 1982 and the bad loans and investments made between 1983 and 1985. It is very difficult to attribute specific losses to specific causes, however. I have seen only two attempts to do so, and both authors acknowledged that their estimates are heavily influenced by bad data and guesswork.[73] These estimates also do not have completely compatible categories or data.[74] Both authors nonetheless suggest that the interest rate losses that thrifts experienced before 1983 will account for perhaps 50 percent of the total cost of resolving thrift failures. Another 25 percent of the cost may be assigned to bad real estate loans and investments made primarily between 1983 and 1985. All other factors—including losses on other assets (junk bonds, for instance), excessive operating costs, fraud, and Bank Board delays in handling insolvencies—account for the remaining 25 percent of FSLIC's losses.

6

Congress Before Deregulation

LEGISLATION PROFOUNDLY AFFECTED the savings and loan business. Laws specified what thrifts could and could not do. Laws determined where S&Ls might obtain funds, how much they could pay for them, to whom they could lend it, and under what conditions these loans could be made. Laws do not just happen, however. Legislation is approved—or defeated—by Congress through the individual votes of the members of the House of Representatives and the Senate. Obviously, thrifts have an interest in what legislators do.

But do legislators have an interest in what thrifts want them to do? Most observers agree that during the 1980s Congress was particularly, and inappropriately, attentive to thrift concerns to the detriment of the public interest. This concern is stated most starkly by former Bank Board chairman Edwin Gray: "The fact is when it came to thrift matters in the Congress, the U.S. League and many of its affiliates were the de facto government. What the League wanted, it got. What it did not want from Congress, it had killed. . . . Every single day that I served as Chairman of the Federal Home Loan Bank Board, the U.S. League was in control of the Congress as an institution."[1] In the next three chapters I attempt to make sense of what Congress did, and did not do, for the thrift business during the thrift tragedy. In doing so, I will examine the debates over what Congress should have been doing and will look at Congress's votes to show what it did. These policy debates and votes cannot be considered apart from political goals or from the economic and institutional context. While it may be the luxury of the scholar to discover the theoretically optimal way to achieve a particular goal, Congress by necessity must grapple with the question: "What should we do now, given the mess we are in?" In general, Congress does not start from scratch in designing policies but works from "present conditions, present policies, and present objectives."[2]

In this chapter I generally omit the anecdotes concerning "who did what for whom" that have filled most other books about the thrift business.[3] I exclude these stories, but not because they are unimportant. It is difficult to be around politics without being impressed by the critical role that personal and idiosyncratic factors play in policy decisions. Yet the public rationales for the policy choices are also important, and these explanations have not generally been presented.

In particular, the reasons given in public can be useful in determining whether Congress acted responsibly. It is worth asking: Did Congress make reasonable efforts to consider the public policy issues, to examine evidence and to evaluate alternatives, and to choose policies that would serve a sensible conception of the public interest? Or did Congress act irresponsibly by ignoring clear and compelling rationales for resolving the thrift business's problems?

In these chapters on congressional debates I do not attempt to measure how much ideas and analyses, rather than constituents and ideologies, actually influenced thrift-related legislation.[4] Instead, I pay more attention to justifications than to motivations because motivations are private and justifications public. As a result, understanding motivations requires data from inside participants' heads, but justifications can be drawn from public sources. It is clearly easier to find out how legislators explain their actions than to determine the thinking that actually guided them.

But public justifications are important not only because they are accessible. They also provide us with information to judge the quality of these decisions in terms of efficiency, equity, risks, and feasibility.[5] After all, neither voters nor scholars can ever truly know what their representatives think, but they can judge what their legislators say and do.

Congressional concerns regarding the thrift business involve numerous highly complex and technical issues. I focus only on the three core issues affecting the financial condition of the thrift business and FSLIC. The first concerns the liability powers of thrifts, which determine where the thrifts can borrow money and how much they can pay for it. The second issue involves thrifts' asset powers, which determine the kinds of loans and investments thrifts can make. The third issue involves deposit insurance and includes such matters as how much insurance thrifts receive, how much they should pay for it, what should be done with insolvent thrifts, and how FSLIC's deficits should be funded. I consider liability and asset powers simultaneously in the first part of this chapter; deposit insurance is examined in the second part.[6]

Liability and Asset Powers

Until the end of the 1970s, thrifts had strict regulations regarding how much they could pay to borrow money and where they could borrow it. In 1966 ceilings were placed on the interest rates that thrifts could pay for deposits, and in 1963 narrow limits were imposed on the ability of S&Ls to collect funds from wholesalers. As a result, most thrift business liabilities were in the form of low interest retail savings deposits or other fixed-rate accounts. As late as 1977, more than 97 percent of thrift business liabilities were accounts *not* earning market rates.[7]

Prior to the 1980s, thrifts were also sharply limited in the kinds of loans and investments they could make; they primarily issued home mortgage loans. Federal savings and loan associations, for example, could not make commercial loans in real estate or construction, could not make consumer loans to any great extent, could not make direct investments, and could not hold commercial paper or offer credit cards.[8] The home mortgage loans they could make had to be fairly small (less than $75,000) and for property close to the S&L's offices. As a result, in 1979 FSLIC-insured associations held about 85 percent of their assets in mortgage loans and mortgage-backed securities (MBS).

The thrift business's average cost of liabilities and its average return on assets between 1965 and 1987 are shown in figure 6.1, and the difference between costs and returns is indicated in figure 6.2.

Between 1965 and 1978 the gap between the cost of liabilities and the return on assets was fairly large and stable.[9] Despite small dents during 1970 and 1974, this was a period of steady profitability for the thrift business. Indeed, the business had been profitable every year since at least 1945. Even during earlier "credit crunches"

FIGURE 6.1

Thrift Interest Costs and Asset Yields, 1970–1987

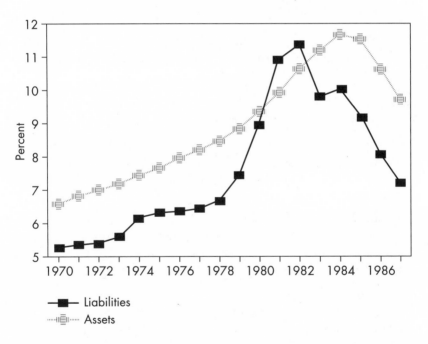

—■— Liabilities

······||≣||······ Assets

Source: For 1970–1979: Andrew S. Carron, *The Plight of the Thrift Institutions* (Washington, D.C.: Brookings, 1982), 15; for 1980–1987: Norman Strunk and Fred Case, *Where Deregulation Went Wrong: A Look at the Causes Behind Savings and Loan Failures in the 1980s* (Chicago: U.S. League of Savings Institutions, 1988), 36.

Note: Interest costs are the average cost of funds, FSLIC-insured savings institutions. Asset yields are the average interest rate on mortgages, FSLIC-insured savings institutions.

FIGURE 6.2

Interest Rate Spread, FSLIC-Insured Thrifts, 1970–1987

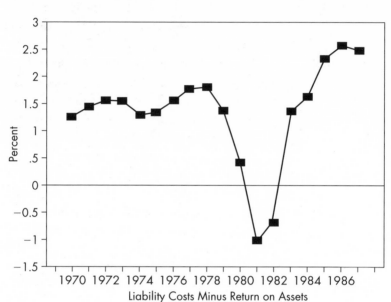

Source: Author's calculations from data in figure 6.1.

in 1966, 1969, and 1974, the gap between interest earned and interest paid closed only slightly.

Notice, however, that liability costs could be highly variable because thrift liabilities tended to have short maturities: a regular savings account, to take an extreme example, could be withdrawn any day without penalty. The average interest rates a thrift pays for its liabilities thus generally reflect what it currently pays. For example, when an S&L raises the interest it offers for savings deposits, it pays *all* depositors this rate, not just the new ones it attracts.

The thrift business's return on assets, in contrast, changes only slowly from year to year. Most thrift assets tend to have fixed rates and long terms, such as the standard thirty-year home mortgage loan. As a result, the average return on a thrift's assets depends heavily on what it has historically earned on these assets. When an S&L raises the rates on its home mortgage loans, for instance, it earns that rate only on the new loans; the existing loans retain their lower rates.

The cost of liabilities thus changes more quickly than does the return on assets (see figure 6.1). This means that even though return on assets increased every year between 1965 and 1983, the gap between returns and costs narrowed each time liability costs increased sharply, as they did in 1966, 1970, 1973–1974 and, in particular, between 1979 and 1981. Even though interest rates were soaring between 1979 and 1981, thrifts could only increase their return on assets gradually. Note also how sharply liability costs fell after 1981, and how thrift business return on assets continued to climb through 1983.

The Politics of Liability Regulation

Politicians are not just concerned about the way things are, but about the way they think things should be. In regulating thrift business liabilities, for example, they had three major goals.[10] The first was to stabilize the financial system, to eliminate "cut-throat" competition among financial institutions by keeping overly aggressive firms from bidding up the price of funds.[11] The second was to promote home ownership by providing a steady and inexpensive flow of funds to thrifts that would then be used for home mortgage loans.[12] These goals were to be achieved by keeping both the interest rates paid on liabilities and the interest rates received on assets low and stable. The third goal was to help the Federal Reserve conduct monetary policy by giving it a tool to control the supply of credit.[13]

Critics of the regulations, however, contended that limits on liability powers would not achieve these goals, would make the problems they were supposed to solve worse, or would create new problems. Interest rate ceilings, some contended, did not eliminate competition among financial institutions but served to increase nonprice competition among regulated institutions and to encourage unregulated financial institutions (such as money market mutual funds, MMMF) to enter the market.[14] In addition, interest rate ceilings on savings deposits caused "disintermediation," in which funds moved out of thrifts and banks and into the hands of competitors when market interest rates were above the interest rate ceilings. As a result, interest rate ceilings were seen as inefficient, because they kept regulated firms from competing on the basis of price, and destabilizing, because they prevented thrifts and banks from easily controlling their flow of liabilities.

Some analysts further contended that interest rate ceilings paradoxically made housing credit less available and more expensive.[15] Whenever market rates rose above the Regulation Q ceilings, the flow of deposits into thrifts diminished so that, all other things being equal, they had less money to lend. As the supply of deposits fell, therefore, thrifts could charge higher rates for the relatively scarce mortgage loans. Alternately, thrifts could raise additional funds by borrowing through the capital markets, but doing so was seen as more expensive than the market price of unregulated deposits.

Interest rate ceilings were also criticized as inefficient for macroeconomic policy.[16] Some believed that the economy was more prone to cyclical variations when interest rate ceilings were used to control inflation. It was believed that, by driving funds into unregulated firms (such as MMMFs) over which the Federal Reserve had little control, Regulation Q diminished the effectiveness of the Federal Reserve's monetary policy.[17]

Perhaps the most important criticism of interest rate ceilings, however, was that they were unfair to the "small saver." Low income households held most of their savings in the form of checking accounts, savings accounts, and low denomination investments such as savings bonds. All these investments were controlled by interest rate ceilings. The higher the level of market interest rates, the greater the gap between the rates that small and larger savers could earn. This amounted to discrimination against the small saver.[18]

The Situation in 1979

Unless Congress chose to ignore financial stability, monetary policy, housing affordability, and consumer equity, it had to consider all these important issues together in deciding what liability powers financial institutions should have. The more market interest rates exceeded the Regulation Q ceilings, the more difficult each issue became. In 1979, short-term interest rates were about six percentage points higher than the legal limit on passbook savings accounts, and this record gap was growing.[19] The financial system was becoming shakier and shakier, the Federal Reserve appeared to be losing control over monetary policy, the housing sector was in a deep slump, and the inequities in the treatment of savers seemed to be growing. Pressures grew for Congress to act.

But what should Congress do? The theories and evidence on each individual issue left legislators a great deal of uncertainty about which policies were appropriate, and these uncertainties were greatly increased when all the issues were considered jointly. There was no consensus, for example, on the way to make monetary policy more effective, or even on the impact that changing financial institution liability powers would have on the Federal Reserve's ability to manage the economy. Experts also disagreed on whether or not interest rate ceilings helped provide a steady and inexpensive source of housing finance, and whether deregulating interest rates would make the situation better or worse.[20] In addition, because thrifts, banks, and other financial institutions were all competitors, it was almost impossible for Congress to concern itself with the liability powers of a single group. Changing the liability powers of any one set of financial institutions would affect the profits (and stability) of the others, and policy makers would have been remiss to ignore these secondary effects.

Let us nonetheless take advantage of a luxury Congress did not have and ignore monetary policy, housing finance, and other financial institutions in determining the liability powers of the thrift business. Let us also limit our attention to one specific, but quite limited, proposal concerning interest rate deregulation—a proposal to create one new kind of deposit certificate—rather than the whole range of liability power issues facing Congress. Even with these radical simplifications, we can see that Congress did not face easy choices regarding the thrift business. But to understand this, we first need to review the context within which Congress acted.

Thrifts and banks faced substantial disintermediation during 1978, when interest rates increased sharply. As a result of this threat, on June 1 the Bank Board (and commercial bank regulators) authorized thrifts (and commercial banks) to offer a "money market certificate" (MMC) with a $10,000 minimum deposit, a maturity of six months, and an interest rate tied to the six-month Treasury bill rate.[21] For the first time since 1966, thrifts could pay market interest rates on at least one form of deposits.

These MMCs had an immediate and massive impact on thrift business balance sheets. Thrifts issued $34 billion in MMCs by November 1978 and $102 billion by November 1979. During this same period, however, the S&L business suffered a decline of $24 billion in passbook deposits and $15 billion in other small certificates.[22] The growth in MMCs, and the transfer of funds out of accounts with interest rate ceilings, sharply raised thrift interest costs (see figure 6.1). Although the thrift business was able to increase its interest income by writing some new loans with the proceeds from the MMCs, the growth in interest income did not nearly compensate for the rise in interest expenses (figure 6.2). As a result, thrift business profits dropped by 83 percent between 1978 and 1980.[23]

Despite the squeeze the MMCs put on thrift business earnings, Senator William Proxmire proposed legislation in 1979 requiring the Bank Board to authorize a new MMC that reduced the minimum deposit to $1,000.[24] The House and Senate both held extensive hearings and floor debate in 1979 and 1980 and amassed thousands of pages of testimony concerning the effect of this proposal (as well more general recommendations for eliminating interest rate ceilings) on the thrift business.[25] These hearings and debates sharpened the focus on two difficult problems.

First, interest rate ceilings discriminated against "small savers" (those who could not afford the $10,000 minimum MMC deposit) when market rates were above the Regulation Q ceilings. Most academic research supported this argument.[26] This point was also persuasively made to Congress by numerous groups claiming to represent the elderly and consumers.[27] Indeed, some criticized the legislation for not going far enough. The spokesman for Public Advocates argued: "We believe the proposed regs are cosmetic. . . . They will . . . result in $2 billion to $4.5 billion additional to consumers over the next year. . . . [But] they are just the tip of an iceberg of problems that will still deprive the consumer of $13 billion to $15 billion in interest."[28]

The idea that interest rate ceilings were unequivocally bad for the "little guy" was not a universally held or substantiated view, however. The AFL-CIO presented data suggesting that low income families in general would be losers if interest rate ceilings were lifted because they would have to pay more for loans and other financial services than they would gain in higher interest rates on their savings. According to its analysis, although net savers would benefit from higher interest rates, net borrowers would suffer losses, and over 50 percent of families held savings deposits of less than $1,000 or had no savings accounts at all.[29]

In addition, if market rates remained high, the short-run financial stability of the thrift business was threatened if even this one new certificate was authorized. Bank Board Chairman Robert McKinney, and later, Chairman Jay Janis, testified before Congress on numerous occasions that authorizing the new MMC would strongly depress thrift business profits. Janis argued that such a certificate would lower thrift business net returns on assets by half, to the lowest levels since World War II, and would double the number of thrifts expected to lose money in 1980 to almost 40 percent. Janis estimated that net return on assets for the business would fall to 0.14 percent in the second half of 1980 if the $1,000 MMC were approved, compared to 0.34 percent if the $10,000 limit were retained. (In contrast, return on assets was 0.84 percent in 1978.) According to Janis, the effect on the thrift business of authorizing these new certificates would be "devastating."[30]

After extensive and intensive debate Proxmire relented, amending his proposal on the floor of the Senate to read that

> upon unanimous agreement the Board of Governors of the Federal Reserve System, the FDIC, and the FHLBB shall reduce the minimum denomination of all certificates of deposit to not more than $1,000 as soon as feasible except that if the Board of Governors of the FRB or the Board of Directors of the FDIC or the FHLBB determines that economic conditions warrant or that such action is necessary to avoid a threat to the economic viability of depository institutions, the reductions . . . shall be postponed.[31]

As Proxmire himself noted, "To the extent that we reduce the money market certificate from $10,000 to $1,000, sure, we accommodate the small saver . . . but it can be at the great expense of the savings and loans. I am aware of that. This amendment would go to that very problem."[32]

That amendment, revised to create a panel also including the secretary of the Treasury and the chairman of the National Credit Union Administration, survived to become part of the Depository Institutions Deregulation and Monetary Control Act of 1980 (DIDMCA).[33] This panel, called the Depository Institutions Deregulation Committee (DIDC), was to implement the gradual elimination of Regulation Q. Congress charged the DIDC with phasing out interest rate controls "as soon as possible," and certainly within a six-year period (ending March 31, 1986).[34] The committee was directed to phase out interest rate controls with due regard to their effect on the housing market and the viability of depository institutions, thrifts in particular. The DIDC was to authorize a $1,000 MMC as soon as possible, though any member of the committee was given veto power over its approval. Congress thus resolved—at least temporarily—the issue of interest rate ceilings by the combination of delegation and instruction.

The Situation After DIDMCA

Despite the enactment of DIDMCA, the thrift business's position continued to worsen between 1980 and 1982. Even though the $1,000 MMC was not created by DIDMCA, the thrift business's return on assets fell to 0.14 percent in 1980 (as Janis believed it would if the certificate were authorized). And that was the good news. Thrift business profitability fell to minus 0.75 percent in 1981 and minus 0.65 percent in 1982, for a total loss of almost $12 billion in those two years. By far the most important cause of these losses was the increase in interest rates that S&Ls had to pay on their liabilities (figure 6.1).[35]

In addition to losing money, thrifts lost deposits. Figure 6.3 shows the net new savings (minus interest credited to existing accounts) and the net new retail savings (excluding certificates in $100,000 minimum certificates) at FSLIC-insured thrifts between 1976 and 1985. Between 1979 and 1981, S&Ls were able to continue growing slowly—even though they lost retail savings almost every quarter—

FIGURE 6.3

New Savings Flows, FSLIC-Insured Thrifts, 1976–1986

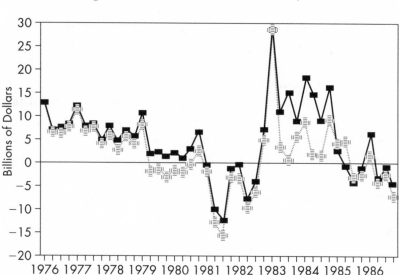

Source: U.S. League of Savings Institutions, *Savings Institutions Sourcebook, 1987* (Chicago: USL, 1987), 27.

because they were able to attract other sources of savings. Beginning in 1981 and continuing through the third quarter of 1982, however, thrifts had net savings losses each quarter. The thrift business managed to attract $6 billion in net new deposits in 1980, but had net deposit outflows of $39 billion in 1981 and $29 billion during the first eleven months of 1982.[36] Even with the MMC, S&Ls were not able to compete effectively for savings deposits. In particular, savers were still eager to take advantage of accounts such as the MMMF, which acted like checking accounts while paying interest.

The DIDC made several efforts to deregulate interest rates in 1981 and 1982. These attempts were extremely controversial, and the savings and loan business fought to slow the committee by lobbying its members and challenging its decisions in court. The business was successful on both counts: the committee withdrew one proposed increase in the ceilings, and two other increases were stopped by the courts.[37]

Congress followed DIDC's progress (or lack thereof) closely, holding at least three oversight hearings in 1980 and 1981.[38] The constant theme of these hearings was that rapid interest rate deregulation would ravage the thrift business and that "the safety and soundness of thrift institutions demands that the pace of deposit rate deregulation be carefully metered."[39] Slow deregulation, however, provided the business with few benefits as long as market interest rates were substantially above the ceilings. A 0.5 percent increase in the passbook savings account ceilings would cost the thrift business an estimated $500 million extra in interest on existing accounts, for example, but would not attract extra deposits because the additional interest did little to close the gap between more profitable investments elsewhere.[40] Carron estimated that thrift business losses would have been twice as large as they were in 1981 if interest rate ceilings had been eliminated, with similar losses coming in 1982.[41]

Congress thus had good reason not to require the DIDC to speed up interest rate deregulation in 1981 and 1982. But Congress could not stop deregulation either. Because market interest rates were so far above the interest rate ceilings, the proportion of S&L liabilities subject to ceilings declined from about 40 percent in 1980 to only 20 percent in 1982, as depositors transferred their funds to higher-paying accounts outside the thrift business. Interest rate ceilings covered an ever smaller proportion of thrift business liabilities.

Congress again addressed interest rate ceilings during consideration of the Garn–St. Germain Act of 1982. This time Congress *required* DIDC to create an insured account for thrifts and banks that would be "directly equivalent to and competitive with" MMMF.[42] Congress further specified that the interest rate ceilings would be eliminated by January 1984. Following the congressional mandate, DIDC approved a new "Money Market Deposit Account" (MMDA) by December 1982. In its first month $43 billion were placed in MMDAs, including $10 billion of new deposits. The MMDA effectively eliminated deposit rate ceilings, and savings again flowed into the thrift business. Thrift interest rate expenses, meanwhile, continued to climb.

How was the thrift business to turn a profit as its interest costs escalated? The simple answer, of course, was that S&Ls had to earn more on their assets. Because most thrift assets were long-term, fixed-rate mortgages that were earning less than the thrifts were paying on their liabilities, S&Ls had to make new investments earning higher interest rates. At the same time that Congress was expanding thrift liability powers so that S&Ls would have to pay market rates for funds, it decided it had to grant them greater asset powers so that they could better earn market rates of return.

The Politics of Asset Regulation

The rationale behind asset regulations closely paralleled that for liability regulations. Because home mortgages were a fairly safe investment, requiring thrifts to invest primarily in them was thought to enhance the stability of the thrift business. Furthermore, compelling thrifts to invest in home mortgages was an attempt to ensure that sufficient funds would flow into that sector.

Modern "portfolio theory" was the primary intellectual challenge to the first rationale. This theory essentially holds that investors can on average earn higher and more stable profits by investing in a variety of assets with varying maturity lengths. Investing in one kind of asset—even "safe" ones such as home mortgages—left the investor too vulnerable to changes in the performance of that asset. Investing in assets with one fixed maturity—such as thirty-year fixed-rate mortgage loans—left the investor susceptible to changes in inflation and interest rates. There was a great deal of empirical evidence supporting portfolio theory. Largely on the basis of portfolio theory, several blue-ribbon commissions had recommended that S&Ls be allowed to diversify their assets.[43]

The economic events of the late 1970s and early 1980s demonstrated that at least one side of portfolio theory was correct. Firms that concentrated their investments in "safe" long-term, fixed-rate assets, as the savings and loan business did, took a beating when interest rates unexpectedly increased (see figure 6.1). Between 1970 and 1979 the gap between what thrifts earned and what they paid averaged a fairly steady 1.5 percent, as both return on assets and cost of funds were increasing. In 1980 this gap almost vanished, and in 1981 and 1982 S&Ls on average paid more for funds than they earned on their investments.

Figure 6.1 also suggests why there was little urgency to expand thrift asset powers before 1980 and great pressure to do so afterwards. As long as S&Ls were maintaining a comfortable interest rate spread, as they were prior to 1979, asset deregulation was primarily of theoretical importance. After 1980 it must have seemed that waiting any longer spelled catastrophe. Because Congress found holding interest rates down to be beyond its control, the most likely way to increase business profitability was to increase the return on assets by allowing thrifts to invest in new, and preferably more lucrative, ways. By the early 1980s, therefore, asset deregulation seemed to be not just a good idea, but an imperative.

The public policies governing the thrift business gradually changed in response to these economic and intellectual changes. Historically, the social contract had been that the thrift business would primarily make home mortgage loans in return for accepting low interest savings accounts. Beginning in 1978, the Bank Board and Congress had been gradually removing regulations on liabilities so that thrifts would have to compete for funds in the open market. Thrift business advocates argued, sensibly, that if thrifts had to compete with other financial institutions for liabilities they should also be able to make the kinds of investments that these other institutions could make.

By the late 1970s, then, there was virtually universal agreement concerning the source of and solution to the thrift business problems. The source: "The thrift institutions' problems derive in large part from the preponderance of a single type of investment in their asset portfolios—the long-term fixed-rate residential mortgage."[44] The solution: "New powers are vital to the future health of thrifts."[45] Additional asset powers for the thrift business were seen as a requirement, not an option. When Senate Banking Committee Chairman Garn asked Andrew Carron, one of the leading independent experts on thrift issues, whether the thrift business could survive without new asset powers, Carron responded: "As an industry that has a role, that has a focus, that plays a major part in the economy, no, it cannot survive."[46]

Congressional banking committees heard a great deal of such testimony during the early 1980s, and not just from the thrift business, or even from the thrift business's regulators. At the same hearing at which Garn questioned Carron, the Comptroller of the Currency, the primary regulator for national banks, stated that "expanded powers are a necessary component of any legislative solution to the current thrift problem."[47] Speaking for the Department of the Treasury, Assistant Secretary Roger Mehle argued that "expanded lending and investment powers must be included in any legislation . . . establish[ing] a structure for the long-term viability of the thrift institutions."[48] Whenever Bank Board Chairman Pratt testified before Congress, he stressed the need for greater asset powers for thrifts.

Unfortunately, almost no one warned Congress that giving thrifts new asset powers posed risks for the thrift business and FSLIC. Indeed, prior to the Garn–St. Germain Act, commentators were virtually unanimous in their belief that asset deregulation would at least modestly enhance the overall profitability of the thrift business, while potentially reducing FSLIC's likely losses.

Despite the widespread intellectual and political support for asset deregulation, the Congress (through the DIDMCA) took only a modest step toward increasing the asset powers of thrifts. For example, it permitted federal S&Ls to invest up to 20 percent of their assets in consumer loans, commercial paper, or corporate debt securities. Before DIDMCA, federal S&Ls were prohibited from making these investments except to a small extent through "service corporation" subsidiaries.[49] Giving thrifts these new powers was not a bold leap into uncharted waters, however. Mutual savings banks (MSB), state-chartered financial institutions primarily in the Northeast that were similar to savings and loans, already had asset powers similar to those authorized by DIDMCA. An Interagency Task Force on Thrift Institutions reported to Congress that "the best evidence available regarding the response of the thrift industry to the expanded asset powers by [DIDMCA] lies in an analysis of the current behavior of [MSBS]."[50] Given the experiences involving asset deregulation in the MSB business, the task force concluded that thrifts in general will *not* move rapidly to take advantage of the asset powers offered by [DIDMCA]. . . . Any shift that might occur would probably be completed only after a considerable period of time. . . . However, this is not to argue that the thrift industry should be prevented from participating in the business loan markets. There may be segments of this market in which the institutions may be able to compete.[51]

The expanded asset powers were thus expected not to save the thrift business from its problems immediately, but rather to provide longer-term stability.

The thrift business indeed took little advantage of its new asset powers between 1980 and 1982. At the end of 1982, for example, FSLIC-insured thrifts held less than 12 percent of their portfolios in "nontraditional" assets.[52] Meanwhile, thrift business conditions continued to disintegrate, as the cost of liabilities increased much faster than the return on assets. Thrift business criticism of the government's policies also increased sharply: "Thrift institutions are in trouble because they did what the government required or encouraged them to do—make long-term mortgage loans at affordable interest rate to home buyers. At the same time, they have been forced to compete for savings at sharply increased deposit interest rates."[53] Texas was held up as a model of the benefits of expanded asset powers. Texas already granted state-chartered S&Ls greater flexibility in making investments, and so these associations were already modestly more diversified than federally chartered thrifts operating in that state.[54] This modest additional amount of diversification apparently gave Texas-chartered thrifts some modest economic protection, however. Although both federal and state thrifts in Texas lost money in 1981 and 1982, the return on assets for state thrifts was minus 0.55 and minus 0.25 compared to minus 0.85 and minus 0.70 for federal thrifts.[55]

When Congress was considering legislation in 1982, only a few still disagreed that further expanding thrift asset powers would improve the business's condition. The Garn–St. Germain Act expanded thrifts' asset powers much further than DIDMCA, yet it did so primarily along the same lines. Garn–St. Germain permitted federal thrifts to invest up to 40 percent of their assets in commercial real estate, doubling the amount that had been allowed by DIDMCA, and allowed thrifts to make an additional 15 percent in other commercial loans. Garn–St. Germain also increased federal thrifts' abilities to hold consumer loans from 20 to 30 percent of assets and increased the types of consumer loans that could be made.

Garn–St. Germain did offer federally chartered S&Ls some new asset powers that federally chartered banks did not have. Although federal thrifts were permitted to hold only 11 percent of their assets in commercial loans, they were allowed to count high-yield, below-investment-grade corporate debt securities (usually called "junk bonds") as part of this 11 percent. In addition, federally chartered thrifts were allowed to make direct investments (that is, buy equity rather than extend credit) in ventures for up to 3 percent of their assets.[56] These changes appeared modest compared to the actions of some states. The Sun Belt states in particular, such as Texas, California, Colorado, and Arizona, went much further than Garn–St. Germain in allowing state-chartered thrifts to make commercial real estate loans, commercial loans, and direct investments.[57]

It does not appear that Congress carefully considered the effect the truly new asset powers (especially direct investments and junk bonds) would have on the thrift business and FSLIC. Neither, as far as I can tell, did other observers. Descriptions of Garn–St. Germain published soon after it was enacted did not warn that particular categories of assets were likely to create larger risks for FSLIC.[58] Given the broad and deep consensus that asset deregulation was a good thing, this is not surprising.

Deposit Insurance

While FSLIC was the deposit insurer for the thrift business, Congress played a large role in determining what kinds of accounts would be covered by the insurance, how large the insured accounts could be, how much the insurance would cost and, to some extent, when FSLIC could take action against an S&L. Because Congress made these key decisions for FSLIC, Congress might be blamed for creating or worsening several of FSLIC's major problems. These problems fall into four categories, which I shall consider in turn.

First, Congress greatly expanded FSLIC's insurance coverage in the 1980s. It is commonly believed that this dramatically increased FSLIC's losses because it allowed shaky thrifts to grow much faster and larger than they should have while ensuring that FSLIC would pick up a larger share of the tab if they failed.

A second concern was that Congress did not allow FSLIC to act as a genuine insurer by charging premiums based on the riskiness of thrifts' loans and investments. Because Congress failed to authorize FSLIC to use risk-based premiums, the argument goes, thrifts made excessively risky investments.

Third, Congress did not ensure that FSLIC had a large enough insurance fund to cover its potential losses, did not make sure that the thrift industry paid the full cost of its insurance, and did not provide FSLIC with adequate funding once it was recognized that FSLIC was broke. These failures allegedly have had the effect of increasing the cost to the American taxpaying public.

Finally, Congress has been accused of meddling with FSLIC's ability to intervene early in failing thrifts to keep them from imposing greater losses on the insurance fund. Throughout the 1980s Congress favored "forbearance"—thrifts judged to be insolvent through no fault of their own, owing to temporary economic conditions, were given time to work their way back to profitability.

In this chapter, I will examine deposit insurance coverage, which was substantially increased by Congress in 1980. FSLIC's size, forbearance policies, and insurance premiums, which became more important during the mid-1980s, will be covered in the following chapter.

Deposit Insurance Coverage

When FSLIC was created in 1935, it was authorized to insure savings accounts for $5,000. The amount of insurance coverage for individual accounts was occasionally increased over the years, and by the 1970s individual savings accounts up to $40,000 were covered.

Perhaps the most controversial provision (in hindsight) in DIDMCA was the one that increased deposit insurance coverage from $40,000 to $100,000 per account.[59] This change has taken on an ominous cast in most reports. For example, after noting that the Senate version of the legislation had raised the cap to $50,000 while the House bill left it at $40,000, Michael Waldman reports that "late at night, senators and representatives broke off their [conference committee] session and retreated to a back room. They emerged with a 'compromise': the cap would be raised to $100,000. According to eyewitnesses, lobbyists from the U.S. League of Savings Institutions pressed lawmakers for the change. Within the secret congressional meeting, Representative Fernand St. Germain, a powerful banking committee member, insisted on the higher level."[60] Raising deposit insurance coverage to $100,000 may or may not have been a good policy as measured by, for example, its contribution to the size of FSLIC's losses.[61] But this does not necessarily mean that Congress was reckless in raising deposit insurance coverage to $100,000 per account. Examining the patterns in congressional expansion of deposit insurance prior to DIDMCA, the consequences of these expansions, and the rationales for increased deposit insurance can help us assess congressional culpability.

DIDMCA, as it turns out, was not the first instance of Congress sharply increasing deposit insurance coverage. During the credit crunch of 1974, for example, Congress had doubled insurance coverage from $20,000 to $40,000 for individual accounts.[62] Furthermore, DIDMCA was not the only case where Congress had raised deposit insurance coverage to $100,000 on particular accounts; it had done so twice previously. In 1974, insurance coverage on public accounts was raised to this level. In 1978, insurance on IRA and Keogh accounts (which cover pension and profit-sharing plans) was also increased to $100,000. The congressional increase in deposit insurance coverage through DIDMCA was thus hardly unprecedented and should hardly have been unexpected. House Banking Chairman Henry Reuss (D-Wisc.) stated in 1979 that he would support an increase in insurance coverage "to whatever is needed to account for present and future inflation levels."[63] DIDMCA indeed appears to have followed the congressional pattern of expanding deposit insurance coverage in size and extending it to particular depositors.

It was also hardly obvious in 1980 that increasing deposit insurance coverage would cost the federal government anything. The dramatic increase in coverage in 1974 (and to a lesser extent in 1978) had not caused the insurance funds of FSLIC (or FDIC) to decline. Indeed, the FSLIC insurance fund continued to grow each year through the 1970s. It might also be noted that, despite the increased coverage, the percentage of thrift deposits covered by deposit insurance actually declined during the 1980s. In 1980, 96.5 percent of thrift deposits were insured; by 1984, only 91.7 percent were.[64]

Good arguments for increasing deposit insurance coverage had also been raised. It is worth remembering that deposit insurance has essentially two rationales: to protect the savings of depositors and to enhance financial stability by eliminating bank runs. The existing insurance coverage limits did serve generally to provide smaller or less sophisticated investors a safe place to keep their funds, though by 1980 $40,000 was not an especially large sum for, say, a retirement age couple who had sold their home and moved into less expensive quarters. But limited deposit insurance did leave depository institutions vulnerable to runs by rational uninsured depositors (as well as frightened insured ones). When depository institutions and the thrift system begin to appear shaky, as they did by 1980, the fear of runs becomes stronger and the rationale for using greater insurance coverage to quell these fears more convincing. From this perspective, increased deposit insurance coverage appears prudent because it reduces the risk of systemwide bank runs.

In addition, only rarely did FSLIC or FDIC actually liquidate a failed institution and pay off insured depositors while allowing uninsured depositors to take losses. More commonly, the deposit insurer used a "purchase-and-assumption" method of resolving failures. In this method the insurer subsidizes the purchase of the failed institution, and all deposits (insured and uninsured alike) are transferred to the acquirer.[65] As a result, "only very unlucky uninsured depositors [in larger banks] or the relatively few uninsured depositors in small banks ever sustain deposit losses as the result of institution failures."[66] Furthermore, since uninsured investors are less likely to lose money if they place their funds in institutions that are "too big to fail" than in small banks or thrifts, large banks have an advantage in competing for uninsured deposits. In practice, then, uninsured depositors are treated arbitrarily and inequitably when their institution fails, while large banks are given a competitive edge over smaller depository institutions through "too big to fail" policies.

These inefficient and inequitable aspects of a deposit insurance system with incomplete insurance coverage and differential treatment of failed institutions were well understood in 1980. To correct these flaws, some analysts indeed were (and still are) calling for 100 percent deposit insurance coverage, in which *all* deposits would be covered.[67] This view was not and is not universally held. Other forms of deposit insurance involving such features as private co-insurance have also been proposed. But no proposal has seemed capable of producing all the outcomes desired.

Thus, in increasing deposit insurance as it did in DIDMCA, Congress did not break new ground. Higher deposit insurance coverage could be—and had been—justified on grounds of both equity and efficiency. No obviously bad consequences had arisen when insurance coverage had been increased in the past. The increase was similar in quantity and kind to ones previously approved by Congress.

If Congress's policy choice was defensible, then what about the way Congress made the choice? Insurance coverage was not increased after extensive hearings, committee markups, and floor debates, but as a last-minute addition to a conference committee report. Was this process an irresponsible way to increase insurance coverage? This is a tougher call. But a noted scholar is worth quoting at length on the issue of congressional conference committees.

The authority of conference committees to modify legislation has long been a subject of great controversy. Conferees must be given substantial discretion to change and create legislative language if they are to find compromises that are acceptable to a majority of both sets of conferees and to floor majorities in both chambers. Rules and precedent provide that only matters of disagreement between the chambers are before the conference. Experience has shown that these constraints are highly ambiguous and difficult to enforce. . . . A conference negotiating differences is [thus] given very wide discretion in crafting a new version [of the bill].[68]

Summary

By 1982, Congress had largely deregulated thrift business liability and asset powers, and had expanded deposit insurance coverage. Thrifts were now forced to pay market rates to obtain funds, but they had a great deal more flexibility in the amount they could raise and the sources from which they could raise it. Thrifts could also make a wide variety of investments previously prohibited to them. The year 1982 marked the height of congressional expansion of thrift business powers. It did not end Congress's concern with the sources and uses of S&L funds, however, or with the condition of the deposit insurance fund. In the following years, Congress considered whether it had given thrifts too many liability and asset powers, or whether the deposit insurance system was adequate for the job of protecting citizens' deposits and preserving financial stability.

7

Congress After Deregulation

ASSET AND LIABILITY DEREGULATION did not end congressional interest in thrift business powers, though it did change Congress's focus. Before 1982, Congress was concerned that too little money was flowing into the thrift business and that thrift business assets were too concentrated in fixed-rate home mortgage loans. In the following years, Congress began to worry that too many funds—especially wholesale funds—were pouring into S&Ls and that the thrifts were investing too many of them in high risk assets.

Liability Powers After 1982: Brokered Deposits

Prior to the early 1980s, thrifts had collected most of their deposits retail from individual savers in local areas in relatively small amounts. Brokered deposits, in contrast, are wholesale funds obtained from a firm that places money for primarily institutional investors. Because deposit brokers are generally quite sensitive to rates of return, thrifts had a limited ability to use brokered deposits as long as interest rate ceilings existed. Furthermore, before 1981 S&Ls could hold no more than 5 percent of all their liabilities in the form of brokered deposits. As a result, the thrift business held an insignificant portion of its liabilities in such deposits.

DIDMCA and Garn–St. Germain, along with Bank Board initiatives, helped changed that. Interest rate deregulation allowed thrifts to bid for brokered deposits by offering higher rates. Increases in deposit insurance coverage (from $40,000 to $100,000 per account) meant that brokers could raise more money faster. Bank Board Chairman Pratt eliminated the 5 percent brokered deposit limit, essentially allowing each thrift to acquire as much funding from brokers as it decided was necessary. Finally, limits on brokers' commissions were removed in 1982. Wholesale funds poured into the thrift business, fueling its growth in 1983 and 1984.

The thrift business grew much more rapidly in 1983 and 1984 than did either the commercial banking industry or the economy as a whole (figure 5.1, above). The thrift business's use of brokered deposits grew even faster, increasing from $3.3 billion to $43 billion (from 0.5 to 4.4 percent of assets) between 1981 and 1984 (figure 5.2, above). During this period, some individual thrifts used brokered deposits to fund extraordinarily rapid growth. The close correlation between thrift growth rates and the use of "nontraditional" liabilities, including brokered deposits, repurchase agreements, and other liabilities, was dramatic (figure 5.3, above).

Many of the most rapidly growing S&Ls failed. For example, the 637 thrifts that FSLIC liquidated or sold between 1986 and 1989 had doubled their assets, from $141 to $283 billion, between 1982 and 1985. The rest of the thrift business grew about half as fast during these three years. Seventy-four of the 637 thrifts grew by over 400 percent. Chief among these "flameouts" were Diversified American Savings Bank in California, which grew from $11 million in 1982 to almost $1 billion in 1985, and Bloomfield Savings and Loan in Michigan, which grew from $2 million to $676 million during this period.[1]

By 1984 the Bank Board had become quite alarmed that rapid thrift growth, fueled by brokered deposits, posed a large threat to FSLIC.[2] It believed that one way to stop rapid thrift growth was to limit the use of brokered funds. Chairman Gray, together with FDIC Chairman Isaac, proposed a regulation that would have limited deposit insurance to $100,000 per depositor. This would have meant that each broker could have no more than $100,000 insured in any one S&L. This regulation would have brought the deposit brokerage business to a quick halt.

The FHLBB and FDIC called for public comment on brokered deposits in November 1983.[3] The agencies received over 240 sets of comments, "with an extremely wide range of viewpoints expressed."[4] Comments from thrifts, banks, and credit unions were fairly evenly split over whether regulations were an appropriate way to limit brokered deposits; for the most part, deposit brokers and academics opposed regulation. The FHLBB and FDIC decided to proceed and, in January 1984, invited comments on their specific proposal to limit deposit insurance to $100,000 per broker per institution. Each agency received over 3,400 comments. About 2,800 individuals who placed deposits with brokers, as well as the brokers themselves, opposed the regulation. A slight majority of the several hundred bank and savings institutions that commented opposed the proposal. The major bank groups supported the proposal. The two main thrift groups, the United States League of Savings Institutions and National Savings and Loan League (NSLL) split, however, with the USL actually favoring the new limits.[5] The Comptroller of the Currency and the Justice Department's Antitrust Division, for their part, questioned the rule's effectiveness and legality.

At this point, thirty-seven members of Congress asked the agencies to defer the rule until Congress could consider the issue. Congress promptly did so, holding hearings in March.[6] Testimony was received from representatives of the thrift, bank, and deposit brokerage industries, the FHLBB and FDIC, the Treasury, the Securities and Exchange Commission, the Comptroller of the Currency, the Federal Reserve, the National Credit Union Administration, former Bank Board chairman Pratt, and academics. With the exception of the FLBB and the FDIC themselves, virtually no one gave unqualified support for the proposal. The Federal Reserve and one academic backed the rule in part. All other witnesses, including former Bank Board chairman Pratt, completely rejected the regulation.

Despite the strong objections raised at this hearing, the FHLBB and FDIC issued their final rules on March 26, effective October 1. A deposit broker immediately challenged the regulation in federal court. In June a federal district court judge issued an injunction to prevent enforcement of the regulations, and in January 1985 the United States Court of Appeals concluded that the FSLIC and FDIC could not discriminate between deposits placed by individuals and those placed by brokers, and that the regulation was thus illegal.[7] The court ruled that only Congress could prohibit insurance on brokered deposits.

The Bank Board and the FDIC then turned to Congress for such legislation. Although legislation was periodically introduced to restrict brokered deposits, Congress did not approve any such legislation for almost five years, when it made modest changes in FIRREA in 1989.[8]

The Congress's unwillingness to provide the financial regulators with the recommended legislation could be construed as an ill-advised favoring of the commercial interests that opposed it. The brokerages that opposed limits included many large Wall Street firms such as Merrill Lynch, Dean Witter Reynolds, Prudential Bache, First Boston, and Goldman Sachs & Co. The individuals who used brokers staunchly defended their right to earn high interest rates while having their funds insured, and individuals who used deposit brokers were likely to be affluent and politically active. The savings and loan business, however, was split on this issue. Although many savings and loans, including the USL itself, supported limits on brokered deposits, the intensity of their support was nothing like the fervor with which brokers and depositors opposed the limits.

Yet congressional reluctance to limit the use of brokered deposits does not mean that Congress simply counted the votes and ignored the issues. Congress gave the brokered deposit issue careful consideration when agencies first proposed their rule, and continued to do so afterwards. Between 1983 and 1988 at least eight congressional hearings or reports examined the use of brokered deposits by thrifts and banks.[9]

More important, congressional committees appear to have made genuine efforts to assess the problems and not just assay their political effects. The House Government Operations Committee, for example, was not content with holding hearings, but performed its own analysis. Its report focused on three key questions: 1) Did brokered deposits cause the alleged problems, and would the proposed regulation reduce the problems? 2) What would the regulation cost, and would its benefits outweigh these costs? 3) Were there other ways to reduce the problems? In short, the committee addressed basic issues of regulatory effectiveness and efficiency.

The committee admitted there were "notable cases of failing or failed institutions that have made extraordinary use of brokered funds."[10] It recognized that many of the problem thrifts and banks continued to experience dramatic growth fueled by brokered deposits. It acknowledged there were persuasive arguments that, because deposit insurance allowed any insured institution to raise large amounts of funds quickly, weak institutions were encouraged to engage in high risk activities.

Still, the overall evidence led the committee to conclude that removing deposit insurance from brokered deposits was "neither necessary nor justified and will probably not be effective in correcting the specific abuses found by the agencies."[11] A principal source of evidence was the data submitted by the FHLBB concerning rapidly growing thrifts (table 7.1).

Several important implications can be drawn from this table. The concerns of the regulators were not unfounded, since there were a number of problem thrifts of all sizes that were growing rapidly, had huge increases in brokered deposits, and held large portions of their liabilities in the form of brokered deposits. Many problem S&Ls, however, managed to grow rapidly even though brokered deposits accounted for only a small and (in the case of the small and medium thrifts) shrinking share of total deposits. This suggests that restricting brokered deposits was unlikely by itself to restrain S&Ls from growing rapidly. Finally, many nonproblem thrifts that were growing rapidly also relied on brokered deposits for their growth while holding much of their total deposits in this form. The available data, in short, suggested that problem thrifts might or might not be relying on brokered deposits for rapid growth and that thrifts relying on brokered deposits for swift growth might or might not be problems.[12]

The committee also noted that Bank Board Chairman Gray relied heavily on "horror stories" in making the case for tight regulatory restrictions on brokered funds. Without disputing the accuracy of these accounts, the committee argued that these cases appeared to

TABLE 7.1

Rapidly Growing Thrifts, 1984
(in percent)

	N	Deposit Growth (%)	Brokered Deposit Growth (%)	Brokered Deposits as Percent of Total Deposits
Problem thrifts relying on brokered funds				
Small	91	302	49	24
Medium	15	84	210	48
Large	6	47	249	20
Problem thrifts not relying on brokered funds				
Small	71	55	-29	9
Medium	70	49	-5	8
Large	7	50	156	6
Nonproblem thrifts relying on brokered funds				
Small	34	81	498	35
Medium	11	102	447	35
Large	5	57	202	34
Nonproblem thrifts not relying on brokered funds				
Small	287	65	-98	5
Medium	104	51	14	5
Large	15	35	46	11

Source: U.S. Congress, House, Committee on Government Operations, *Federal Regulation of Brokered Deposits in Problem Banks and Savings Institutions*, Report, 98th Cong., 2nd sess., 26.

Note: Rapidly growing thrifts are those whose annualized rate of deposit growth from December 31, 1983 to March 31, 1984 exceeded 25 percent. Problem thrifts are those with supervisory rating of 4 or 5 (on a scale of 1–5, with 1 representing the most sound institutions) at March 31, 1984.

Deposit growth was principally from brokered funds if the increase in brokered funds was more than 50 percent of the total growth.

include flagrant abuses in addition to whatever problems occurred from the use of brokered deposits. In the judgment of the committee, the Bank Board should therefore focus on identifying and controlling specific instances of abuse rather than imposing unnecessary, ineffective, and harmful regulations on sound and unsound thrifts alike.

These instructions were reasonable but, paradoxically, impractical. The Bank Board, as we have seen, found it difficult to use its discretion to control thrift behavior and so preferred to apply rules to restrain thrifts. Given the aggressiveness with which individual thrifts fought the Bank Board's attempts to apply its discretion in the absence of clear rules, we may conclude that the regulators' desire for rules was practical but not, alas, convincing. Within their own domains, both Congress's and the Bank Board's approaches were understandable. Discretion is better than rules because it can focus on abuses; rules are better than discretion because they establish enforceable and fair standards. There is no easy way to solve this rules vs. discretion dilemma.

Despite rejection in the courts and Congress of efforts by the Bank Board and the FDIC to limit deposit insurance for brokered deposits, the agencies continued to press for rules to constrain the use of these funds. At the same time the Bank was unsuccessfully attempting to withhold deposit insurance from brokered deposits, it also issued a rule that limited the use of brokered deposits by FSLIC-insured thrifts whose net worth was less than 3 percent of liabilities.[13] These thrifts were not allowed to obtain more than 5 percent of their liabilities through deposit brokers; if they already held more than 5 percent in brokered deposits when the rule was implemented, they could not increase that amount. This rule was not challenged in court, and congressional monitoring showed that the regulation was effective. For example, a study by the House Government Operations Committee in 1986 found that after implementation, brokered fund growth among problem institutions (those identified in table 7.1) "completely stopped . . . suggest[ing] that rapid brokered deposit growth can be effectively controlled by supervisory efforts."[14] Although some problem institutions did continue to grow rapidly with brokered deposits, most of these had received waivers from their regulators to do so. The Government Operations Committee nonetheless urged the FHLBB and FDIC to avoid broad regulations and "to redirect their regulatory attention more narrowly at specific areas of abuse."[15] Congress took no legislative steps to change FHLBB policies on the brokered deposit issue, however.

The Bank Board also took a more direct route toward limiting rapid thrift growth, whether fueled by brokered deposits or by other liabilities. In early 1985 the Bank Board implemented regulations that imposed strict growth ceilings on thrifts with low net worth.[16] Thrifts that met their net worth requirements could grow up to 25 percent annually without regulatory permission and more than 25 percent with permission. Congress did not interfere with this rule and the rule worked (figure 5.1). Thrift business liabilities had been growing more than twice as rapidly as those in commercial banking in 1983 and 1984, but returned to comparable levels in 1985 and 1986. Congress continued to monitor the use of brokered deposits through several other hearings, but took no further actions on this issue.

Asset Powers after 1982: Direct Investments

As Congress intended and most experts recommended, the thrift business used the asset powers given to it by DIDMCA and the Garn–St. Germain Act in an attempt to bolster its earnings by making new types of investments. The most controversial of the newly permitted assets were direct investments, in which the thrift takes an ownership stake in a project rather than just lending the project money. By 1985 the thrift business held about $30 billion, or about 3 percent of its total assets, in direct investments.

The controversy concerned the effect of direct investments on the profitability of the thrift business, and ultimately, on the health of the FSLIC. Some believed direct investments were the business's salvation. *Savings Institution* magazine reported at the end of 1984 that the fastest-growing S&Ls had the highest percentage of direct investments in real estate development, the highest returns on assets, and the highest reported net worth.[17] On the other hand, the Bank Board was finding that same year that direct investments were causing some S&Ls large losses. Several large thrifts (most notably Empire Savings and Loan in Texas) had gotten into big trouble because of direct real estate development investments. Bank Board Chairman Gray reported that 70 percent of FSLIC's caseload now had asset problems "usually consist[ing] largely of raw land or half-completed real estate projects"—in short, direct investments.[18]

The Bank Board subsequently attempted to protect FSLIC by proposing a rule to limit the ability of S&Ls to make direct investments.[19] This regulation restricted direct investments by thrifts to 10 percent of a thrift's assets or 200 percent of its net worth, whichever was greater. Any direct investments over these amounts would have to gain regulatory approval and be accompanied by a capital infusion worth 10 percent of the investment's purchase price. Although this proposal actually increased the ability of federally chartered thrifts to make direct investments (Garn–St. Germain had limited direct investments to 3 percent of assets), it was designed primarily to restrain state-chartered thrifts in states such as Arizona, California, Florida, and Texas.

The Bank Board received 252 public comments on the proposed regulation. Over 200 comments opposed the rule as unwise or illegal: unwise because it would make the thrift business's profitability and capital problems worse, and illegal because it exceeded the Bank Board's statutory authority to regulate state-chartered institutions. The board made modest changes to the proposal, but decided to implement it despite widespread opposition.[20]

Congress began examining the proposed Bank Board regulations (and thus direct investments themselves) in hearings held by the House Government Operations Committee in February 1985.[21] The committee reviewed thirteen statements, seventeen studies, and twenty-four selected public comments from federal regulators, academics, and financial institutions—almost eleven hundred pages of testimony—and produced no consensus.[22] As the Bank Board's director of policy development admitted, "We didn't have the convincing knock-'em-dead evidence" to support the rule.[23] For every study the Bank Board presented to bolster its case that direct investments needed to be limited, an outside study rejected the need for such a regulation. Some studies "demonstrated that greater proportions of direct investments by institutions would increase the risk of loss to them and the FSLIC fund."[24] Other studies found that "direct investments did not contribute to the extraordinary failures of S&Ls over the period or to the further weakening of associations. To the contrary, the evidence presented indicates that direct investments reduced the risk of FSLIC payouts."[25] Some prominent financial experts supported the rule, while others opposed it. Federal Reserve Chairman Paul Volcker submitted a letter urging the proposed regulation be tightened even further.[26] Future Fed Chairman Alan Greenspan, in contrast, wrote that the rule's limitations "are unsound in principle and will prove to be harmful in practice."[27]

After these apparently inconclusive hearings, Representative Frank Annunzio (D-Ill.) introduced a resolution that instructed the Bank Board to delay implementation of the direct investment rule by six months. A total of 223 members—more than half the House—cosponsored this resolution, and Annunzio's Financial Institutions Subcommittee proceeded to hold hearings on it.[28] Although Annunzio contended that the Bank Board was "acting too hurriedly" in implementing the rule, his main argument was that no regulation was needed: "I realize there have been abuses of the direct investment lending rule, but I also feel that the FHLBB has the ability to deal with these problems on a case-by-case basis."[29] Bank Board Chairman Gray rejected this argument entirely:

> With all due respect to you ladies and gentleman on the subcommittee, the responsibility for the mounting losses to the FSLIC—losses that we are now seeing from bad assets resulting from what have turned out to be bad direct investments—would fall squarely on the shoulders of the Congress itself, to the extent that such a delay [as the resolution proposed] would impair our ability to deal with such problems.[30]

Federal Reserve Chairman Volcker and FDIC Chairman Isaac concurred in separate letters supporting the Bank Board's rule. Despite the fact that a majority of the House had signed Annunzio's resolution, it was never voted out of the subcommittee. Congress took no legislative action on the direct investment rule, and the Bank Board implemented the regulation as planned.

Congress had not yet finished its oversight of direct investments, however: the Government Operations Committee issued a report in

October 1985 based on the seemingly inconclusive hearings it had held earlier that year.[31] As in the case of brokered deposits, this report critically assessed the available evidence and drew conclusions based on these assessments. After reviewing skeptically the direct investment studies presented in its earlier hearings, the committee concluded that "it is simply not possible at present to make reliable statistical estimates of the risks faced by thrifts generally from direct investments . . . or of how these risks affect overall portfolio risk and insolvency risk."[32] Furthermore, quantitative analyses faced "inherent limitations . . . no matter how reliable the data" because economic risk "does not derive from simple and easily studied random processes of the sort that statisticians can analyze with their standard mathematical methods."[33] The committee, in short, found that neither the regulation's opponents nor its advocates could offer convincing empirical evidence.

The committee nonetheless made several judgments on the basis of theoretical reasoning and flawed evidence. It rejected the view that unrestricted direct investments would reduce the number of thrift failures and concluded instead that the "higher portfolio risk inevitably means some increase in failures among institutions whose direct investments are not successful."[34] The committee acknowledged, however, that because direct investments were on average highly profitable, the thrift business should be encouraged to make such investments at "controlled" levels. But because FSLIC bore the cost of S&Ls that failed due to unsuccessful direct investments, yet gained no financial benefit from thrifts that invested successfully, the committee recommended that steps be taken to ensure that FSLIC did share in the equity gains of profitable thrifts. Until such reform occurred, the committee found that the Bank Board's direct investment regulation was "an appropriate and necessary restriction."[35]

The Deposit Insurance Fund

Historically, Congress has determined the insurance premiums that FSLIC charged insured thrifts. The premiums Congress authorized did not produce nearly enough income to keep the FSLIC solvent in the 1980s, however. Congress has been unwilling to impose premiums on the thrift business that were high enough to pay all FSLIC's expenses. As a result, Congress has had to use general revenues—taxpayer money—to meet FSLIC's obligations. Furthermore, Congress was reluctant to fund FSLIC in 1986 and 1987, and ultimately authorized much less than was necessary for FSLIC to handle appropriately all insolvent thrifts. The conventional view is that the ultimate cost of the thrift tragedy to taxpayers will be much higher than it needed to be because Congress did not act promptly and forcefully to give FSLIC the resources it needed. More important, many have accused Congress of acting irresponsibly in not fully funding FSLIC.

This section focuses on congressional response and considers three issues that Congress had to decide. How big should FSLIC's insurance fund be? Who should pay for the insurance, and how much should they pay? How quickly should FSLIC have been funded, and how much funding should it have been given?

The Size of the Insurance Fund

FSLIC's insurance fund has proven much too small to cover its losses during the 1980s. But this does not necessarily imply that Congress was negligent in determining how large FSLIC's reserve fund should be. Examining FSLIC's history and comparing FSLIC with its peer insurance fund, the FDIC, can help illustrate why.

Several facts about this history are worth noting. FSLIC *never* suffered an annual loss before 1980. Although FSLIC had to handle individual savings and loan associations that went bust, FSLIC *always* had greater yearly income than expenses. As a result, FSLIC's insurance reserve grew every year for forty-five straight years.[36]

Furthermore, FSLIC's insurance fund, as measured by its reserve-to-insured-liabilities ratio, was higher than FDIC's in each year between at least 1970 and 1982 (figure 7.1). FSLIC's reserve fund did decline from 2.05 to 1.28 percent as a percentage of insured liabilities between 1970 and 1980. This decline, however, is entirely attributable to the policy decision made in the early 1970s that the fund was too large, and that 1.25 percent was the appropriate target. Even at this level, however, FSLIC's fund was larger relative to insured

FIGURE 7.1

FSLIC and FDIC Reserves, 1970–1988

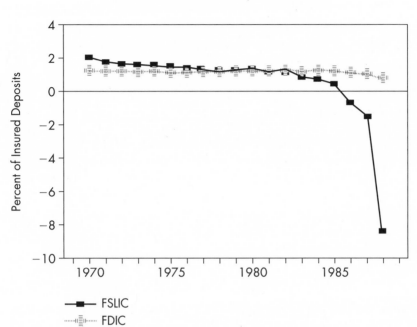

Source: U.S. League of Savings Institutions, *Savings Institutions Sourcebook, 1987* (Chicago: USL, 1987), 73; Federal Home Loan Bank Board, *1984 Annual Report* (Washington, D.C.: FHLBB, 1984), 8; Federal Deposit Insurance Corporation, *1993 Annual Report*, July 1994, 141.

liabilities than it had been in the thirty years from FSLIC's inception until 1965. In short, prior to 1980 there was little evidence that FSLIC's insurance fund was too small, and there were no arguments made that it needed to be increased. As one scholar wrote at the time, "the FSLIC fund through 1979 appears to have been grossly larger than was necessary."[37]

FSLIC's insurance fund fell precipitously during the mid-1980s (figure 7.1). In 1983, FSLIC's reserves totalled $6.4 billion dollars. By 1987, FSLIC was estimated to be $13.7 billion in the hole, a $20 billion dollar loss in four years.[38] Until about 1990, this hole increased dramatically, with virtually every estimate. This means that an "adequate" FSLIC fund would have been not two or three times as large as the reserve in 1983, but perhaps ten times as large. A deposit insurance fund large enough to handle all the necessary demands would have been far outside all precedent in United States history. Given FSLIC's experience up to 1980, it is hard to imagine a persuasive argument for creating such a large deposit insurance fund. It seems perverse to fault Congress for not making FSLIC build such a large fund.

Who Should Pay?

As it became increasingly clear in the 1980s that FSLIC did not have enough money to pay its bills, Congress tried to decide who should pay them. The dominant view is that thrifts persuaded Congress that the business should not pay, and so the American public did. One popular anecdote has an unidentified thrift lobbyist speaking to Bank Board Chairman Ed Gray in 1986, when Congress was considering legislation to aid FSLIC: "Listen, Ed, in 1989 we'll have a new administration running things. By that time everyone will know this problem is so big that the industry can't pay for it. The taxpayer will have to pay for it then, not the industry."[39] Yet an examination of the net income of FSLIC and the thrift business during the 1980s demonstrates that it would have been *impossible* for thrifts to have covered FSLIC's expenses (table 7.2). Between 1981 and 1988, FSLIC lost over $60 billion more than the thrift business's net income. Only in three years (1983–1985) did net income for the entire business exceed FSLIC's net losses. In other words, the thrift business's *entire* net income during this period would not have been enough to pay FSLIC's expenses. Under no circumstance was Congress going to be able to raise enough money from the thrift business to pay all FSLIC's expenses.

But how much money should Congress have tried to raise from the business? The policy answer to this question hinged on matters of efficacy and equity. Congress would have been ill advised to raise deposit insurance premiums if doing so would make the situation worse for the thrift business and FSLIC. Congress was also quite aware that its deposit insurance policies should be fair (in the sense of treating like firms alike). Yet it was almost impossible for any policy to meet these conditions and also raise substantial revenue.

TABLE 7.2

Net Income of FSLIC and FSLIC-Insured Thrifts, 1981–1988 (in $ billions)

	FSLIC	Thrifts
1981	0.0	−4.6
1982	0.1	−4.1
1983	0.0	1.9
1984	−0.8	1.0
1985	−1.1	3.7
1986	−10.9	0.1
1987	−8.6	−7.8
1988	−66.0	−13.4
Total	−87.3	−23.2

Source: Federal Home Loan Bank Board, *Annual Report*, various years; Office of Thrift Supervision, *Combined Financial Statements, FSLIC-Insured Institutions*, 1988, iii; U.S. General Accounting Office, "Resolving the Savings and Loan Crisis: Billions More and Additional Reforms Needed," testimony prepared for the U.S. Congress, Senate, Committee on Banking, Housing and Urban Affairs, 6 April 1990, 22.

Consider efficacy. From 1950 to 1985, each thrift paid premiums equal to $1/12$ of 1 percent of insured deposits. This brought FSLIC about $700 million in 1985. In 1985 the Bank Board also imposed an additional $1/8$ of 1 percent "special assessment" on insured deposits, which raised an extra billion dollars.[40] It was unclear how much further insurance premiums could be increased before they started generating less revenue and greater costs for FSLIC. Profit margins for the thrift business in the mid-1980s were extremely narrow, yielding 0.39 percent return on assets in 1985 and 0.09 percent in 1986. The special assessment already equalled approximately one-fourth of the profit for the entire thrift business in 1985 (which was by far the most profitable year of the decade for the business) and was greater than the profit in 1986. Further raising insurance premiums across the entire business would have pushed some thrifts deeper into insolvency, increasing FSLIC's resolution costs.[41] Raising insurance premiums would have also induced some thrifts—the healthier ones—to change charters and become banks (which still paid only $\frac{1}{12}$ of 1 percent for their insurance); these banks would no longer pay premiums to FSLIC.[42] Thus, raising thrift deposit insurance premiums, rather than improving FSLIC's condition, could have made it worse.

Now consider equity. Increasing deposit insurance premiums would have further increased the disparity between the rates thrifts and banks paid. The special assessment meant that thrifts already paid 150 percent more per insured dollar than did banks; deposit insurance rates gave banks a competitive edge. In addition, increasing premiums across the board would have increased inequities within the thrift business (in terms of paying a "fair share"). Solvent, profitable thrifts argued, understandably, that they should not have to pay higher premiums to fund the losses of their insolvent and unprofitable peers.[43]

In 1986 and 1987, Congress determined that it should not and could not raise deposit insurance premiums to help provide FSLIC with the funds it needed. Congress nonetheless attempted to raise funds for FSLIC through thrift business resources so that it would not have to use general revenues. The Competitive Equality Banking Act (CEBA) called for the Federal Home Loan Banks (whose shareholders were the thrifts) to use up to $3 billion of their net worth to buy stock in a new entity, the Financing Corporation (FICO). FICO was to use this money as collateral to borrow up to $10.8 billion by issuing thirty-year bonds. The interest from the $3 billion was to pay off the principal on the bonds, and premiums from the thrift business were to be used to pay the interest on them. FSLIC's 1987 recapitalization was thus entirely funded by the thrift business.

In 1989, however, Congress did decide in FIRREA to raise the deposit insurance premiums for S&Ls. Under the assumption that the surviving part of the business would be healthier in the future, FIRREA scheduled thrift premiums to rise an additional 10 percent, from 20.83 to 23.0 cents per $100 of deposits, between 1991 and 1993.[44] FIRREA also taxed the net worth and the future profits of the Federal Home Loan Banks.[45] All things considered, Congress probably could not have raised much more from the thrift business during the 1980s to pay FSLIC's bills.

Why Did Congress Take So Long to Recapitalize FSLIC?

The Congress received its original request in April 1986 from the Reagan administration to "recapitalize" FSLIC by letting it borrow an additional $15 billion over five years. Congress did not pass a "recap" bill for sixteen months, and then CEBA provided FSLIC with only $10.8 billion, of which no more than $3.75 billion could be borrowed in any single year. Congress then waited to provide FSLIC with additional funding until 1989 (and FIRREA), when it granted FSLIC another $50 billion.

Congress has been almost universally condemned for acting too slowly and for providing FSLIC with too little money during 1986 and 1987. Most accounts place special emphasis on the ability of key politicians to stall the legislative process on behalf of the thrift business. Pilzer writes that House Speaker "Wright kept the FSLIC recapitalization bill locked in committee for more than six months."[46] Mayer quotes a letter to Bank Board Chairman Gray in which Senator David Pryor (D-Ark.) wrote: "I have put a 'hold' on the Senate recapitalization bill . . . [until] you will correct the abuses which have been taking place in Arkansas and other states."[47] Waldman notes that Wright put a similar hold on the legislation, pulling it from a scheduled floor vote.[48] These accounts also suggest that Congress, by granting FSLIC much less than the administration recommended, willfully provided it with grossly inadequate resources. As James Ring Adams puts it, "CEBA was a national scandal."[49]

The causes of this delay and stinginess have been traced to the influence of the thrift business over Congress. Again, Pilzer writes that Wright "was a willing tool of the powerful thrift industry lobby."[50] Adams states FSLIC's recap "involves a Congress willing to sacrifice the public good to the narrow interests of cronies and big contributors."[51] Waldman argues that CEBA "was a major victory by the S&Ls over the taxpayers—one of the most blatant and shameful instances of Congress favoring a powerful industry over the needs of the public."[52] The consequences of Congress's actions are presumed to have been a large escalation in the ultimate cost to the taxpayer.

These writers are correct, as far as they go. Individual politicians *did* seek to delay FSLIC's recap, the thrift business *did* lobby Congress effectively to limit the amount FSLIC could raise, and these limits *did* increase the total cost. But as we shall see, these details nonetheless *did not* have much of an impact on the length of time it took the bill to pass or the total cost of restoring FSLIC.

It is not possible to define the "right" amount of time that Congress should take to consider legislation. The length of deliberations often depends on a proposal's complexity and urgency. Legislation that is complex takes longer to consider; legislation that is urgent can be handled more quickly. The recap bill was highly complex and did not seem especially urgent, at least not in 1986. Rather than consider complexity and urgency separately, we will consider them within the sequence of events that occurred between the initial introduction of legislation in 1986 and its final passage in 1987.[53]

On May 22, 1986, FSLIC recap legislation was introduced into the House by Banking Committee Chairman St. Germain (D-R.I.) and ranking Republican Wylie (R-Ohio). This legislation to recapitalize FSLIC with $15 billion, which closely paralleled the administration's proposals, used "a complex borrowing arrangement."[54] This arrangement involved a transfer of Federal Home Loan Bank capital to a new "Financing Corporation" (FICO) that would sell bonds to private investors and then use the proceeds of these sales to aid FSLIC. As Lawrence White, a member of the Bank Board at the time, notes, "Many in Congress did not understand this plan . . . and simply saw [it] as more government borrowing and spending, which they wished to avoid."[55]

As complex as the FSLIC recap proposal itself may have been, it was among the least complicated problems the Congress faced. On June 4, 1986, the Congressional Budget Office (CBO) concluded that the administration's recap bill would add about $12 billion to the federal budget deficit. The Gramm-Rudman-Hollings antideficit law required legislation adding to the deficit to be offset by reductions in some other area. Even though the treasury department and the Office of Management and Budget disagreed with CBO's conclusions, this judgment stopped FSLIC's recap in its tracks. House Banking Committee Chairman St. Germain refused to cut $12 billion from programs within his committee's jurisdiction and so cancelled a planned June 24 markup until CBO's objections could be resolved.[56]

In the Senate, meanwhile, Banking Committee Chairman Garn (R-Utah) had no interest in passing an FSLIC recap bill in isolation from other financial reform measures. Garn instead introduced comprehensive legislation on June 24 that "would have reached virtually every corner of the financial services industry."[57] His proposal would have banned "non-bank banks," a recommendation strongly opposed by the financial giants such as Sears and Merrill Lynch, which operated such banks.[58] It would have allowed bank and thrift holding companies to enter into lines of business (such as selling municipal bonds, mutual funds, and mortgage-backed securities) from which they had been banned since the Depression. It included consumer protection measures such as credit card interest rate disclosure and check-hold limitations. Garn warned he would "absolutely not" consider piecemeal legislation from the House.[59] St. Germain, for his part, insisted that these banking issues should each be addressed individually, not as part of omnibus legislation.

As it turned out, Garn got less than he wanted and St. Germain more than he had planned. The Senate Banking Committee passed a much slimmed-down version of Garn's proposal on August 7, 1986. This bill contained only the FSLIC recap and a provision allowing out-of-state acquisition of ailing banks. "It was apparent to me there was simply no hope of passing a comprehensive bill because of resistance in the House," Garn admitted.[60] Senator William Proxmire (D-Wisc.) insisted, however, that he would filibuster any legislation that did not close the non-bank bank loophole. Proxmire maintained that the government's ability to sell or merge failing thrifts would be severely hampered if companies could enter new geographical markets by establishing non-bank banks. According to Proxmire, the non-bank bank loophole had to be closed to protect FSLIC.

In the House, FSLIC's recap was voted out of subcommittee by voice vote on July 19, but languished in committee for two months. On September 17, Gray wrote St. Germain to remind him of FSLIC's urgent needs. At this point St. Germain finally moved, but in doing so his committee added two measures to FSLIC's recap that had already been approved in separate legislation by the full House. These measures, which limited the time a bank could hold customers' checks and contained wide-ranging authorization for federal housing programs, were strongly opposed by the White House.[61] The House Banking Committee then voted 47–1 to approve the FSLIC recap, together with the other measures, on September 23.[62] The full House was scheduled to vote on the recap on September 29. At this point Wright, concerned about the treatment of Texas thrifts, temporarily pulled the bill off the calendar. He placed it back on the calendar one week later, and the House approved the bill by voice vote.

The Senate had not yet acted, however. On October 17, Garn was able to fashion a compromise bill, since Proxmire had agreed to drop his non-bank bank amendment. The bill that emerged was so heavily watered down that it dropped even the FSLIC recap provisions. But because of other delays normal at the end of a session, the Senate did not approve its banking measure until 4 P.M. on the day Congress was to adjourn. The Senate sent this bill to the House, where Senate leaders expected that the measure would be amended to once more include FSLIC and bank regulatory provisions and would then be returned. On this last day of the session, however, the House was virtually adjourned and operated under unusual parliamentary procedures that prohibited amendments, roll call votes, or consideration of controversial legislation. Discovering this, the Senate quickly passed another measure that included a one-year, $3 billion FSLIC recap together with some other banking provisions, and by 7:30 P.M. sent this bill to the House. St. Germain, acting on the basis of two caucuses of Banking Committee Democrats, refused to consider any measure that separated housing, consumer protection, and FSLIC's recap. St. Germain concluded that

> the Senate waited until the final hours to move anything and then ignored key consumer, housing, and regulatory issues, to the detriment of the public interest. Clearly, the Senate hoped to force the House into a take-it-or-leave-it position. We are not going to accept or have shoved down our throats at the last minute of this session anything that we do not agree to. Nothing is going to be railroaded through this House.[63]

At 9:34 P.M. on October 18, the House adjourned for the year, and the FSLIC recap died.

There was little controversy in 1986 surrounding the need for FSLIC recapitalization, the amount FSLIC should receive, or the form the recap should take.[64] The USL had not yet even stated an official position on the issue. The controversial "holds" put on legislation by Wright (and Pryor) created, at most, minor delays in the voting, especially in contrast to the "hold" that occurred while the budget dispute with CBO was settled. It appears that all the delays in the House made little difference in any case because it was the Senate that waited until it was too late to enact a law. Yet the Senate's procrastination seems to have had almost nothing to do with the proposed recap itself. It seems to have had almost everything to do with policy differences within the Senate, and between the Senate and House, concerning major financial issues.

Lawrence White, a Bank Board member between 1986 and 1989, has summarized congressional handling of FSLIC's recap in 1986:

> Congress felt no sense of urgency and proceeded to consider [the recap] at a leisurely pace. First, the inability of the FSLIC to liquidate or place insolvents with acquirers was not seen by Congress as a crisis. Second, neither the Bank Board nor the Reagan administration presented the problem to the Congress or the public as one of crisis. This was done, at least partly, to avoid creating headlines that might scare depositors and lead to runs on insolvent and solvent thrifts alike. Also, the full depth of the problems of the troubled thrifts . . . were not yet apparent to the agency or to the Treasury leadership.[65]

The next year brought some new characters and an even more complex plot. The Democrats had taken control of the Senate, and Proxmire had replaced Garn as Banking Committee chairman. Like Garn, Proxmire introduced legislation to recap FSLIC as part of a comprehensive banking reform. This reform again contained several highly controversial proposals. As in the previous year, Proxmire wanted to close the "non-bank bank" loophole; this proposal was again strongly opposed by some of the nation's largest corporations.[66]

Unlike Garn, however, Proxmire wanted to slow financial deregulation by imposing a moratorium on most banks' entry into securities, insurance, and real estate businesses, thus extending provisions of the Depression-era Glass-Steagall Act. Proxmire's recap plan called for allowing FSLIC to raise $7.5 billion.[67]

The administration called Proxmire's proposals "highly objectionable" because they imposed further restrictions on financial institutions, and urged the Senate to consider FSLIC's recap separately. The White House threatened to veto the legislation if it did not increase FSLIC's funding or if it did include the other provisions. Proxmire, however, was adamant that FSLIC's recap should not be considered in isolation, and that all his provisions were essential for a successful restructuring of the financial services business. Proxmire also argued that failing thrifts would not be easily sold unless the government closed the non-bank bank loophole.[68] Proxmire and the Senate moved promptly to approve his bill, spending less than six weeks from its introduction on February 17 to floor approval on March 27.

Enter Forbearance

In the House, what had once been easy became hard. Although the whole House had approved FSLIC's $15 billion recap by voice vote the previous year, it now ran into significant opposition. When the House Banking Committee held hearings on FSLIC recap on January 21 and 22, the USL now proposed an alternate plan that limited the recap to $5 billion over two years and contained "forbearance" provisions for failing thrifts. Forbearance was the term used for giving shaky thrifts more time to recover if they they were well managed but suffered from local economic conditions beyond their control. The National Council of Savings Institutions urged, in contrast, that the $15 billion recap be passed immediately.

Two arguments were made for providing FSLIC with less money than the administration wanted and for granting forbearance to marginal S&Ls. The first concerned equity. At the beginning of 1987 members of Congress increasingly passed along complaints to Banking Committee members about thrift regulators' "arbitrary and capricious" actions.[69] As Doug Barnard (D-Ga.) told Chairman Gray at the

FSLIC recap hearings held in January 1987, "There have been some questions that individual home loan banks have been overly rigorous and arbitrary in their supervisory actions, including the closing of certain savings and loans."[70] Texas Attorney General Jim Mattox threatened to sue "to stop use of federal regulatory procedures that discriminate against [Texas] savings and loan associations." Mattox continued, "We don't understand why the New York banks are given so much leeway, particularly in the bad foreign loans they've made, but on Texas loans we can't get the same forbearance and understanding."[71] The importance of fair regulatory treatment was compounded by the fact that the FHLBB regulators worked for a Republican administration, yet Texas thrifts were prominently involved in raising money for the Democratic party.[72]

The second concerned "just deserts." A large proportion of thrift business problems was concentrated in Texas and the other states in the Southwest. Thrifts in these states claimed that their difficulties were linked to the broader economic problems of their states and that they had no part in causing these problems. "It was argued that [the regulators] prevent lenders and borrowers from developing strategies to allow them to recover from severe economic conditions caused primarily by a downturn in the real estate, energy and agriculture markets."[73] Thrifts in other states, for their part, were not especially eager to pay for a problem they believed was not of their own making.

A third argument concerned cost. The thrift business contended that granting failing thrifts forbearance would save FSLIC money and avert its need for general revenues. The theory was that many thrifts would eventually regain solvency if the government did not take them over. As USL President Joe Morris put it, "Soundly operated institutions, if given some time, can recover from the temporary effects of economic adversity. We are proposing that they be given some time."[74] By granting forbearance, it was claimed that FSLIC would save money twice. It would escape the initial cost of liquidating or merging bankrupt thrifts. In addition, the argument went, whenever FSLIC liquidated a thrift in an economically distressed area, it "would further depress local real estate values, compounding problems for remaining insured depository institutions and making the depression worse."[75]

It is admittedly a challenge to take the thrift business's self-serving arguments seriously in the "kill the crooks" atmosphere of the 1990s, especially since there actually were so many swindlers involved in S&Ls during the 1980s. But consider the empirical and theoretical evidence available to Congress at the time.

Thrift business problems were indeed heavily concentrated in Texas. At the end of 1987, almost one-third of all thrifts insolvent by RAP standards, and 40 percent of insolvent thrift assets, were in Texas thrifts.[76] Almost half of all Texas thrifts were insolvent but still operating.[77] Even the solvent Texas thrifts had an average net worth of about 3 percent, which was the minimum amount the Bank Board required. In short, virtually the entire thrift business in Texas was already insolvent or on the verge of insolvency.

The economic situation did contribute to this concentration of thrift business problems. Figure 7.2 shows an index of two key economic indicators, commercial real estate and domestic crude oil, that affected the viability of S&Ls in Texas and the Southwest.

Commercial real estate values in the South and in the United States as a whole rose in tandem between 1977 and 1983. After that, commercial real estate prices remained fairly stable nationally in 1986 and 1987, but they took a beating in the South and especially in the Southwest.[78] Domestic crude oil prices, which play a large role in the Texas economy, fell even farther and faster. Since many real estate projects were predicated on rising oil prices, falling oil values spelled almost certain problems for real estate investors.

It is easy to see how a Congress interested in protecting economically important constituents at the expense of the general public may have been persuaded to favor the thrift business on the basis of equity and just deserts. Whether thrifts "deserved" forbearance from the regulators is one question. But whether it was in the taxpayers' interest to allow insolvent or nearly insolvent thrifts to remain open is another. The answer seems to have been a resounding no.[79] Forbearance has become badly discredited, and few people defend it today.[80]

It is again helpful, however, to judge forbearance by the evidence available to Congress in 1987. Forbearance had already been tried for the thrift business, it appeared to have been successful, and it was also being used by banking regulators. The principal data supporting

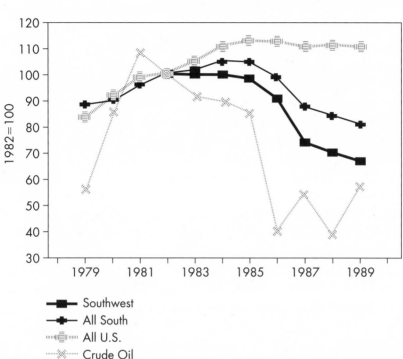

FIGURE 7.2

Commercial Real Estate and Crude Oil Prices, 1977–1989

— Southwest
— All South
All U.S.
Crude Oil

Source: Lawrence White, *The S&L Debacle: Public Policy Lessons for Bank and Thrift Regulation* (New York: Oxford University Press, 1991), 111.

the efficacy of forbearance come from a GAO report released in September 1986.[81] Because the GAO is usually considered to have been a prudent voice for FSLIC and the thrift business, it is worth considering this report in some detail. It illustrates the complexities and uncertainties concerning forbearance.

The GAO noted that FSLIC had actually been practicing forbearance since 1982, when it began to allow many insolvent thrifts to remain in business. In December 1982 there were 222 insolvent thrifts in operation. By the end of 1985, about one-fourth of these thrifts had been merged or liquidated, one-fourth had recovered their solvency, and almost half (107) were still insolvent. An additional 360 thrifts had become insolvent after December 1982 and remained bankrupt in December 1985, bringing the 1985 total to 467 insolvent but operating thrifts.

The GAO attempted, first, to estimate the costs of liquidating all 107 insolvent thrifts that remained insolvent between 1982 and 1985. The GAO then estimated the costs for waiting until 1987 before liquidating the 367 thrifts expected to remain insolvent at that time.[82] The costs of liquidating thrifts can vary over time, depending on changes in interest rates and the values of the thrifts' assets. Because the GAO did not have information on asset values for each thrift, it was able to estimate only the effect of changes in interest rates on liquidation costs.

The GAO's analysis produced several major findings regarding the costs of past and future forbearance. It estimated that FSLIC potentially saved between $4.6 and $5.2 billion due to changes in interest rates by *not* liquidating the 107 insolvent thrifts between 1982 and 1985.[83] In other words, declining interest rates meant that it might have been about $5 billion less expensive for FSLIC to liquidate these 107 thrifts in 1985 than it would have been in 1982. The GAO was not able to estimate, however, the change in the asset values of these thrifts over the three-year period. If these assets had dropped by more than about 3 to 4 percent in value each year, FSLIC would have been worse off by waiting. But because most insolvencies that occurred prior to 1983 were caused by problems in interest rate, not in assets, it appears that forbearance saved FSLIC money through the mid-1980s.

The merit of forbearance in the future was even less certain and depended heavily on interest rates and asset values. The GAO simulations predicted that FSLIC would lose over $1.4 billion by delaying liquidation of the 367 insolvent thrifts from December 1985 until December 1987 if interest rates did not change over that period. Using several assumptions that substantially simplified the analysis, the GAO also estimated that delaying liquidation from 1985 to 1987 could *reduce* FSLIC's costs by as much as $4.5 billion or *increase* them by over $8 billion.[84] Once again, the GAO was careful to point out that, to the extent that asset values declined, FSLIC's expenses would grow. This was of special concern because it was recognized that most recent thrift insolvencies were caused by asset, not interest rate, problems.[85]

The House attempted to examine these issues during hearings in January 1987. St. Germain agreed to hold additional hearings in March regarding the allegations of regulator misconduct, and the Banking Committee subsequently assigned staff (two former GAO auditors) to investigate the complaints. The investigators found that some regulators had operated in an "inflexible, intolerant fashion." Overall, however, the investigators found that the regulators had acted appropriately, given the nature of the region's problems. Others testifying at the March hearings concurred that "the regulators made a good case and the savings and loan operators did not."[86]

Despite the evidence presented at these hearings, on March 31 St. Germain (backed by Speaker Wright) offered the Financial Institutions Subcommittee his plan to recapitalize FSLIC with $5 billion over two years and forbearance provisions, as a substitute for the $15 billion, five-year plan without forbearance provisions he had introduced at the beginning of the session. The forbearance provisions mandated that a "well-managed" thrift with a net worth of at least 0.5 percent of assets "shall not be closed." Thrifts would also be allowed to appeal regulatory decisions about the value of their assets.[87] The subcommittee voted 23–20 to reject St. Germain and preserve the $15 billion plan. On April 1, however, the full committee voted 25–24 to lower the recap amount to $5 billion.[88] The deciding vote was cast by St. Germain himself as a proxy for the absent representative Walter Fauntroy from the District of Columbia.[89]

Because the full committee rejected the subcommittee's proposal; did so by virtue of a proxy cast for a delegate who did not even have full voting rights; did so in favor of the proposal backed by the S&L business; and did so in apparent disregard for the true needs of FSLIC, this vote has been seen as a substantial misuse of power.[90] It is therefore useful to review the points made by the committee's own report.[91] The report notes, first, that differences in the borrowing authority granted by each proposal were not large in absolute terms: the administration's bill would have raised $3.5 billion each year compared to $2.5 billion each year by St. Germain's proposal. (Neither amount, as it turned out, would have been nearly large enough to handle FSLIC's insolvencies.) It notes that "the bill as reported reflects the Committee's awareness that $5 billion is only a beginning.

At the end of the two year period, the Committee, in all probability, will be called upon to authorize further financing." (It was, in fact, called upon to authorize such financing and did so; it would have had to do so regardless of which proposal was accepted.) While the majority believed that the amount approved was insufficient for the entire task, they were also concerned that the Bank Board did not have adequate personnel to spend more effectively. What proved most misguided in hindsight was the view that giving the Bank Board any more funding would give it "a mandate . . . to close troubled thrifts rather than work with the institution's management to restore the institution to economic vitality." The report notes finally that "the closeness of the full Committee and Subcommittee votes is indicative of the difficulty of the judgment call involved."[92]

The committee report also gave those who made the judgment to support the full $15 billion recap a chance to air their views. The sixteen members who signed the "strongly dissenting" portion of the report argued that St. Germain's proposal "directly contradicts the overwhelming amount of testimony" and was "woefully inadequate" to address an "emergency situation." The dissenters concluded by harshly criticizing the majority who had voted to reduce FSLIC's funding:

> Those Members who lack the desire to address the true extent of the problem and who believe they can wait two years to muster their resolve are betting that the situation will not deteriorate. Not only is such a bet imprudent, it wagers the savings of Americans across the country on what is a long shot at best, rather than protecting the stability of the deposit insurance system and those depositors who depend on that insurance to safeguard their life savings.[93]

It can hardly be said that the Banking Committee ignored the seriousness of the issues surrounding FSLIC's recap.

When the bill came to the House floor, St. Germain and Wright reversed themselves again. This time, St. Germain proposed an amendment to restore the $15 billion figure, and Wright spoke on behalf of it. "I've changed my mind," Wright announced April 28 on the House floor, urging his colleagues to vote for the full $15 billion "to see this problem through" and "to ensure the public confidence."[94]

Other Democratic and Republican leaders continued to speak against the larger recap, however.[95]

Both a Republican president and a Democratic Speaker now called for the House to approve the $15 billion recap. Yet, incredibly, majorities of both parties rejected an amendment to restore the higher figure and the proposal failed by a vote of 153-258. The House approved its $5 billion recap bill with forbearance provisions by a vote of 402-6 on May 5, about six weeks after the Senate passed its version. The Senate rejected the House measure and reiterated its support on May 14 for a $7.5 billion recap and Proxmire's other provisions concerning non-bank banks. Because of the differences between the two bills, "most lawmakers predict[ed] a long and bitter fight [in conference committee] over substantial differences between the two FSLIC proposals."[96]

The prediction was accurate. The conference committee did not even begin meeting until June 23 and took more than another month to reach final agreement. The committee initially approved an $8.5 billion recap—above the level approved by either chamber—with reduced forbearance provisions. On July 29 the conferees agreed to raise FSLIC's borrowing authority still further to $10.8 billion, apparently to avoid a threatened presidential veto of the lower amount.[97] The House and Senate agreed to the conference report on August 3 and 4, respectively, and President Reagan signed the bill into law on August 10, 1987.

Summary and Conclusions

Congress deregulated thrifts' liabilities in the 1980s by eliminating all ceilings on the interest rates that S&Ls could pay for deposits and by allowing S&Ls to obtain deposits from a wide variety of retail and wholesale sources. Congress first attempted to do this in the Depository Institutions Deregulation and Monetary Control Act of 1980 (DIDMCA). Through this law Congress created the Depository Institutions Deregulation Committee (DIDC), comprising the main financial regulatory agencies, and instructed it to lift interest rate ceilings progressively while attending to the impact of such actions on the thrift business. When the thrift business effectively blocked DIDC's actions, Congress took direct action by requiring DIDC immediately to authorize an account that would compete directly with institutions not subject to interest rate ceilings.

On balance, the interest rate deregulation in DIDMCA and Garn–St. Germain was a sensible approach to a thorny problem. The evidence in 1980 was very strong that rapid elimination of Regulation Q would threaten thrift business viability and depress the housing industry. Legislators might be forgiven for concluding on the basis of careful analysis that it was not good public policy to savage major sectors of the economy, even as the USL, NAR, NAHB, and AFL-CIO were reminding them as constituents that it was not smart electoral politics to do so. On the other hand, the data increasingly suggested that interest rate ceilings would not serve permanently to stabilize the thrift business. Furthermore, the evidence was quite clear that interest rate ceilings discriminated against small savers. The AARP, NRTA, NOW, Public Advocates, Consumer Union, and the Gray Panthers wanted Regulation Q eliminated, and Congress understandably saw the merit to these equity arguments.

To resolve these conflicting forces and policy uncertainty, Congress in DIDMCA delegated authority over interest rate controls to a committee of the officials in the best position to understand the situation, to appreciate the alternatives, and to evaluate the consequences of these alternatives.[98] Congress's instructions that this committee should move "as fast as possible" but "with due regard for the effect" of its policies were not easy to follow, however. These congressional directives reflected the multiple policy goals that Congress hoped to achieve. When the DIDC was unsuccessful in using this mixed mandate to remove interest rate ceilings, Congress gave it explicit instructions to do so. Congress gave DIDC these directions when it became increasingly apparent that interest rate controls were both unfair to depositors and destabilizing to the thrift business.

Funds started pouring in to the thrift business once liabilities were deregulated, and a number of S&Ls began growing rapidly. The Bank Board attempted to impose a number of regulations to limit excessive growth. One rule probably would have eliminated virtually all brokered deposits by removing their deposit insurance coverage. A second regulation limited the ability of marginal thrifts to grow rapidly through brokered deposits. A third rule did not target brokered deposits, but limited growth from any source while allowing better capitalized thrifts to grow more quickly.

Congress rejected the first regulation and allowed the Bank Board to impose the others. These congressional decisions were sensible. The logic and evidence supporting the first and broadest regulation were weak, and therefore Congress did not provide the regulators with the legislative authority to implement such a rule. Congress recognized that rapid growth by weak thrifts posed dangers to the deposit insurers and encouraged the regulators to restrict such growth, as the other two rules did.

These decisions also suggest that Congress did not surrender to the thrifts that wanted unconstrained growth or to the deposit brokers who sought the unregulated ability to sell deposits. Congress instead attempted to differentiate between "good" and "bad" growth and thus between different classes of thrifts and their rights to brokered funds. Congress did not send a message to the thrift business that all S&Ls had the right to unlimited growth: sound thrifts were to be permitted to grow more rapidly than unsound ones. Congress did not tell the brokerage industry that it had the right to sell unlimited deposits to all S&Ls: brokers were allowed to market only a modest quantity of deposits to unsound thrifts. Given the available information and reasoning, it is not obvious what Congress should have done differently.

As with liabilities, thrift asset powers had been limited to provide financial stability and to support housing. By the early 1980s, it was uncertain whether asset regulation was serving either goal. The central tenet of modern portfolio theory—that investments can yield higher and more stable returns if they are diversified instead of concentrated in one even relatively safe investment—was broadly accepted. Asset deregulation was not a partisan issue either in Congress or in the executive branch during the late 1970s and early 1980s. President Carter had supported expanded asset powers for thrifts in 1979 and President Reagan did likewise in 1982. Virtually everyone was for them, except those businesses (such as banks) that stood to face new competition. The argument for expanding thrift asset powers became especially compelling once thrifts' liabilities had been deregulated. Congress acted by modestly expanding thrift asset powers in DIDMCA and then increasing them much further in the Garn–St. Germain Act.

Some of these new asset powers, such as the ability to make consumer or commercial real estate loans, were not especially controversial when Garn–St. Germain was enacted or even later. The same cannot be said for direct investments (and some other investments, such as junk bonds).[99] Direct investments that went sour have created large losses for the thrift business and hence for FSLIC, and Congress has been blamed for approving these asset powers. Congress, to be sure, apparently did not closely consider the impact that some new asset powers could have on FSLIC's reserves. In particular, there apparently was no public debate in the period leading up to Garn–St. Germain about the possibility that direct investments or junk bonds might create additional losses for FSLIC.

The ability of S&Ls to make direct investments and trade junk bonds did become controversial in the years after Garn–St. Germain, however, and the Bank Board devised regulations to limit their use. Congress reconsidered these issues, and the proposed regulations, in a number of hearings and reports. These reports showed that the evidence supporting (and opposing) the regulations was inconclusive. Congress nonetheless permitted the Bank Board to implement its regulations as "appropriate and necessary."

Congress raised deposit insurance on individual accounts from $40,000 to $100,000 in 1980. Though many have denounced this change, these new deposit insurance ceilings did little to increase FSLIC's losses. In raising insurance coverage, moreover, Congress followed a historical pattern that had not previously resulted in losses for FSLIC. Furthermore, there was legitimate intellectual support for making deposit insurance coverage not just broader, but universal.

The congressional delay in recapitalizing FSLIC was not unusual and due primarily to the variety and complexity of the problems. Individual legislators, eager (and sometimes too ready) to protect thrifts in their district, delayed proposals until their concerns were heard. More broadly, committee leaders disagreed about what to do and how to do it. They disagreed about who should pay and how payment should be made. More important still, the leaders disagreed about basic issues of legislative strategy—in particular, whether FSLIC's refinancing should be handled in isolation or as part of a broader reform of the financial system. Budget issues and concerns about regulatory capacity weighed heavily. Even the fact that each house of Congress sought to impose its view on the other slowed the process down. As a result, the recap bill tortuously made its way into law. Still, at most the delays increased FSLIC's losses only modestly.[100]

Congressional support for forbearance is also easy to understand. For purely selfish reasons, members of Congress will typically want to come to the aid of local businesses when they can. But there are also broader reasons for legislators to seek to assist marginal thrifts. A public-spirited representative would want to be assured that thrifts were treated uniformly across the country, so that neither local economic nor political conditions put local thrifts at a disadvantage. A civic-minded legislator may seek to keep borderline thrifts in business in order to preserve local employment and financial opportunities. A fiscally prudent politician might conclude—with good evidence—that forbearance could provide a low cost method of protecting borrowers and lenders. After all, forbearance had worked to protect individuals and the public during the Depression and the early years of the 1980s.

Congress did not stop the thrift tragedy from unfolding, but neither did it ignore it. Throughout, Congress deliberated, considering various public goals and the ways to achieve them, examining evidence, and evaluating alternatives. Such deliberation did not usually make the choices easy and clear. Public goals—such as providing savers with market yields and borrowers with affordable mortgages, or keeping thrifts profitable while focusing on home finance—were not always compatible. The evidence about the ways to achieve these goals was often ambiguous or misleading. The empirical relationship between brokered deposits and thrift problems was unclear, making it difficult for Congress to act. In contrast, the relationship between direct investments and thrift profits did seem clear, but the conclusion that investments increased profits proved wrong. Conflicting goals and incomplete, if not incorrect, evidence made choosing among alternative policies perplexing.

Congress did not disregard its oversight responsibilities. It does appear that congressional oversight was alerted by "fire alarms" rather than produced by "police patrols"; that is, oversight was triggered when someone reported a problem, rather than being initiated by active congressional monitoring.[101] On important issues regarding thrift liabilities, assets, and deposit insurance, the fire alarms sounded and congressional committees held hearings and issued reports. While congressional oversight did raise issues for debate, it often did not produce solutions to the problems it discovered. When oversight did yield clear problems and solutions, action was usually forthcoming.[102]

Congressional action was not always immediately forthcoming, however. Sometimes Congress acted swiftly; often, it did not. In general, the speed of the congressional response appears to have been influenced by the complexity and salience of the issue and the consensus about the solution.[103] The more complicated and obscure the problem, and the more divisiveness about the solution, the longer it typically took Congress to act. When the problem was important and a clear consensus existed regarding solutions, Congress could act swiftly. Unfortunately, during much of the thrift tragedy the issues were complex and esoteric, and the solutions open to debate.

8

Congressional Voting

PERHAPS CONGRESS IS BETTER AT DELIBERATING than at voting. Perhaps all its consideration of the issues was cast aside when it came time to cast votes. When all was said and done, perhaps members of Congress simply voted the wishes of the thrift business. To assess these possibilities, we now examine congressional voting behavior during the thrift tragedy.

The idea that Congress was especially solicitous of the thrift business is based on two related propositions: first, money talks, as do constituents; and second, Congress listens to both. Both propositions are firmly rooted in the public choice tradition.[1] According to this view, members of Congress are primarily motivated by their desire to remain members of Congress. Raising money for campaigns and generating support among constituents are both means to this end.

Critics of the congressional role in the thrift tragedy have been particularly concerned about the impact of S&L campaign contributions on congressional activity (and inactivity).[2] As Michael Waldman, director of Congress Watch, wrote: "The S&L disaster couldn't have happened without a posse of thrift allies on Capitol Hill—lawmakers purchased by campaign contributions, personal gifts, entertainment, and speech fees."[3] Common Cause has conservatively estimated that thrifts gave almost $12 million in political action committee (PAC) and individual campaign contributions to congressional candidates and political party committees during the 1980s.[4] As Charles Keating himself said, when asked if his campaign contributions influenced legislators, "I want to say in the most forceful way I can: I certainly hope so."[5] Before concluding that the Congress was indeed the best one thrift money could buy, however, let us reflect on the kinds of voting decisions that elected representatives face.

Congressional Voting

Are members of Congress influenced by public spirit or by self-interest in their voting decisions? Usually, they are influenced by both. Members can easily believe that what is good for their country is good for their political careers, and vice versa. Legislators may also find it obvious that what is good for their constituents is good for the public; in fact, they may consider the public for most purposes to be their constituents. Since one of the primary jobs of elected representatives is indeed representation, a member of Congress might believe that faithfully following the wishes of the district's electors is the best way to pursue the public good.

But there are several ways that policy preferences of the public and those of its elected representatives can coincide or conflict (table 8.1). Usually, legislators will experience little conflict in making their voting decisions, since public and personal interests coincide (case 1). At times, legislators will vote with public opinion (i.e., constituent preferences) even though they may personally believe the public interest calls for them to vote against it (case 2). More rarely, a legislator will vote for a proposal even though public opinion opposes it (case 3). A fourth possibility, that the public has no real policy preferences, is quite common, and in that instance the representative can vote either way without much public pressure (case 4); alternatively, the public but not the representative has a preference, and the official can easily vote with the popular sentiment (case 5). A final case, in which the public has conflicting views about the public interest, also occurs frequently. In this case, the legislator will inevitably please some constituents and anger others (case 6).

Note that both the public spirit perspective and the public choice perspective can explain each of these outcomes; therefore,

TABLE 8.1

Interpretations of Legislative Voting

Case	Public's Preference	Official's Preference	Official's Vote	Interpretation
1	Proposal A	Proposal A	Proposal A	*Public spirit*: Official votes for public interest. *Public choice*: Official votes to maximize personal political gain.
2	Proposal B	Proposal A	Proposal B	*Public spirit*: Duty to constituents overrides personal policy preference. *Public choice*: Personal ambition overrides personal policy preference.
3	Proposal B	Proposal A	Proposal A	*Public spirit*: Duty to public interest overrides constituents' preferences. *Public choice*: Official expects to fool constituents; expects they will forget; or expects other political benefits exceeding costs.
4	None	Proposal A	Proposal A	*Public spirit*: Official votes for public interest. *Public choice*: Official votes to maximize personal gain.
5	Proposal A	None	Proposal A	*Public spirit*: official votes for public preference. *Public choice*: Official votes for public preference.
6	Conflict over Proposals A and B	Proposal A	Proposal A	*Public spirit*: Official votes for public interest. *Public choice*: Official votes to minimize personal damage and maximize personal gain.

voting patterns do not allow us to test directly which view is correct. Still, the public spirit view is more persuasive, for two reasons. When the public and the legislator agree, when the public has no preference, or when the official has none (cases 1, 4, and 5), no difficult choices need be made: by voting in the public interest, the representative at the same time serves self-interest. For these cases, the public spirit and public choice perspectives cannot be distinguished (except in their assumptions about human behavior).

Two other cases are more difficult for public choice advocates to explain. Elected officials do on occasion vote against constituent wishes (case 3). While the public spirit approach would find this perfectly natural, public choice advocates must look still deeper for the selfish reason behind the vote. For example, they may posit that the official hoped the constituents could be fooled or would forget the vote. According to their view, even political suicide must justify some personal ambition.

A more common, and important, situation occurs when constituents have sharply conflicting views about which policies are best (case 6). Here the self-seeking politician could engage in complex mental calculations to determine which vote would minimize costs and maximize benefits; but this cost-benefit calculation is made all the harder in that public opinion constantly shifts, so that yesterday's maximization might be today's minimization.[6] A public-spirited official, in contrast, can "do the right thing" and get no more blame (and perhaps less, to the extent that voters value honesty and consistency) than the calculating official.

It would seem that the most troublesome case, from the public spirit perspective, occurs when representatives vote against their personal policy preferences and for the public preferences (case 2). Yet the traditional theory of representation makes the argument that public officials should not put their own beliefs above the views of those they represent, that doing so is not service, but hubris.[7] One need not be a hypocrite or a schemer to ignore personal beliefs and vote with public opinion. An elected representative may do this out of a sense of duty.

How does money change the situation? For the most part, not at all.[8] To see this, substitute the phrase "campaign contributor preference" for "public preference" in table 8.1. In cases 1, 2, and 5 the representative will act just as before, and either public spirit view or the public choice perspective could easily explain this behavior. To be sure, case 3 seems unlikely to occur often, since contributors are usually unwilling to give a large amount of money to those who vote against them and politicians are reluctant to vote against those who contribute to their campaigns. Case 4 is not really an issue, since politicians do not normally receive contributions from those without policy preferences.

The most important, and potentially troubling, situation would occur when campaign contributors prefer one policy and the broader public favors another (a variant of case 6). How, then, will the representative vote, and how should the vote be cast? Unfortunately, the answers are still not clear. The official may favor either the donors or the public, and may do so for reasons relating either to self-interest or to the public interest. While it might seem that the self-interested politician would vote for the contributors' interests, the official may nonetheless vote for the public if doing so is seen as a way to gain additional popular support. While it might seem that the public-spirited legislator would vote for the popular interest, the politician might yet favor the monied class over the people for the traditional conservative rationale that the public is served best when wealth is served first.

Thus, a study of congressional voting patterns cannot resolve whether legislators were motivated by self-interest or by public spirit. What it can do is identify the "objective" factors to which representatives responded in their voting decisions. Voting studies can help reveal whether (though not why) legislators were influenced by such things as partisan affiliations, campaign contributions, and constituent demographics as they cast their votes. Of particular concern here is the congressional response to the thrift business.

Prior Studies of Congressional Voting

Scholarly studies of the effect of business interests on legislative voting have three common weaknesses that limit their usefulness. The first concerns the choice of the votes to be explained (the "dependent variable"). Most researchers have focused either on a particular "key" vote or have constructed a general "index" including multiple votes.[9] Since legislators often have a variety of reasons for voting for or against any given proposal—especially the often highly conflictual ones that typically comprise "key" votes—interest group influence may not show up on any specific vote.[10] Whether or not interest group influence appears to be important might also depend on the researcher's choice of the "key" vote to study.[11] The opposite problem exists for voting indices, however. The specific influences on particular votes may be "washed out" when many votes are aggregated into one index.[12] Neither a key vote nor a voting index allows the researcher to determine whether interest groups have repeated influence across many votes.

A second deficiency of congressional voting studies is that they usually focus on only one legislative chamber, most commonly the House of Representatives. There may be statistical reasons for doing this, but the substantive basis behind such a research strategy is less clear. Votes in one house have no legislative impact unless the other house concurs.[13] It is thus important to look at both the House and Senate in determining interest group influence on legislation.

A third weakness involves the indicator of business interests. Typically, a single, short-term measure of business influence—such as campaign contributions from the relevant interest group during a single election cycle—is used to assess the effect of the business on congressional voting.[14] This ignores the possibility that there may be multiple, conflicting, or longer-term relationships between the legislator and members of the interest group. A more sophisticated view would consider that business groups are often internally divided, that legislators are sensitive to these divisions, that legislators may respond to numerous signals from different portions of the interest group, and that representative and constituents can develop relationships that are more durable than a single electoral cycle.

Despite the widely held view that the thrift business controlled the Congress, only a single published study has examined the influence of thrifts on voting, and this study looked at only a single vote in the House of Representatives.[15] The authors, Romer and Weingast, take a public choice view of Congress and apply it to a House vote concerning a proposal by Banking Committee Chairman St. Germain in 1987 to increase FSLIC's borrowing authority from $5 to $15 billion.[16] Although Romer and Weingast emphasize the importance of congressional structure and incentives on legislative behavior, their results do not strongly support their assumptions.[17] Most interestingly, the two most important influences on voting were political party and member ideology, which I believe have more to do with political beliefs and commitments than incentives or structure.[18]

The research presented here attempts to identify and measure the factors concerning the representatives and their constituencies that influenced congressional voting on S&L issues during the thrift tragedy. It improves on previous research by examining numerous individual roll call votes, by analyzing votes in both the House and the Senate, and by including multiple measures that characterize the thrift business. In this chapter I summarize the main elements of this research and its conclusions; technical details are contained in appendix 4 and the footnotes.

Congressional Votes on Thrift Issues

For this study I examined the floor votes in the House of Representatives and Senate on the four laws enacted between 1979 and 1989 that most directly affected the financial condition of the thrift business.[19] These laws are: the Depository Institutions and Monetary Control Act (DIDMCA, 1980); the Garn–St. Germain Depository Institutions Act (1982); the Competitive Equality Banking Act (CEBA, 1987); and the Financial Institutions Regulatory Reform and Enforcement Act (FIRREA, 1989). A total of twenty-one roll calls were analyzed, ten from the House and eleven from the Senate.[20]

These votes encompass a wide variety of issues, from broad "omnibus" legislation (bills containing numerous provisions) to extremely narrow concerns (such as whether the current chairman of the FHLBB would need to be reconfirmed as the chairman of the OTS when the OTS replaced the FHLBB). Several roll calls involved proposals that would have changed the treatment of nonthrift financial institutions;

these were included because the institutions were often the thrifts' competitors. Two kinds of roll call votes pertaining to these four laws were excluded from this study, however. I omitted roll calls in which the overwhelming majority voted together because, in such cases, there was no variation to study: if everyone votes the same, it is impossible to identify the factors that influenced the voting.[21] Four roll calls (two each in the House and Senate) were excluded because they involved the treatment of spending (but not the spending itself) under the Gramm-Rudman budgetary restrictions. I eliminated these votes from the analysis because they did not directly concern thrift issues. One House Banking Committee vote of special interest is also discussed separately in appendix 4.

Thrift Business Influence on Congressional Voting

Members of Congress may be influenced in their voting decisions by members of the thrift business acting either as contributors or as constituents. While most of the publicity has focused on the influence of S&L campaign contributions, a less dramatic possibility is that Congress was responsive to thrift business interests because the business was widely decentralized, economically important, and philosophically valued—three traits that enhanced the business's political power. At the beginning of the 1980s over four thousand thrifts were dispersed around the country, so that every member of Congress had one or more thrifts as constituents. The thrift business held almost $1 trillion in assets. Thrift constituents typically were prominent local business people and were often allied with other significant local business owners such as home builders and realtors. They also operated businesses that helped fulfill the American Dream: home ownership. As Representative Charles E. Schumer (D-N.Y.) noted, "The power of the U.S. League [the largest thrift organization] occurs not so much from the money they give, but because they represent institutions in every congressional district." Representative Bruce A. Morrison (D-Conn.) added that thrifts "say they *are* housing. They make the American dream."[22] In this section, I explore the potential influence of campaign contributions and then of thrift constituencies.

Thrift Business Campaign Contributions

Scholars have devoted considerable effort to examining the effect of interest group campaign contributions on congressional voting. Even though the view that politicians are self-interested dominates social science, most scholarly research concludes that contributions have little influence on voting behavior.[23] These findings are probably not convincing to those outside the research community.[24] Given the widespread and commonsensical belief that money does indeed influence politics, perhaps the models that show campaign contributions have no impact on voting, rather than the conventional wisdom they reject, need to be questioned. Remember, however, that demonstrating a link between contributions and votes need not imply that representatives have voted against the public interest.

Researchers looking at this issue have typically sought to determine whether campaign contributions from a particular interest group (or groups) to a particular candidate during a particular electoral season influence that legislator's votes during the upcoming legislative session.[25] This implies both that "short-term money" affects "short-term votes" and that "interest groups" have unified political goals. Although this may sometimes be true, there are good reasons why politics does not always work that way.

A legislator who has received large campaign contributions from a group over time, and who is indeed heavily influenced by these contributions, may not receive very much money from the group during any particular election, for example. The candidate, if in a safe seat, may not need the contributions; the interest group, upon judging that seat relatively safe, may direct its resources elsewhere. As a result, in considering only the impact of contributions during a single electoral cycle, researchers may be led to misstate the effect on voting behavior.

Furthermore, a legislator who has received large contributions, and who is influenced by them, may not vote the contributors' interests on any particular roll call. The contributors may not need the legislator's vote if their favored measure is sure to pass (or even sure to fail); the legislator, in seeing that the measure has enough votes (or lacks so many), may vote against the contributors despite their generosity.

Consequently, any single roll call vote may understate campaign contributions' influence on legislative voting.

Legislators, moreover, are attentive to their political base—those who have helped the candidate in the past and those who are likely to do so in the future. These past and future orientations are closely linked. Legislators would have no special reason to vote the preferences of campaign contributors from the previous campaign unless they expected to receive additional electoral support in the future. There is thus no compelling reason to use prior donations as the sole measure of the influence of campaign contributions on votes. It may make more sense to look jointly at contributions the legislator receives before and after the vote.

An alternate way of studying the relationship between campaign contributions and congressional voting would thus include both longer-term measure of contributions and multiple votes. A long-term measure of campaign contributions, containing data from several election cycles, would reduce the idiosyncrasies of a single election, incorporate the effect of potential contributions on voting behavior, and perhaps illuminate more stable relationships between interest groups and legislators. For these reasons, I shall examine the impact of all reported campaign contributions from the thrift business between the years 1981 and 1990 to each member of Congress.[26]

Using total thrift campaign contributions for the entire decade to determine business influence over Congress also has a few weaknesses. For the earliest votes examined (1979), it is entirely a prospective measure (all contributions were received after the vote); for the latest votes analyzed (1989), it is primarily a retrospective measure (all contributions were obtained before the vote). If the impact of contributions on voting behavior is either primarily retrospective or primarily prospective, this variable may not accurately portray the relationship between money and votes at both ends of the period. If, however, legislators honor longer-term relationships with interest groups, this variable will have little impact on the analysis.

This indicator of campaign contributions also covers differing lengths of time for different representatives. Representatives in 1980 who continued to serve through 1990 would have had the entire decade to accumulate campaign contributions from the thrift business, for example, while legislators elected in 1988 would have had contributions from only one election cycle. Average campaign contributions per election could serve as an alternative variable. It is not clear whether legislators are more likely to be influenced by the total contributions they receive from the thrift business or from their average contributions during an electoral cycle.[27]

An additional problem with the use of total thrift campaign contributions as a measure of thrift influence is that it excludes legislators who did not remain in office through 1990. This is not much of a problem for voting data from 1989, but many legislators serving in 1979 and 1982 (and, to a lesser extent, in 1987) were no longer in Congress at the end of the decade. It is theoretically possible that the legislators who retired, who were beaten, or who died before 1990 were fundamentally different from those who remained in office at the end of the decade. For better or worse, this does not seems to have been the case.[28]

Combining all thrift campaign contributions into a single measure of thrift influence creates a problem. Even within a single business, contributors can have differing interests. Big thrifts and small thrifts, or profitable and unprofitable ones, can have conflicting legislative goals. Now suppose two legislators received the same amount in contributions from the thrift business, but one legislator received money primarily from large thrifts and the other mainly from small thrifts. If a vote pitted the interests of large and small thrifts against each other, and each legislator voted the way the major contributors preferred, it would incorrectly appear that contributions did not influence voting outcomes because similar total contributions produced both yea and nay votes.

There is no good solution to this problem.[29] The broader the definition of "interest group" used for counting campaign contributions, the more likely it is that contributions will have no apparent effect on legislative voting because of divisions among the contributors. The more narrowly defined the interest group, the fewer will be the legislators who have received contributions, and the fewer the votes in which the group will be interested.

In this study, I added together campaign contributions received by a legislator from all thrift PACs and from all individuals identifying themselves as affiliated with S&Ls. Thus, a significant relationship between thrift contributions and congressional voting does not simply mean that "money affects votes" but that contributors generally are unified *and* that legislators respond to them. If no relationship is found, in contrast, it might be because contributions are unimportant or it might mean that contributors disagree about how the vote should be cast.

Thrift Business Constituencies

The thrift business is often depicted as unified in its political goals. Yet the "business" is not a single entity, but an assortment of several thousand (more or less, depending on when one looks) individually owned and operated businesses. These businesses did share many similarities until the 1980s and were amenable in many cases to promoting a single political agenda. S&Ls were generally small, simple, stable, profitable, and (financially) conservative.[30] Note the word "generally," however. Even at the beginning of the thrift tragedy there was a diversity of opinion within the thrift business on political issues of importance to that business, because thrifts varied in size, profitability, and commercial strategy.

The differences among thrifts within the S&L business increased enormously during the 1980s. Many thrifts became larger—much larger—than their peers. The variation in average thrift assets from state to state increased from about $110 million to $430 million between 1979 and 1989; average assets also increased by almost the same amount during this period.[31] Profitability also varied substantially among thrifts, and variations in profitability increased dramatically over the course of the decade. In 1979, average thrift profitability in the average state was $0.8 million, and profitability varied by $0.9 million from state to state. In contrast, by 1989 average thrift profitability (or rather, deficit) in the average state was minus $4.5 million, and the variation across the states was $14.4 million.

It should come as no surprise that different thrifts can have different political interests. Although a wide variety of differences may be politically relevant, differences in size and profitability are most likely to be important. Large and small thrifts can be expected to disagree over a number of political issues. Large thrifts usually sought new powers because they wanted to expand further; small thrifts typically opposed changes to the status quo because they feared new competition. Similarly, profitable and unprofitable thrifts often sought different legislation. Unprofitable S&Ls generally favored policies that helped keep them in business, while profitable associations found that they could benefit if their insolvent competitors were allowed to fail.[32]

If legislators are sympathetic to the condition of the thrifts in their districts, they are also likely to be attentive to the sheer number of them. Each thrift has a voice—especially through its owner and directors—and may petition the government for redress. Since thrifts are likely to agree on many political issues, the more thrifts in a legislative district, the greater an impression they may be able to make on their representative.

To examine whether the characteristics of the thrift business that varied from place to place affected congressional voting, I included the number, size, and profitability of thrifts in each political jurisdiction in the analyses of the roll call votes. Thrift size was defined as the average total assets of thrifts by state or by congressional district. Thrift profitability was measured by the average net income of a thrift by state.[33] A final indicator of thrift business influence was the total number of S&Ls per state or the average number per congressional district.

Partisan and Ideological Influences

With all the attention paid to the thrift industry's alleged control over Congress, it is easy to forget that a legislator's party affiliation is likely to be the dominant influence on many votes. Partisan influence is especially important to members of Congress because the party reflects the representatives' individual ideologies and their organizational commitments. Representatives usually vote with their party because, from their point of view, it is both good policy and good politics.

Partisan affiliation is the one factor in the analysis that we can be sure influences congressional voting. What will be interesting to explore, therefore, is the substantive question: Is either party more culpable for passing legislation that contributed to the thrift tragedy?

Estimating the impact of partisanship by itself cannot answer this question. It can, however, help identify the particular issues on which the parties voted differently.

Some scholars have included measures of the representative's political ideology other than partisanship in their assessments of legislative voting patterns. In general, these indices of ideology are closely related to partisanship and, as a result, including both brings little additional information to the analysis.[34] Moreover, the relationship between political ideology and attitudes toward the thrift business is unclear at best. Conservatives and liberals alike may find principled reasons to support (or oppose) legislation aiding S&Ls.[35] I thus omitted political ideology from this study.

I did include the legislator's region which, in this case, was a more relevant measure of attitudes toward the thrift business. Regional differences have historically been important in American politics, and it seems unlikely to be any different here. Certainly publicity about thrift business problems—and controversies—has focused on such states as Texas, California, Florida, Colorado, and Arkansas. Politicians and thrift owners throughout the "Sun Belt" seem to have had distinctly different attitudes about how business in general, and the thrift business in particular, should be run, compared to their northern and eastern peers. Accordingly, this analysis identified legislators as coming either from one of the eighteen Sun Belt states or from one of the thirty-two other states.[36]

The Analysis

I have identified several "objective" factors that might influence members of Congress as they voted on legislation affecting the thrift business. A legislator's political party or regional background might have made it more likely that the vote would be cast for (or against) a proposal. Similarly, the number, size, or profitability of the thrifts that were in a legislator's constituency might have influenced that politician's votes; the campaign contributions received from the thrift business might also have affected these votes. It is relatively easy to measure these objective factors and to estimate their influence on voting behavior.

Other, more "subjective" factors (such as the personal beliefs of the legislators) also influence congressional voting, of course. Since these factors are difficult, if not impossible, to measure, they are not included in the statistical analysis presented below. The practical significance of including some variables and omitting others is that the importance of the included factors will tend to be overstated and the influence of the omitted factors understated. In other words, the results presented below probably exaggerate the true influence of the thrift business on congressional voting.

I determined the thrift business's influence on congressional voting in several steps. First, I estimated the impact of thrift, partisan, and regional factors on voting behavior for each roll call.[37] Second, I identified the factors that frequently had an impact on voting behavior across all the roll calls. Third, I calculated the average impact of these variables on congressional voting. These steps allow us to judge the typical importance of each individual factor on the legislators' votes. Fourth, I estimated the influence of all the thrift variables together, and then the partisan and regional variables. This step helps us assess the importance of the thrift business compared to the other political factors on voting behavior. Finally, I estimated the influence of all these objective factors combined, in order to determine how important all the objective factors were in congressional voting on thrift legislation.

The Results

It is clear that partisan affiliations, region, and thrift constituencies all considered together affected congressional voting on the twenty-one roll call votes on thrift legislation. On average, if one knew a legislator's party and region, the amount in campaign contributions received from S&Ls, and the characteristics of the thrift business within the constituency, one could correctly predict the legislator's vote about 80 percent of the time.

The thrift factors usually influenced congressional voting, though it appears they affected the Senate less frequently than the House. In eight out of the ten roll calls in the House of Representatives the thrift business variables almost certainly influenced the votes.[38] In contrast, the thrift variables together appear to have had an impact on only six out of the eleven votes in the Senate, and we have reason to be less confident of this impact.[39]

The political factors (party and region) together were usually influential on both House (eight out of ten) and Senate (ten out of eleven) votes. In at least two House and one Senate roll call, however, partisan and regional considerations seem to have had at most a weak influence on outcomes.[40] In the three instances when party and region were not influential, thrift-related variables did apparently affect the votes.

It is possible to make a rough estimate concerning the relative importance of thrift and political factors on congressional voting. In both the House and the Senate the political factors dominate, though the House was somewhat more sensitive than the Senate to its thrift constituencies. In the House, the political factors account for about 80 percent of the total explanatory power of the models, while thrift factors contributed the remaining 20 percent. This probably understates the average importance of thrift factors, however, because partisan factors were overwhelmingly influential on three votes.[41] When these votes were omitted from the analysis, thrift and political factors had about a 50–50 split in importance. Political factors also account for almost 80 percent of the explanatory power in the Senate. Unlike the House, however, political factors still contribute more than two-thirds of the influence on voting in the Senate even if the three votes in which the political factors are most prominent are omitted.

These results suggest that representatives and senators may have responded to somewhat different factors when casting their votes, at least on legislation affecting the thrift business. Constituent factors—that is, the characteristics of the thrifts within the congressional district—appear to have been somewhat more important in the House than in the Senate. Partisan and regional factors may have influenced voting more commonly in the Senate, though representatives were also often influenced by these factors. These results fit the image of a House equally concerned with parochial and partisan matters, and a highly partisan Senate somewhat less concerned with local interests.

Different factors did influence different congressional votes.[42] In the House, political party, region, thrift business campaign contributions, the number of constituent thrifts, and the size and profitability of constituent thrifts all routinely affected roll call votes. The same factors had an impact on voting outcomes in the Senate, though campaign contributions and thrift size appear to be important less often in that body. It is highly unlikely that each of these individual variables (with the possible exception of campaign contributions and thrift size in the Senate) appeared to be important unless they truly were.

While not every variable was important on every vote, each variable influenced voting outcomes on at least several votes. The most common variables affecting voting in the House were political party and region, which each influenced eight out of ten roll calls. Thrift business variables also sometimes shaped voting outcomes, with each variable affecting between three and five of ten roll calls. Political party and region also were the variables most commonly shaping Senate votes, with party having an impact on six of eleven votes and region on five of eleven. The thrift-related variables influenced voting in the Senate on as few as two or as many as five out of eleven roll calls.

House Republicans were more likely than House Democrats to vote for two proposals that might have reduced FSLIC's (and ultimately the taxpayers') total losses had they been adopted. In 1982, Republicans voted 135–22 in support of an administration measure that would have provided assistance (in the form of interest-bearing promissory notes) to thrifts with low net worth. Assistance would have been based on a sliding scale so that only a portion of a thrift's losses would have been made up. Democrats opposed this proposal 186–19. After this proposal was defeated, Democrats voted 188–17 to support an alternate measure that guaranteed the net worth of all marginal thrifts at 2 percent; Republicans, however, also supported this plan 84–74.

In 1987, House Republicans were also more likely than Democrats to support a floor amendment to increase FSLIC's recapitalization from $5 to $15 billion, which would have allowed FSLIC to close down more insolvent thrifts. Democrats opposed this amendment 160–78, even though it was proposed by St. Germain, the Democratic chairman of the Banking Committee, and supported by Speaker of the House Jim Wright. Still, a 97–73 majority of Republicans also opposed the amendment.[43]

Partisan affiliation in the House had no measurable influence on the final roll calls concerning DIDMCA or FIRREA. And even though Democrats were more likely than Republicans to have voted in support of the Garn–St. Germain Act, and Republicans had a higher probability than Democrats of supporting FSLIC's $15 billion recapitalization, a majority of both parties voted for the former and against the latter. Given these outcomes, it is easy to see how neither Democrats nor Republicans have been able to use thrift-related legislation for partisan advantage.

In the Senate, the Republicans took a more pro-deregulatory stance than the Democrats on at least three occasions.[44] In each case, a motion was made to remove controversial measures from a bill and to approve a "clean" bill focusing on just one issue. In 1979, Republicans were more likely than Democrats to support omnibus financial reform legislation, though 50 percent of the Democrats also supported the omnibus measure. In 1987, Republicans were much more willing than Democrats to provide new powers to financial institutions other than thrifts. Still, it is not clear from this that the Republicans are any more (or less) culpable than the Democrats for the thrift tragedy.

The average impact of each individual factor on voting behavior in the House and Senate, and the variation of these impacts on the various votes, are summarized in table 8.2. Several important implications can be drawn from this table.

The effects of individual variables are substantial. For example, the legislator's political party had a 28 percent impact on the likelihood of voting for or against thrift-related legislation in the House. In other words, if a House Democrat voted for a proposal, a House Republican was 28 percent more likely to vote against it (all other factors being equal). Similarly, the voting probabilities differed by 18 percent between House legislators from Sun Belt states and those from non–Sun Belt states; by 18 percent between districts with larger thrifts and those with smaller thrifts, or between districts with more profitable thrifts and those with less profitable ones; by 10 percent between districts with more thrifts and those with fewer; and by 8 percent between legislators who received larger amounts in thrift campaign contributions and those who received smaller amounts.[45]

The impact of each variable also differed substantially from vote to vote: each variable was quite important on some votes and quite unimportant on others. This can be seen by comparing the standard deviations of the effect of the variables on congressional voting to their mean impact: they are nearly the same size. This implies, for example, that it is nearly as likely that party will have a 60 percent effect on voting probabilities as that it will have no impact at all, or that region will have a 35 percent impact or no influence.[46]

The House and Senate are quite similar regarding the relative importance of the different variables, as indicated by the degree (not necessarily the frequency) of their effect on roll call votes. In both houses, party is the most important variable affecting voting, and campaign contributions are the least important. In neither body, furthermore, do campaign contributions have a trivial impact. In both the House and the Senate average thrift income, thrift assets, region, and number of thrifts within the jurisdiction ranked second to fifth in order of the degree of impact on congressional voting.

TABLE 8.2

Mean Effect of Individual Factors on the Probability of Voting for Thrift-Related Legislation, 1979–1989

Vote	Party	Region	S & L			
			Funds	Number	Assets	Income
House	0.28	0.18	0.08	0.10	0.18	0.18
(%)	(.31)	(.17)	(.08)	(.16)	(.26)	(.28)
Senate	0.38	0.15	0.06	0.15	0.20	0.25
(%)	(.34)	(.15)	(.09)	(.16)	(.24)	(.20)

Note: Standard deviations in parentheses.

Conclusions and Implications

At the beginning of this chapter I argued that legislators could vote their constituents' (or campaign contributors') preferences for self-interested reasons, for public-spirited reasons, or for some combination of both. An analysis of roll call votes, moreover, could do little at best to determine which motivation dominated. It is nonetheless possible to identify some objective factors which might have influenced congressional voting on thrift issues, to test whether these factors actually were important and how important they were. While these tests will not show what was in the minds of the legislators, the results can help us assess the health of the political system.

We have seen that legislators were sensitive to the concerns of their savings and loan constituents. Senators and representatives tended to vote the interests of the thrift associations within their state. The campaign contributions of these thrifts were indeed one factor—but not the only one—affecting their votes. Congressional voting was also influenced by the number, size, and profitability of thrifts within the legislative districts.

Thrift interests were not uniform, however. In particular, it is misleading to suggest there was a single "thrift interest" to which legislators were sensitive. In many cases large and small S&Ls, or profitable and unprofitable thrifts, or even those who made campaign contributions and those who did not, had different views about appropriate legislation, and Congress reacted to these differing preferences. Legislators with many, large, or profitable thrifts in their jurisdictions voted somewhat differently than did representatives whose constituent thrifts were few in number, small in size, or lacking in profits.

It should be emphasized that legislators responded to factors other than thrift interests when they voted. Legislators tended to vote like others in their party and from their region, and the parties and regions tended to differ from each other. The legislator's party typically was the most important factor influencing congressional votes.

Furthermore, the voting patterns in the House and Senate were neither exactly the same nor entirely different. Representatives seem to have paid attention more often in their voting decisions to their thrift constituents than did senators. Both senators and representatives were most influenced by partisan factors, were moderately affected by thrift constituent characteristics, and were influenced by campaign contributions to a lesser extent.

These conclusions "hardly point to a political system that has failed." Whether members of Congress are motivated by self-interest, the public interest, or both, they represent their constituents and these constituents have diverse interests. Local interests are not the only influence on policy, however, since the political party of the legislator is the single most important factor affecting congressional voting. The House and Senate weigh party and constituents somewhat differently, yet neither chamber ignores either factor in making its decisions. This sounds like representative government, American style.

9

Concluding Words

THIS STUDY BEGAN by contrasting the public choice and public spirit views of politics in general and the thrift tragedy in particular. It concludes with the argument that the public spirit perspective gives a more accurate account of these politics. The thrift tragedy did not occur due to the self-interested motives of public officials. Instead, FSLIC failed despite the public-spirited behavior of politicians and bureaucrats.

The institutional structure of the FHLBS had little to do with FSLIC's failure. It is not at all clear that, had the FHLBS been designed differently, FSLIC's losses would have been substantially reduced. With notable exceptions, the officials within the different parts of the FHLBS attempted to fulfill their mission as they understood it, and the organization of the FHLBS by itself did not prevent officials from doing their jobs. Nor did it alone guarantee they could do them. The structural elements of the FHLBS most responsible for the thrift tragedy were the rules imposed on the thrift business. Without question, the policies in place at the end of the 1970s all created the conditions for the thrift tragedy to begin. These policies required (or encouraged) thrifts to make long-term, fixed-rate mortgage loans; limited thrifts' ability to diversify their portfolios; placed restrictions on thrifts' powers to obtain deposits from diverse sources and pay market interest rates for them; and provided federal insurance on savings deposits. Without doubt, the policies adopted in the beginning of the 1980s that empowered thrifts to pay whatever they wished for funds and to invest these funds in virtually any project allowed the tragedy to grow and spread. With certainty, these policies were adopted to benefit the public by making homes affordable, savings safe, and thrifts stable.

The resources of the FHLBS were not adequate to the task. FSLIC's losses would have been reduced if the FHLBB had had more and better staff and if the insurance fund had been better funded. From this it may be tempting to draw the "Vietnam War lesson": if only we had dedicated ourselves to victory, victory would have been ours. This conditional, being neither provable nor falsifiable, is open to debate forever, but some observations about it might serve as grounds for consensus. A few more resources would not have changed the outcome. Any additional spending would have done little good unless it had been used effectively and, given the strategies prevailing at the time, it is not clear that it would have been so used. There was strong and widespread opposition (some legitimate, some not) to massive increases in spending. Given the uncertainty of the effectiveness of additional spending and the demand for funding for other government programs, it should be little wonder that public officials were reluctant to spend more than they did.

Policy choices were rarely easy during the thrift tragedy, nor were they easily made. At times politicians and bureaucrats deliberated—that is, debated goals, gathered evidence, and considered alternatives—at great length before acting. They deliberated less when goals, evidence, and alternatives seemed clearer. In general, the greater the deliberation the poorer the timeliness, and the greater the speed in which decisions were made the less deliberation occurred. Because officials can hardly be both swift and deliberate, it would be easy to show that officials acted either too slowly (when they deliberated at length) or too rashly (when they made decisions quickly). Yet a broader and fairer look at officials' decisions during the thrift tragedy provides evidence that, in general, they decided cautiously when no consensus existed and quickly when one did: they deliberated when the solutions were not clear and acted when they were.

Congressional committees conducted substantial oversight on the thrift business during the 1980s. The committees heard testimony, reviewed studies, and produced reports—but rarely took action. The primary reason for this is that the testimony and studies were often conflicting or ambiguous. The fact that oversight seldom led to action does not imply congressional inattentiveness, or worse, negligence. It does remind us how much easier it is to hear about problems than to solve them.

Throughout the thrift tragedy a wide variety of voices were heard within the Congress. Our examination of the congressional debates showed that elected representatives listened to elements within the thrift business, but the politicians also considered the demands of bankers, brokers, developers, realtors, home builders, home buyers, the elderly, and even the "small savers." Even within the narrower examination of congressional voting, the evidence indicates that Congress responded to various elements within the thrift business. These voices, however, did not always form a chorus, since members of Congress representing small, or unprofitable, or a limited number of thrifts often voted differently than members with more, larger, or more profitable S&Ls as constituents. To be sure, campaign contributions also affected congressional voting but, of all the influences from the thrift business, they were the least significant influence. FSLIC's failure thus did not occur owing to the lack of representation; if anything, congressional responsiveness to the diversity of interests—savers, borrowers, lenders—within society made the thrift tragedy more likely to begin and more difficult to stop.

Politicians and bureaucrats generally made good faith efforts to limit the thrifts' collapse or reduce its impact. Officials' lack of success in preventing FSLIC's failure does not imply they acted exclusively, or even primarily, out of selfish motives. Even public-spirited officials, acting in society's interests as best they can, cannot always prevent tragedies from occurring.

The fact remains that the federal government will spend about $180 billion (in present value 1991 dollars) between 1980 and 1996 to clean up all the insolvencies in the thrift industry.[1] This expense has been variously called a "monumental disaster," a "catastrophe," a "fiasco," and a "debacle." Aren't these assessments alone enough to damn the officials who allowed it to happen? Not necessarily. FSLIC's losses, though tragic in its dramatic content, were hardly disastrous in human consequences.

A Monumental Disaster?

What, after all, makes FSLIC's failure catastrophic? It cannot be expense alone. Although any federal policy that costs as much as FSLIC's failure (an average of $11 billion annually over the sixteen-year period between 1980 and 1996) is not exactly trifling, neither is it uncommon among national programs. The major federal programs—defense, income security, and health care, for example— cost vastly more, of course. Yet less familiar programs are also more expensive than deposit insurance has been. Over the same period, the average costs for income support programs for farmers will run almost $15 billion each year.[2] The federal government spends considerably more each year on allowing individuals to deduct the interest paid on home mortgages than it expends annually on FSLIC's failure, and apparently will do so in perpetuity.[3] Much bigger "catastrophes" go virtually unnoticed. Every year the federal government fails to collect well over $100 billion in taxes it is owed.[4] Each year during this period the federal government will pay as much in interest (an estimated average $220 billion) on the federal debt as it will spend on the entire thrift "disaster."[5] This debt, it should be remembered, is the result of the government collecting too little revenue for too large obligations—the same situation that occurred with FSLIC.

Many people believe that the government spends far too much on farm payments, mortgage interest deductions, and interest on the federal debt.[6] Perhaps it does, though the consensus for eliminating subsidies for either farmers or home buyers is hardly universal. Consensus would probably be greater for reducing the government's interest payments. Doing this, however, would require higher taxes or lower spending and, as experience has shown, neither is easily accomplished.[7] At any rate, federal spending on farmers, home buyers, or bond holders is not a disaster, nor is it usually designated one.

If it is not the size of the federal spending on thrift resolutions that is cataclysmic, then perhaps the distribution of this spending is. While no good data exist about this distribution, we can be certain of two things. First, the benefits were tilted heavily towards the more affluent. Deposit insurance is an entitlement program without a restrictive means test; therefore, everyone with an insured deposit is protected regardless of wealth or income.[8] The affluent received the bulk of deposit insurance's benefits because, although most insured accounts at thrifts were fairly small, most of the insured money was in fairly large accounts.[9] Second, even though benefits are tilted toward the wealthy, millions of individuals received benefits either directly or indirectly.[10] More than 20 million depositors held accounts at S&Ls that failed during the 1980s, and all these deposit holders are beneficiaries of FSLIC. Many of those who performed services for failed thrifts, obtained loans from them, or sold property to them also indirectly collected deposit insurance payments. Deposit insurance payments were, like our nation's wealth, both narrowly concentrated on the wealthy and widely dispersed among the less affluent.

These two distributional aspects of the deposit insurance program once again parallel the experience of numerous other federal programs. Farm support programs are justified as a way to help the "family farmer"—and many family farmers do get help from them—but "the great bulk of farm subsidies has gone to the richest farmers and the biggest agribusinesses."[11] And just as deposit insurance provides the most benefits to the biggest accounts, farm subsidy programs yield the largest payoffs for the largest farms. Similarly, the home mortgage interest deduction "mainly benefit high-income people who own expensive homes."[12] The net distributional effect of federal interest payments are less clear, although it is beyond dispute that gross interest receipts increase with individual wealth.[13]

Individuals will disagree about the ethical and political principles that support these distributions. Many will believe that policies so tilted toward providing benefits to the affluent do not serve the best interests of the nation's citizens or its economy. But the distributional aspects of the thrift "catastrophe" are common in American public policy. Such distributions are indeed widely accepted by the public.

Another reason that the thrift tragedy might be a "monumental disaster" concerns its economic impact. The CBO has attempted to estimate this impact by using a simulation model of the United States economy.[14] CBO suggests that the GNP may have been reduced by a total of about $200 billion (in 1990 dollars) between 1981 and 1990, and the overall loss may approach $300 billion by the end of the 1990s.[15] According to this study the main reason for the forfeited GNP is that "the S&Ls channeled some of the nation's investments into inefficient and sometimes worthless projects, rather than into productive investments such as new factories and new equipment. This reduction in the nation's capital stock causes potential GNP to be lower than it would be otherwise."[16] The same has also been said about the other programs.[17] Farm subsidies have been denounced for diverting resources away from more efficient uses (i.e., too many crops are grown).[18] The mortgage interest deduction and other housing subsidy programs have been said to "preempt private sector investment resources, and this absorption has an inhibiting effect on productivity and economic growth" (i.e., too many houses are built).[19] The economic impact of federal spending on defense, health care, income transfers, and deficits on economic growth must be much more severe than the thrift "catastrophe" because these expenditures are so much larger and have lasted so much longer.

The claims that the size, distribution, and economic impact of FSLIC's losses are not uniquely large, unfair, and depressing may sound like the faintest praise ("of all the tumors, that one is my smallest"). But the examples presented above hardly exhaust the possibilities. Numerous federal programs that have proven broadly popular have cost more, have had more biased distributions, or have imposed greater burdens on the economy. Admittedly, that does not diminish the magnitude of FSLIC's losses, but it does help put them in perspective. In economic terms the government spending on the thrift tragedy was a moderately large, mildly redistributive, and modestly inefficient residential and commercial development program.

A final indication that FSLIC's losses are not catastrophic is the effect on people's lives and the public's reaction to the losses. Some observers have been perplexed that the public has not become outraged over the thrift mess. The apparent public indifference is sometimes attributed to the complexity of the issues or the enormity of the losses. How could the public truly become angry over matters too difficult to understand and too expensive to comprehend?

This view understates the public's abilities and overstates the thrift tragedy's magnitude. Some large and complex issues, such as inflation, unemployment, health care, or crime can produce huge public responses because they perceptibly affect people's lives. Millions of individuals are hurt when economic or social conditions worsen, and the public often responds politically to such threats. With relatively few exceptions, however, the public was not directly damaged by FSLIC's failure.[20] In truth, FSLIC *prevented* the losses from becoming catastrophic to the public by ensuring that individuals did not lose their savings. The public did not perceive a disaster because there was none.

The political consequences of the thrift tragedy are also modest. There was no wholesale rebellion against elected politicians. FSLIC's failure played a negligible role in the 1988 and 1992 presidential elections and few congressional races have focused on thrift issues. Perhaps the worst political consequence of the thrift tragedy is the continued erosion of popular faith in elected officials. Responsibility for this erosion is mixed. Some politicians have earned the scorn they have received. Yet the public choice and popular views—by blaming both the guilty and the innocent in their castigation of public officials in general—have also contributed to the growing cynicism.

Political Reforms

Many financial reforms have been proposed to prevent another thrift tragedy from occurring. Many of these reforms are no doubt sound, though their size and the distribution of costs and benefits, their compatibility with other public goals, and their economic and political feasibility are of course subject to debate.[21]

Less attention has been devoted to political reforms, and the theoretical rationale for these reforms has been less developed. Before considering some individual proposals, let us reflect on the reform messages of the public choice view and the public spirit view in general.

The public choice belief about political reform is clear. Since officials are immutably self-interested, reforms must be designed so that officials seeking to advance their own benefits will, as a side effect, enhance the public good.[22] There is much to commend this view. After all, a basic element of representative democracy is that politicians must compete for votes: individuals seeking office are driven by self-interest to provide the greatest benefits to the greatest number of voters. This conversion of self-interest into public interest through the ballot box is part of the genius that gives democracies an edge over authoritarian governments.

But the limits to self-interest as a guiding principle of politics and political reform should be obvious. Two limits in particular bear mention. First, no existing political system relies entirely on converting self-interest into public interest. If individuals were only self-seeking, elections would quickly degenerate into mob rule (by the public) and demagoguery (by the politicians).[23] Second, real political reform would be almost impossible. If all reform proposals are judged exclusively by the criterion "does it help me?" then why should we expect political actors to adopt any reforms that benefit the public at large?[24] The public choice view of politics thus leads inexorably to a catch-22. Politics are flawed because individuals are self-interested, but, because individual self-interest dominates, efforts to reform politics are futile.[25]

The public spirit view toward political reform is more direct. It contends that officials seek the public interest and suggests that reform proposals can be made and debated on their own merits. Officials and the voters at large can choose or reject proposals based on whether or not they can be expected to improve the public welfare, not just on how they affect the individuals making the decisions. The power of this view can also be seen through the miracle of real elections. Successful candidates are often the ones who offer the most compelling vision of the public interest, and the voters choose among candidates based on these visions. This belief in offering alternative ideas about the general welfare and trusting citizens to choose among them is another indispensable element in democratic government.

The public spirit perspective is optimistic about the prospects for political reform. It assumes that government officials (and the public) typically want to improve public policy and that this reformist attitude makes improvements possible. But it also recognizes that reforms may come slowly, since individuals disagree about which changes will actually serve the public interest, and may work poorly, since our understanding of policy consequences is uncertain and incomplete.

While the public spirit view may be more optimistic than the public choice view about the prospects for political reform, it is less (naively) optimistic about the policy consequences of reform. If individual self-interest can be properly channeled through an appropriate set of rules, the public choice view suggests, decisions beneficial to society will automatically arise as a side benefit of individual decisions. An "invisible hand" of politics, like that presumed to exist within free markets, is the holy grail sought by public choice scholars. The public spirit believes this quest for the holy grail is quixotic; it doubts that any set of rules will lead automatically to policies beneficial to the public. Political systems are imperfect and imperfectible. Because our views of the public interest conflict, because our knowledge of policy tools is flawed, and because our situation constantly changes, policy tragedies would continue to occur even if all individuals were perfectly public spirited. If all individuals are merely selfish, such tragedies are sure to occur yet more often.

Reforming Congress

Despite the lavish helpings of blame that have been heaped on Congress for its role in the S&L mess, few observers have new ideas about how to improve congressional behavior regarding the business.[26] Some extol the perennial favorite, campaign finance reform.[27] The argument is that politicians would make policy decisions more favorable to the public at large if they were less dependent on campaign contributions from "special interests." The evidence that campaign finance reform would work to reduce policy errors, as the proponents contend, is sparse, and the prospect that such reforms would bring unintended consequences is nearly certain.[28]

Other reformers have called for reducing Congress's influence over the regulators so that they would be more free from political influence. The desire for a bureaucracy removed from politics is understandable. Whenever an agency misfires, Congress can be said to have exercised too much influence over it; except, of course, in those cases where the bureaucracy acts too independently of the duly elected legislature. In these cases of bureaucracy "running amok," Congress is seen as having exercised too little control over the administrative apparatus. Depending on the moment, then, Congress is advised to exert less or more control. Debates over the proper relationship between Congress and executive branch agencies appear to be a permanent feature of politics in the United States.

This tension between too much and too little political control of the bureaucracy is not entirely ignored by the public choice reformers. Kane, one of the harshest critics of the congressional role in the S&L mess, acknowledges that "members of Congress should remain free to win reasonable regulatory adjustments for aggrieved constituents."[29] His reform proposal is also reasonable: "All efforts to win forbearances for individual constituents should be reported to the House and Senate ethics and banking committees" and these reports should be made public.[30] As a proposal for good government, who could argue against it? Yet it has two significant weaknesses. In the past, FSLIC's losses were due primarily to policy commitments and policy conflicts and not to the individual interventions of members of Congress; listing interventions would thus have saved FSLIC little. Its future effectiveness is also open to question. If politicians are as cynically self-interested as Kane argues, it would be a simple matter for them to evade the rule. That is, if public choice theory is correct, this reform would be useless. Yet if politicians are public spirited, such a rule might be helpful because it would require legislators to make explicit any belief they had that assisting specific constituents is beneficial to the general public.

Another popular reform proposal calls for "honesty in budgeting." According to this line of reasoning, a primary political reason that FSLIC's losses grew so large was that Congress was willing and able to ignore them as long as it did not have to actually pay for them. Congress, in essence, treated FSLIC like a credit card in which losses were not reported when they were incurred (i.e., when the charge was made) but only when they were paid (i.e., when the check was sent). Again, Kane has a proposal: "The annual implicit and explicit cost of [FSLIC's] guarantees [must] be henceforth reported as part of the official budget of the United States. It must no longer be possible for these costs to develop outside of the ordinary process used to control aggregate government spending."[31] Again, whether or not this reform makes sense depends in part on the motives of politicians. Projections of the deficit are already included in the budget each year: Congress (and the president) already know they are incurring greater obligations than they are willing to raise taxes to pay. It is a mystery why adding deposit insurance's "explicit and implicit" obligations to the budget would inspire self-interested politicians to become more fiscally prudent.[32] If politicians are public spirited, however, they will care about the size and distribution of spending, taxes, and deficits. In this case, Kane's reforms might at least encourage further debate about fiscal responsibility. Since legislators already have commitments about these matters, it is important to recognize that the debates will not necessarily change policies swiftly and dramatically (though they might).

We already have one congressional reform: elections. The purpose and benefits of elections are unclear, however, if all politicians are merely self-interested. From the public choice perspective, don't all legislators deserve equally to be voted out? Are any candidates worthy of being voted in? But if at least some politicians are public spirited, the vote, used judiciously, can improve the general interest. Elections should help distinguish between those who seek and those who abuse the public good. Members of Congress who have abused their public trust by placing their own interests above the public interest should be voted out of office, as some have been.[33] Those who faithfully perform their public obligations should strongly be considered for reelection.

The main reason few congressional reforms have been suggested (or adopted) to prevent another thrift tragedy is that few reformers can, first, link a systematic problem to a particular policy or procedure, second, demonstrate that a specific reform remedies the problem, and third, establish that this reform will not create worse problems. These are tough standards, but they should be carefully considered by those interested in improving congressional performance.

Reforming the Bureaucracy

Although there has been a shortage of reform proposals for Congress, there has been a surplus of them for the Bank Board. These proposed reforms have involved three bureaucratic issues: structure, resources, and powers. Many of these proposals have already been adopted through the Financial Institutions Recovery and Reform Act (FIRREA) of 1989.[34]

The FIRREA altered the structure of the FHLBS in two principal ways. It separated the three functions of the Bank Board—regulation, credit, and insurance. It eliminated the Bank Board and moved its regulatory functions (including chartering) into the newly created Office of Thrift Supervision. The OTS, moreover, was not to be an independent agency (like the Bank Board) but a bureau within the Department of the Treasury (like the Office of the Comptroller of the Currency).[35] The FSLIC was pulled out of the FHLBB, renamed the Savings Institutions Insurance Fund (SAIF), and merged with the Federal Deposit Insurance Corporation (FDIC).[36] A Federal Home Financing Board (FHFB) was established to oversee loans made to thrifts by the district FHLBS.[37] Finally, FIRREA created the Resolution Trust Corporation (RTC), directed and staffed by the FDIC, to dispose of insolvent thrifts.

From a public-spirited viewpoint, the reasons for these reforms are clear. The FIRREA attempted to rationalize the financial system by moving toward arranging agencies by function and not by business. Rather than having entirely separate government systems for banks and thrifts, regulators were now placed with regulators (OTS and OCC within Treasury) and insurers with insurers (FSLIC within FDIC). Many reformers had long advocated this functional consolidation and opposed the market specialization of the government's financial agencies; in particular, observers had been critical of the joint regulatory and insurance functions of the Bank Board.[38] Moving the OTS into the Treasury and merging the FSLIC with the FDIC were also attempts to reduce the influence of the thrift business over these offices (and, not incidentally, to increase their credibility). By moving the OTS into the Treasury and the FSLIC into the FDIC, Congress was responding to criticisms that the Bank Board had been too susceptible to influence from the thrift industry and (perhaps) from the Congress itself.[39]

It is open to debate whether these reforms were needed or will be effective.[40] Good arguments were made for them, but institutional interests (the thrift business and the Bank Board) opposed them. It is difficult to see how these changes were motivated purely by self-interest on the part of members of Congress (unless politicians suddenly found it politically useful to listen to ideas and to ignore interests).

Although Congress and the administration were reluctant to provide FSLIC with large amounts of new funding in the mid-1980s, they had changed their tune by the end of the decade. The FIRREA authorized $50 billion in funding for handling insolvent thrifts. Since then, the administration has requested and Congress has approved billions in additional funds for resolving thrift failures. While not providing the deposit insurers with a blank check drawn on the federal treasury, the politicians have made an enormous commitment of financial resources to liquidate, sell, or subsidize bankrupt thrifts and protect insured depositors.

It is possible that members of Congress found self-interested reasons for providing FSLIC with only $11 billion in 1987 and more than ten times that amount a few years later. Perhaps individual calculations changed, and what was once politically unpopular became politically fashionable. The popularity of most policy proposals does fluctuate over time. Yet public support for (or even awareness of) refinancing FSLIC was almost nil and large portions of the thrift business did not exactly champion the refinancing. Why, then, would Congress change its policies so dramatically? One possible answer is that, during the 1980s, Congress was convinced neither of the severity of FSLIC's problems nor of the need for taxpayer assistance; but by 1989, Congress recognized both severity and need and responded accordingly. At both times, in other words, Congress as a whole did what it considered best, not just what was most expedient.

The FIRREA also took several steps to increase the enforcement powers of OTS. It expanded the ability of OTS to issue cease and desist orders and to remove the directors and officers of thrifts for even "prospective losses" or other actions that could lead to bankruptcy. It gave FDIC additional authority to end or suspend deposit insurance at unsafe thrifts. It increased the civil and criminal penalties it could impose on thrift personnel for regulatory violations.

By strengthening enforcement powers, Congress loosened the constraints on the regulators. Loosening these constraints should increase the regulators' ability to restrict excessive risk taking at thrifts and banks. The way regulators use these new powers will determine how effective they are. Because Congress did not actually define the actions that lead to prospective losses, for example, the regulators will have fairly wide discretion in how they use their cease and desist orders.

One Simple Reform

A central theme of this study has been that Congress and the Bank Board attempted to promote the public interest during the thrift tragedy. Congress was responsive and responsible in its behavior, and the Bank Board for its part faced enormous problems with limited tools. Still, Congress and the Bank Board could have done a better job at developing and implementing policies to reduce FSLIC's losses without sacrificing other goals.

Congress could have used the traits that were already its strengths: listening, deliberating, and responding. These strengths would have served better, and been better served, had Congress received better advice on how to resolve the problems of the thrift industry and the FSLIC. Lack of high quality guidance was not the result of a lack of effort on Congress's part, however. Congress cast its net widely in seeking counsel about thrift issues. Yet it did not often receive the advice it needed from the source it should have come from: the Bank Board.

The Bank Board did give Congress plenty of advice. But it did not do the two things it should have done. The Bank Board should have shown Congress that the Board knew what needed to be done. It also should have shown Congress that the Board could be trusted to know what needed to be done. These are two different things. Congressional debates show that many people tell Congress that they know what to do and, of course, some of them actually do. But to whom does Congress actually listen? Facts, theory, and political savvy certainly make an argument more credible. Many in Washington seem to possess these in more than small measure. As a result, Congress tends to pay greater credence to those who consistently show over time that they are giving solid advice.

The Bank Board did not, and could not, convince Congress that its advice was most important. The reasons for this have little to do with the incentives or integrity of individual board members. A more important reason is that the Bank Board was composed of inexperienced individuals who served short terms. Between 1965 and its demise in 1989, only one Bank Board chairman served even one full four-year term.[41] No Bank Board members between 1979 and 1989 had worked in management positions in the agency they became responsible for directing. Given these conditions, how could the board have spoken authoritatively about policy and administration?

The Bank Board's lack of expertise hampered its ability to advise Congress in a couple of ways. Its lack of expertise meant that the Bank Board was less likely to actually give sound policy advice. Yet even when the Bank Board did make solid recommendations, its lack of experience meant that Congress found it more difficult to trust the board's judgment. A Bank Board that was more experienced and more skilled would have been better able to provide authoritative advice to Congress.

What advice might a more mature and accomplished Bank Board have been able to give? A veteran board should have recognized the magnitude of FSLIC's losses earlier and so pressed for more funding sooner; this could have saved some money. A board with more experience should have understood more quickly the dangers posed by thrifts that tried to manipulate the system, and persuaded Congress that these thrifts had to be stopped; this also could have saved money. More skilled and experienced boards might have given Congress different messages about deregulation; this could have saved a *lot* of money. This is an important, and controversial, point.

A Bank Board with a deeper knowledge of the thrift industry and the FHLBS should have given Congress the message that *more* deregulation was needed earlier (in the 1960s and 1970s) and *less* was needed later (in the early 1980s). The empirical support for this view is that about half of the total losses suffered by FSLIC were incurred prior to deregulation (when thrifts lost money due to rising interest rates) and about a quarter of the losses occurred after deregulation (when thrifts lost money by making bad loans). Had thrifts been better able in the 1970s to diversify their portfolios and hedge against interest rate swings, most of FSLIC's losses could probably have been avoided: this would have required more deregulation in that decade. Had thrifts been given less leeway during the 1980s to make reckless investments, a substantial portion of FSLIC's expenditures could have been prevented: this would have required less deregulation in that decade.

It is one thing to contend that a more expert Bank Board should have done certain things. It is another to show that they would have done so: in fact, that cannot be demonstrated. But there are some good reasons for believing that such a board would have done the right thing.

On the one hand, the recognition that the tightly regulated thrift industry was highly vulnerable to interest rate increases was becoming more widespread during the 1970s by those who took the broader view. In 1972, the Hunt Commission recommended that S&Ls be given broader asset and liability powers. In 1975, the Financial Institutions and the Nation's Economy study, commissioned by the House Banking Committee, again recommended limited balance sheet deregulation before it was too late. The committee was looking for a reason to deregulate. The Bank Board could have forcefully given it that reason. It did not. It testified mildly and did not deregulate on its own, as in many ways it could have. To the extent that experience leads to wisdom rather than timidity, an experienced Bank Board would have taken the chances offered it to durably help the thrift industry, the taxpaying public, FSLIC, and ultimately the board itself.

On the other hand, the deliberations over deregulation that occurred within Congress during the late 1970s and early 1980s were almost all about policy, not administration. Congress, lobbying groups, and academics all appeared to be more interested in debating what to do than how to do it.[42] This makes sense, given the skills and interests of these participants. But someone has to speak for administration, and no one should be in a better position to do so than those who administer. These administrators, if they are competent, know when to say: "We can do this, but we cannot do that." In the early 1980s, when Congress was preparing to deregulate the thrift industry, it needed to hear what the Bank Board could and could not do. The Bank Board did not give it this information, because it did not have the administrative experience to make these judgments. If the Bank Board had had more experience, it would have been in a better position to inform policy.

The argument that the thrift industry needed more deregulation earlier and less deregulation later is not likely to be popular. Those with opinions on the issue are typically either for or against deregulation. Advocates of deregulation point to the pre-deregulation losses as evidence for that position, while the opponents focus on the post-deregulation costs. Both sides are partially correct. Too much regulation did make the thrift industry incapable of coping with dramatic changes in the economy. And yes, too little regulation made the thrift regulators incapable of coping with dramatic changes in the thrift industry. But whether deregulation could have been helpful to the S&L business depended largely on its form and timing. Skilled administrators would have been in the best position to understand this.

One simple political reform should be considered. It does not call for major changes in congressional operations or bureaucratic structure or resources. It requires neither legislation nor reorganization. This proposal calls only for more expert individuals to be appointed as the directors of the major government agencies such as the Bank Board. While "expertise" can be interpreted in many ways, I mean by that term that the appointees have served a substantial period within the organization they are nominated to lead *and* that they have distinguished themselves in this service. Financial agencies and other parts of the bureaucracy will usually work better if they are directed by individuals who have mastered their methods and understand their missions.[43]

This reform does not hold out the promise that a self-correcting system can be created, as some advocates of public choice reforms seem to believe.[44] This reform will not always work. Highly skilled leaders do make major mistakes. Unless bureaucrats are different from people in all other occupations, however, we should expect that, on average, the more skilled will perform better than the less skilled.

The public choice and public spirit views paint differing pictures of the thrift tragedy and, more broadly, of American politics. The public choice view assumes the worst about public officials yet is optimistic about the future. It suggests that, although self-interested officials today systematically damage the public interest, institutions can be reformed so that officials' selfish motives are turned (unwittingly) to the public advantage.

The public spirit view is less pessimistic about the present but also has a less utopian vision of the future. The good news is that most officials already tend to promote the public interest as they see it. The bad news is that these good motivations do not eliminate public problems. Indeed, the thrift tragedy occurred in part because of the policy commitments of public officials and because of an inability among officials to agree on the solutions. No amount of political reform in a democratic system will cause policy commitments and policy disagreements to vanish. Policy tragedies will always be with us. Once this is understood, we can devote our public spirit to softening the pain they cause rather than blaming all public officials.

Appendixes

Notes

Index

Appendix 1
The Thrift Business

Let us imagine a hypothetical savings and loan association and focus on the essential elements of the thrift's operating statement and balance sheet. The operating statement indicates the income, expenses, and profit (or loss) of the thrift, while the balance sheet presents the assets (i.e., loans and investments), liabilities (deposits and other borrowings), and net worth (or equity). The operating statement and balance sheet are linked because liabilities create expenses, assets produce income, and profits (or losses) can increase (or reduce) net worth. This model is highly simplified, but it illustrates the key accounting principles that must be comprehended if FSLIC's losses, and its inability to reduce them, are to be understood.

Thrift Balance Sheets

The assets, liabilities, and net worth of a hypothetical S&L are shown in table A1.1. The assets a thrift holds are the loans and investments it has made.[1] Thrift liabilities are primarily insured deposits.[2] The net worth of the thrift is defined simply as the difference between the value of the thrift's assets and its liabilities. The balance sheet of the healthy thrift roughly matches the status of the S&L business as a whole in 1979.

TABLE A1.1

Hypothetical S&L Balance Sheet
(in $ millions)

	Healthy S&L	Marginal S&L	Insolvent S&L
Assets (loans)	$100	$94	$75
Liabilities			
(insured deposits)	94	94	94
Net worth	6	0	–19
Net worth ratio	6.0	0.0	–25.0

Net worth is nonetheless a concept of fundamental importance for the health of an S&L. A healthy thrift will have more assets than liabilities, and thus a positive net worth. Generally speaking, the greater the net worth, the healthier the thrift. In general, the health of a thrift is reported as the ratio of net worth to total assets so that the health of thrifts of different sizes can be compared. In a marginal thrift assets and liabilities are equal, so the net worth ratio is zero. An insolvent thrift has more liabilities than assets, and thus a negative net worth.

It is important to note the difference between the "market" and "book" value of items on the balance sheet. The market value of the assets and liabilities represents the price they would fetch at any given moment if they were sold on the open market. The book value, in contrast, is the value for which they were traded at the moment of the sale.

At the time a transaction is made, the book value of the item (the amount recorded on the thrift's accounts) equals the market value of that item (the amount for which the item could currently be sold). The market value of thrift assets and liabilities can fluctuate over time, however. Yet as long as the thrift holds the assets and its loans continue to be repaid, the thrift is allowed by "generally accepted accounting principles" (GAAP) to report its assets at their book value. (The GAAP approach, incidentally, is used by virtually all industries, except investment banks and pension funds, and not just by thrifts.) As long as the economy is fairly stable, market and book values should closely parallel each other. If economic conditions change dramatically, however, the market and book values of assets can diverge a great deal.

When a thrift makes a $100 million loan, the loans would in theory be backed by $100 million in collateral. This implies that, if the borrower did not repay the loan, the thrift could take ownership of the asset, sell it for $100 million, and repay its depositors. But because the market value of balance sheet items can change, the thrift might not be able to receive book value for any asset it sells.

Thrift Operating Statements

Thrifts receive income from the interest paid on the loans they have made and incur expenses on the interest they must pay on the deposits they hold. Traditionally, the largest source of income for thrifts was the interest they received for the mortgage loans they made. Thrifts also receive income (from fees) by providing loans and other financial services, or from selling their assets. Although interest payments are the largest single expense thrifts have, they of course must also pay other normal business expenses such as salaries, rent, insurance, and taxes. The net income of the thrift is essentially the difference between the income it obtains from assets and the expenses it pays on liabilities. A profitable thrift, of course, has more income than expenses.

The operating statement of the profitable thrift in table A1.2 approximates the thrift business average in 1979. In that year, the thrift business received about 88 percent of its income from interest payments, 4 percent from fees, and the rest from other sources. It spent 83 percent of its income on interest payments, 10 percent on other operating expenses, and had 7 percent net income. The profitable thrift could use its net income to increase the net worth of the thrift, or it could distribute it to the owners, employees, or customers of the thrift. Similarly, an unprofitable thrift could meet expenses by drawing upon its net worth—that is, until the net worth was gone.

The operating statement of the marginal thrift illustrates the impact of rising market interest rates (such as those experienced in the early 1980s). These rising interest rates eliminated the profits of the thrift business, since thrift interest expenses rose much faster than interest income during this period. Of course, the more interest rates rose, the greater the decline in net profits. The operating statement of the unprofitable thrift shows the impact that asset problems can have on thrift income. In this scenario, interest from assets has fallen below interest from liabilities due to the fact that some borrowers are no longer paying interest on their loans. These illustrations do not imply, of course, that a thrift will suffer deficits only because of bad assets and not because of rising interest rates. Changes in asset values or interest rates can each reduce or eliminate thrift profits.

TABLE A1.2
Hypothetical S&L Operating Statements
(in $100,000)

	Healthy S&L	Marginal S&L	Unprofitable S&L
Income			
Interest	$88	$90	$79
Fees	4	4	4
Other	8	8	8
Expenses			
Interest	83	92	83
Other	10	10	10
Net income	7	0	-2
Profit margin[a]	7.0%	0.0%	-2.5%

a. Ratio of net income to total income.

Thrift Income and Net Worth

The net income and net worth of a thrift will thus change as interest rates and financial values change. If interest expenses rise faster than interest income, then net income will fall (everything else being equal); if asset values decline more than liabilities, net worth will fall. Of course, interest rates and financial values are closely related. If an asset (say, a house) falls in value so much that the borrower decides not to repay the mortgage loan, then the thrift that made the loan will lose the interest income from the loan and will also have an asset that has fallen in price. Thrifts can thus become insolvent either through changes in interest rates or in asset values.

If a thrift has to sell an asset below book value in order to raise income to meet expenses, or if it has foreclosed on a loan that the borrower will not repay, the thrift must "write down" the value of its assets to show the amount of loss it has suffered. In either case, the amount of assets the thrift holds, and its interest income, are reduced. The marginal thrift in table A1.1 has either sold assets for a loss or written them down in value from $100 million to $94 million, for example, while the insolvent thrift has either written down or sold for a loss $25 million worth of assets, reducing its total from $100 million to $75 million.

In a healthy thrift, the net worth belongs to the owners. In the example in table A1.1, the owners of the healthy thrift could sell the $100 million of assets, pay off the $94 million of liabilities, and pocket the $6 million of net worth. In an insolvent thrift, however, the negative net worth belonged to FSLIC. The owners of the insolvent thrift would find themselves $19 million short if they tried to repay the $94 million of liabilities by selling off all the assets. But in the United States the legal liability of corporations (such as thrifts) and their owners is limited to their investment in the firm: the owners are not personally responsible for the debts of an insolvent business. This means that the owners would not have been required to come up with the $17 million to repay the depositors; therefore, absent deposit insurance, the depositors would have suffered losses. Since the United States does have deposit insurance, the deposit insurer—FSLIC—would have been responsible for paying the depositors. For FSLIC to avoid losses, it must take control of thrifts before their net worth drops below zero.

A final note: thrift balance sheets and operating statements were extremely fragile. At the end of the 1970s, a typical thrift had a 6 percent net worth and a profit margin of 7 percent. If interest rates drove up operating expenses, or if asset values fell, thrift profits and net worth could evaporate almost overnight. The typical thrift had a small margin of error before insolvency.

Appendix 2
Thrift Failure Case Studies

Hundreds of thrifts failed during the 1980s, and a handful of these failures were highly controversial and highly expensive. The names of these institutions and their operators—especially Charles Keating at Lincoln, David Paul at CenTrust, Jarrett Woods at Western, David Wise (and more notoriously, Neil Bush) at Silverado, Ernest Fleischer at Franklin, and Eddie McBirney at Vernon—have made headlines. These individuals have been alternately characterized as brilliant, innovative businessmen who built financial empires and as devious, sinister criminals who used their institutions to rob the public. Both images, perhaps, are true: in financial matters, the dividing line can be difficult to determine. These men were usually considered brilliant and innovative when they were getting rich, sinister and devious when they were going broke. Most of the attention these men and their institutions have received has focused on particular personality traits or episodes that presumably reveal something about their financial insight or moral blindness.

Regulators, being human, undoubtedly also made judgments about the fitness of these individuals to run federally insured depository institutions. These judgments, in turn, unquestionably influenced the regulators' willingness to impose sanctions on these operators. Yet the capacity to impose sanctions ultimately rests on the regulators' ability to produce evidence to support their judgments in the face of the operators' efforts to avoid them. These operators were certainly not passive in the face of regulatory efforts to discipline them, since they could also afford better (or at least more expensive) legal and financial talent to thwart regulatory control.

The regulators were neither ignorant of nor inattentive to the problems of these institutions. Attention did not necessarily mean swift and costless resolution, however, as these case studies show. Each case illustrates a different problem the regulators faced in assessing thrifts' safety and soundness. In each case the thrift claimed—and presented substantial evidence in support of this claim—that it was solvent and profitable when it was in fact bankrupt.

CenTrust Savings Bank, Florida

CenTrust had $1.9 billion in assets in 1982 when it was bought by David Paul.[1] Paul scorned thrifts' old way of doing business and argued that the only way for Centrust to make profits was for it to rapidly move into new financial investments. By 1988, Paul had turned CenTrust into the largest thrift in Florida and the Southeast, with $10 billion in assets. CenTrust expanded dramatically by amassing brokered deposits and used these funds to make substantial investments in junk bonds and other securities. From 1984 through 1988, CenTrust showed a profit each year of between $36 and $93 million, and in one of those years, *Forbes* listed the thrift as one of the most profitable companies in the United States.[2]

Paul spread money around, liberally. Between 1987 and 1989, the CenTrust Foundation gave $1.7 million to various causes (including the Carter Center established by former president Jimmy Carter) and CenTrust's political action committee gave another $328,000 to political campaigns.[3] Yet federal regulators had been suspicious of CenTrust's operations under Paul from the start. The members of FHLBB's staff (especially those working out of the Atlanta District Bank) had initially recommended denying his application to purchase the thrift because of what they had concluded was an unrealistically optimistic business plan. Paul's plan was ultimately approved, however, because no other offers were made.[4] When Paul bought CenTrust, its $1.9 billion in assets were written down to market values. This write-down reduced CenTrust's earning assets by $525 million and replaced them with an equal amount of "goodwill." In other words, when Paul took control of CenTrust it had a market net worth of *minus* 28 percent.

In 1984, thrift regulators concluded that, because of its aggressive business practices, "CenTrust would have to be scrutinized exceedingly closely."[5] Regulators conducted seven full or "special limited" examinations of CenTrust over the next six years.[6] These examinations were difficult: "From the beginning, the FHLB of Atlanta regulators had a strained and contentious relationship with CenTrust and its CEO, David Paul. Examinations were conducted under extremely adversarial conditions and the examiners reported being frustrated by inordinate delays in getting information and financial data."[7] Despite the close scrutiny CenTrust received, the value of many of its business transactions was far from clear from an accounting perspective.

Consider one technical dispute concerning the treatment of investment securities. Generally accepted accounting principles allow thrifts to value these securities in two ways. If the thrift buys them with the intent of holding them until they mature, then it is allowed to carry them on its balance sheet at their book value. Because it expects to receive par value for this security when it matures, the thrift in this case would not need to adjust the value of the security on its books with changes in its market price. On the other hand, if the thrift actively trades these securities, GAAP calls for the thrift to value them at market price on its books. Accounting disputes occur when there is disagreement about the security holder's intentions, and "accounting literature and regulatory bulletins are far from clear on this issue even today."[8]

Regulators believe there is considerable evidence that CenTrust was attempting to have it both ways through a process known as "gains trading." In essence, CenTrust would agree to buy securities at a given price at a given time. If the market price of the securities was above the given price, CenTrust would immediately resell the securities and pocket the difference as profit. If the market price was below the given price, CenTrust would hold the securities in its portfolio and carry them at book value. As the FHLBB noted, "The practical effect of this practice is the recognition of profit on the winners and deferral of losses on the losers by putting them in portfolio."[9]

The practical effect was great. In fiscal 1987, CenTrust claimed a $60.6 million profit—virtually its entire profit for the year—from its winners in gains trading, while it was able to conceal $81.6 million in "unrealized" losses from such trading. Although the regulators attempted to make CenTrust recognize the losses from these trades, it refused. In a crucial decision, CenTrust's outside auditors (the accounting firm of Deloitte, Haskins & Sells) determined that the firm did not need to post these losses under GAAP. CenTrust thus received unqualified approval of its financial statements from its outside auditors on this issue.[10] The thrift regulators were "reluctant to overrule the auditors in view of the controversy surrounding the issue and the lack of a clearly articulated national policy."[11]

After the accounting issues were sorted out, CenTrust's fortunes deteriorated rapidly, and in 1989 it reported a loss of $119 million. The thrift was finally put into receivership by the RTC on March 9, 1990. An RTC investigation accused Paul of doing more than engaging in debatable accounting practices. Ultimately, he was convicted on ninety-seven counts of securities and banking fraud for using $3.2 million of CenTrust's money to remodel his home and for creating false profits in a round of securities parking deals with the Bank of Credit and Commerce International. He is now serving a long prison sentence.[12] CenTrust's failure cost FSLIC about $1.7 billion, making it the second most expensive thrift insolvency (after Keating's Lincoln).

Ironically, accounting standards adopted by Congress in the FIRREA ultimately made it possible for the regulators to seize CenTrust.

Western Savings Association, Texas

Western was a traditional thrift, engaged almost exclusively in making home mortgages, when Jarrett E. Woods Jr. bought all its outstanding stock in August 1982.[13] Woods transferred all the stock to his personal holding company (Western Capital Corporation) and established WS Service Corporation (WSSC) as a wholly owned subsidiary of Western to engage primarily in acquiring, holding, and selling real estate investments. Western made its acquisition, development, and construction loans through WSSC.

Like CenTrust, Western expanded rapidly (from $34 million to $2 billion between 1982 and 1986), obtaining brokered deposits by offering above market rates of interest.[14] During this period, Western became heavily involved in making highly speculative ADC loans and investments. These transactions contained high up-front fees, giving the appearance of large profits. Thrift system regulators found many of Western's practices to be "unsafe and unsound," and in July 1984 issued a permanent cease and desist order to prevent Western from continuing its reckless activities. As part of this order, Western was required to have an outside auditor review its ADC loans quarterly.

Arthur Young and Company was the firm hired by Western to make these special quarterly audits and its year-end consolidated audits.[15] Arthur Young agreed to audit Western in 1984 and 1985 according to generally accepted auditing standards (GAAS) and presented its statements in accordance with GAAP. The accounting firm also agreed to "plan the examination to search for errors and irregularities . . . that would have a material effect on the financial statements" and to notify the FHLBB's district director of examinations of any apparent misappropriations.[16]

Arthur Young's audits showed that Western had stockholder equity worth about $42 million at the end of 1984 and $49 million at the end of 1985, and that Western had been profitable in both years. In each year Arthur Young issued its "unqualified opinion" that the audits were in accordance with GAAS and the statements fairly represented Western's financial position in accordance with GAAP. Despite this picture of apparent health, the Bank Board declared Western insolvent and took control of the thrift in September 1986.[17] At the time, Western was the third largest thrift taken over by regulators.

In 1990 the FDIC (as the successor to the FSLIC) sued Arthur Young to recover damages of $560 million for "negligent performance" in its audits of

Western. The FDIC claimed that Arthur Young overstated Western's profits by a remarkable $168 million in 1984 and $113 million in 1985.[18] Western was in fact deeply in the red, with a negative net worth of about $100 million in 1984 and $200 million in 1985, according to GAAP. The FDIC claimed further that Western made approximately $1 billion in additional loans in 1985 and $300 million in 1986, causing an additional $560 million in losses. FDIC contends that "most if not all" of these losses would have been avoided if Arthur Young had conducted the audit properly. But because Arthur Young had given Western its stamp of approval, the Bank Board allowed the thrift to continue policies that were causing it to lose large amounts of money. Furthermore, Arthur Young's portrayal of Western as successful and solvent helped Western's board of directors oppose regulatory intervention. Indeed, when Western was taken over in 1986, Woods argued that his thrift still had a net worth of $50 million, an equity well above Bank Board requirements. Calling the takeover an "overreaction," Woods sued to "set aside the unconscionable, unlawful and unconstitutional taking of Western" by the Bank Board.[19]

FDIC's charges against Arthur Young echo those usually made against the regulators themselves. FDIC claimed that Arthur Young had not adequately evaluated audit risks, had deficient technical proficiency, lacked an independent mental attitude, had failed to exercise due professional care, and had violated numerous standards of field work. Two of the most significant allegations against Arthur Young are outlined below.

The first concerns profits from sales of real estate investments. Western, through its subsidiary WSSC, bought and sold real estate. Arthur Young certified that Western had a net profit of nearly $23 million in 1984 and $20 million in 1985 from such sales. However, the FDIC claimed that, in essence, Western often lent the entire purchase price—including the down payment—to the buyer, so that the buyer committed no personal funds and accepted no risk through the purchase. Because the funds for the sale originated with Western, the "profits" came from Western's own money. Most, if not all, of Western's profits from such deals were thus illusory, and the FDIC claims that Arthur Young should have realized this.[20]

The other point of contention between the regulators and the outside auditors concerned Western's provisions for bad loans and investments. Financial institutions are required as a matter of prudence to set aside funds in a reserve account to cover loan defaults and investments that turn out badly. This implies that the institution—and its auditors—must estimate the number of loans and investments likely to go sour. Since funds put into these reserve accounts are not counted as profits, banks and thrifts may be tempted to put too little in them; it is the auditor's responsibility to ensure that loss reserves are adequate. To back a loan portfolio of $770 million in 1984, Western had put $8.5 million aside for loan losses; in 1985, with a loan portfolio of $1.27 billion, it set aside $23.6 million. These reserves were equal to 1 percent and 1.8 percent of loans, respectively. Western made no provision at all for investment losses.

The FDIC's lawsuit claimed that "these provisions were grossly inadequate" and that Western should have set aside at least $150 million for loan losses in addition to $70 million for investment losses over the course of those two years. It further claimed that Arthur Young was negligent in not requiring Western to do this. In making this accusation, the FDIC contended that "all of the 200 largest loans maturing at Western in 1985 were extended, modified, or otherwise restructured [and that] not one loan was paid off with funds derived from a source other than Western itself."[21] While the Bank Board might have had the legal power to declare Western insolvent long before it did, it was reluctant to use this power, given that Western and its (reputable) accountants asserted the thrift's soundness.[22]

Silverado Savings and Loan, Colorado

Silverado may be the best illustration of the perplexities involved in regulating the thrift industry in the 1980s.[23] Silverado, like many other thrifts, was losing money and almost insolvent in 1979 when Michael Wise bought it. Wise chose to grow his way out of the difficulty. Between 1980 and 1983, the thrift grew from $83 million to $371 million in assets, primarily by buying other small thrifts. Silverado almost tripled in size in 1984, to $953 million in assets, and grew by another 50 percent in 1985, to $1.5 billion, making it one of the ten fastest-growing S&Ls in the country.

The rapid growth in these years was fueled primarily by commercial real estate loans. Silverado reported profits in almost every year, and in every year income from loan fees and the sale of loans and securities exceeded net income. Silverado, in short, was making money by growing and trading, not by making and holding home mortgages.

Silverado was not ignored by the FHLBB examiners during these years. It had regular examinations every year in addition to special examinations in which its loan and underwriting policies were given additional scrutiny. The examiners were almost never satisfied with the results of these exams and, as Lowy notes, the examiners "rendered accurate reports, and those accurate reports caused letters to be written, meetings to be held, and charges to be made and defended against."[24] Yet Wise was almost always able to persuade the regulators that, though Silverado was suffering some growing pains, it was basically sound—or would be sound after its business plans were fully implemented. Wise, moreover, did not give the impression of being a quick-change artist. He had quickly moved up in the leadership of the USL, the Federal Reserve Board had appointed him as president of its thrift advisory council, and he served as a director on the Topeka FHLB.[25]

Silverado's rapid growth, furthermore, was permissible under the regulations: the S&L met its net worth requirements in each year through 1987. Silverado was able to report large profits and keep its RAP net worth above the level required for its growth, for two reasons. Like Western, it made huge amounts of commercial real estate loans (at one point, 66 percent of its assets were in such loans) and claimed the up-front fees. Like CenTrust, it participated in gains trading by selling its best assets. In addition, Silverado bought land at high prices (recording the land on its books as an asset) from individuals who then used part of the proceeds on the sale to buy the S&L's preferred stock (of course, no formal quid pro quo existed). The value of this stock, even though it was essentially financed by Silverado, was reported as net worth to the firm.[26]

As Colorado's economy faltered after 1985, Silverado's real estate loans started going bad in increasing numbers. To keep from having to write off these loans in 1986, Silverado pooled them together and sold securities backed by the collateral of this pool.[27] Because it was able to sell some of these securities to its "best" customers, Silverado claimed it did not need to establish loan loss reserves for the assets that backed the securities. These financial arrangements were legal, and Silverado's accounting firm claimed that GAAP permitted earnings from the sale of the securities. The FHLBB disagreed and did not allow Silverado to claim earnings from the sale of these securities under RAP.

Under increasing scrutiny from the regulators, Silverado's directors signed a "supervisory agreement" in 1987 in which they pledged to make home mortgage loans for the most part and to stop making commercial real estate and land loans.[28] The "home mortgage loans" they made were actually purchases of securities backed by home mortgages guaranteed by the government. These "home loans" were, once again, legal but speculative, and not exactly what the regulators had in mind. By the end of 1988, Silverado owned about $600 million worth of these securities, which lost over half their value when short-term interest rates increased at the end of that year.[29]

Silverado fought with the regulators and with the accountants. The firm Ernst & Whinney had done Silverado's books since the mid-1970s, but between 1983 and 1986 the relationship had become ever more contentious.

Finally, in 1986, Silverado dumped Ernst & Whinney in favor of Coopers & Lybrand, claiming that Ernst & Whinney's fees were too high and that they needed to "enhance the appearance of impartiality and independence" (because one of E&W's top auditors had come to work for Silverado). Coopers & Lybrand issued a glowing report at the end of 1986.[30]

Nevertheless, Silverado's real condition continued to deteriorate, and in December 1989 the thrift was finally seized by the regulators and declared insolvent.[31] At that point, Silverado had $2.3 billion of assets on its books, and its failure was expected to cost the government about $1 billion.[32]

Franklin Savings and Loan, Kansas

Franklin was a small S&L in Ottawa, Kansas. When it was losing money in 1981 due to the high interest rates, Ernest Fleischer, who had been an investor at Franklin since the early 1970s, bought the $200 million thrift. Fleischer pursued growth aggressively. By 1985, Franklin had $2 billion in assets. By 1989, Franklin was the largest S&L in the region, with assets valued at $11 billion. Less than $2 billion of its $11 billion in liabilities were retail deposits: the rest were nontraditional borrowings.

Fleischer sought to control the interest rate risks that had decimated the S&L industry by adopting a variety of "hedging" strategies.[33] These hedging strategies did not involve home loans, which made up only $200 million out of its $11 billion. Most of Franklin's assets were in securities based on government-guaranteed home loans. Franklin's rapid growth did not violate the Bank Board's net worth standards because the thrift made large profits by trading these securities.

The problem with Franklin was that the Bank Board and private accountants did not agree on how to value Franklin's hedging strategies. In 1989, the OTS (the Bank Board's successor) and Franklin's auditors (Touche, Ross), both using GAAP, had a $330 *million* disagreement concerning Franklin's net worth. GAAP, as it turned out, did not indicate exactly how losses from hedging strategies were to be measured.

OTS, claiming that Franklin had insufficient net worth, seized Franklin in February 1990. Franklin, of course, sued, claiming that Franklin had a net worth of $388 million. Although Fleischer himself admitted that even he did not fully understand all the hedges, United States District Court Judge Dale Saffels ruled in Franklin's favor and ordered the OTS to give Franklin back to its stockholders.[34] This decision has since been overturned by the Tenth United States Appeals Court and the OTS has again been given control over Franklin.[35] The RTC also filed a $163 million suit against Franklin's directors, alleging negligence and breach of fiduciary duty. Fleischer, for his part, filed a countersuit against the RTC, seeking $820 million in compensation because the RTC had "dissipated" Franklin's assets.[36] These suits were still pending in June 1995.

Lincoln Savings and Loan, California

Charles Keating bought Lincoln in 1984.[37] While Lincoln had a market value net worth of minus $40 million or more, it had enough RAP net worth to grow from $1 billion to $2 billion in the first year Keating owned the thrift. Keating's business plan called for Lincoln to continue its home building business, but Lincoln made virtually no home loans, investing instead in takeover stocks, junk bonds, hotels, financial futures, and high risk loans. As a result of this strategy, Lincoln recorded profits in every quarter between 1984 and 1986, with all its income coming from loan fees, the sale of loans and securities, and tax benefits. Much of this income was allowable under GAAP. Alan Greenspan, soon to become chairman of the Federal Reserve Board, wrote a letter to the regulators in the San Francisco District Bank describing Lincoln as "a financially strong institution that presents no foreseeable risk to the Federal Savings and Loan Insurance Corporation."[38] Other prominent economists, lawyers, and accountants also vouched for Lincoln.

Lincoln and the FHLBB disputed almost everything in an extraordinarily bitter relationship. Much of the conflict involved asset appraisals. FHLB regulators from the San Francisco district office began investigating Lincoln in 1986 when they began to suspect that Lincoln was making too many risky investments. By 1987 Lincoln had grown to $3.9 billion, and the district regulators had finished their examination. Although Keating complained bitterly about their appraisals, the regulators found "substantial irregularities" and recommended that the Bank Board seize control of the thrift. The board did not do so, and instead made an unbelievably bad decision to transfer responsibility for supervision to the main office in Washington. Throughout, Lincoln's auditors continued to certify the S&L's books.[39]

When the Washington office finished its examination of Lincoln at the end of 1988, it also demanded that Keating relinquish control. Instead, Keating threw Lincoln's parent company (American Continental) into bankruptcy on April 12, 1990, and regulators took control of the thrift the following day. Keating, arguing that Lincoln still had a net worth of $500 to $700 million, sued the government to regain control. The contest revolved around the value of Lincoln's assets. Keating claimed that, to justify seizing the thrift, "regulators arbitrarily wrote down Lincoln's $1.4 billion loan portfolio by 50 percent and slashed the worth of its extensive land, hotel and stock holdings by 75 percent."[40] After twenty-nine days of testimony, Judge Stanley Sporkin threw the case out of court, arguing that "it is abundantly clear that [Lincoln's] officials abused their positions. . . . Their actions amounted to a looting of Lincoln. This was not done crudely. Indeed, it was done with a great deal of sophistication. The transactions were all made to have an aura of legality about them."[41] Between the time San Francisco finished its examination and Washington finished its own, however, Lincoln's assets had grown to $5.5 billion. The regulators declared that its failure would cost the government $1.85 to $2.2 billion. The delay in closing down Lincoln cost FSLIC a bundle.[42]

How did Lincoln survive for so long? If its transactions had the air of legality about them, its owner had the manner of a bully: "Keating tried to intimidate everybody. He hired lawyers, accountants, and lobbyists in enormous numbers and discarded them when they became lukewarm about his tactics. He threatened suit whenever anyone questioned his position. He never cooperated. . . . Meanwhile, Keating piously insisted that he was a legitimate businessman who was being victimized by overzealous regulators."[43]

Conclusions

The five S&L failures briefly described here were among the most public and costly of the entire thrift tragedy. While each thrift was brought low by a different investment strategy, all the failures have common elements that typify the Bank Board's real political problems during the 1980s.

Each thrift (except perhaps Western) was led by a powerful owner. These men were rich, aggressive, and confident. They were—or attempted to be—pillars of the community as they worked for a variety of "good causes."[44] To be sure, they all spread their money around among politicians, but they also shared their wealth with civic organizations and within their social circles. These were not dope-smoking, gun-toting thugs: they epitomized many of our society's values.

All the thrifts embarked on innovative investment strategies. It was probably unclear to almost everyone—participants, observers, and regulators—what the ultimate financial impact of these strategies would be. The accounting and legal status of these schemes was uncertain. It was difficult for regulators to demonstrate that these strategies were destructive (or illegal), especially when they appeared to be working well (in terms of generating profits).

The owners were not patsies. They asserted that what they were doing was both legal and profitable. They contested virtually every move the regulators made to limit their discretion. Because they (and their thrifts) were wealthy, they were willing and able to hire the most promising lawyers and accountants money could buy. Because their investment strategies were innovative, they were willing and able to defend their thrifts against the challenges of the bureaucrats.

These thrifts and their owners had wealth and power, they were innovative, and they defended their actions vigorously. Only an uncommonly strong, skilled, and confident agency could have controlled them.

Appendix 3
A Brief Political History of Refinancing FSLIC[1]

1985

October   Bank Board Chairman Edwin Gray asks Congress to approve a $3.5 billion plan to recapitalize FSLIC.

1986

January   Deputy Treasury Secretary George Gould endorses Bank Board program to recapitalize FSLIC.

February 24   GAO reports that FSLIC has a potential liability of $17 billion, although it has only $6 billion in its insurance reserve. The Bank Board strongly disputes this report.

April   Reagan administration unveils $15 billion recapitalization plan.

May 22   Measure introduced by House Banking Committee Chairman St. Germain (D-R.I.) and ranking member Wylie (R-Ohio) in House to provide FSLIC with $15 billion.

June 4   The Congressional Budget Office (CBO) concludes that FSLIC recap would add about $12 billion to the federal deficit. Banking committees cannot increase spending without making comparable reductions in programs under their jurisdiction. St. Germain cancels markup until CBO objections are resolved.

June 24   Senate Banking Committee Chairman Garn (R-Utah) introduces omnibus banking bill.

July 17   CBO complaint settled. House Financial Institutions Subcommittee approves $15 billion FSLIC recap by voice vote.

August 13   Senate Banking Committee approves "stripped-down" FSLIC recap legislation. Bill Proxmire (D-Wisc.) threatens to filibuster unless non-bank bank amendment is added. Phil Gramm (R-Tex.) and William Armstrong (R-Colo.) threaten filibuster if the bill contains House-passed housing authorization.

September 10   Senate Banking Committee Chairman Jake Garn (R-Utah) undergoes major surgery and does not return until the final week of the session.

September 15   Jim Wright (D-Tex.), Steve Bartlett (R-Tex.), John Bryant (D-Tex.), and Martin Frost (D-Tex.) call Bank Board Chairman Gray to his office and complain about regulatory treatment of Texas thrifts.

September 23   House Banking Committee approves $15 billion FSLIC recap 47–1 after the proposal is amended. The amendments include housing and consumer protection provisions that the administration strongly opposes.

September 29   Bill scheduled for floor vote in the House. Wright puts hold on the bill, pulling it from the calendar.

October 3   Senator David Pryor (D-Ark.) puts hold on the bill in the Senate until the Bank Board agrees to reforms.

October 7   Bill passes House by voice vote, approving the full $15 billion.

October 17   Garn persuades Proxmire to drop his non-bank bank amendment.

October 18   Senate bill amended to remove most controversial provisions; FSLIC recap also removed. Passed by voice vote and sent to House under expectation that House would amend it and send it back.

     House operating under parliamentary restrictions that prohibited amendments, roll call votes, and controversial legislation. Refuses to consider Senate bill.

     Senate amends and passes another bill that includes a one-year, $3 billion FSLIC recap and other provisions.

     House Democrats refuse to consider this measure also.

     Congress adjourns without reconciling House and Senate measures.

1987

January 6   FSLIC $15 billion recap reintroduced in House.

January 20   USL presents $5 billion FSLIC proposal.

January 21–22   House and Senate Banking Committees hold hearings on FSLIC recapitalization. House Banking Chairman St. Germain schedules subcommittee markup on H.R. 27 for February 3 and full committee markup for February 10.

January 29   St. Germain meets with Speaker House and other Texas representatives and postpones indefinitely the markup of FSLIC recap.

February 17   Senate Banking Chairman Proxmire introduces comprehensive reform legislation, including $7.5 billion for FSLIC.

March 3–4   House Banking Committee holds additional hearings on FSLIC. GAO testifies that FSLIC is insolvent by over $3 billion, although it retains $1 billion in current reserves.

March 17   Speaker Wright appears before a caucus of Banking Committee Democrats, asking them to reduce FSLIC funding.

March 27   Senate approves S. 790, which provides FSLIC with $7.5 billion over two years. S. 790 includes other highly controversial banking issues.

March 31   House Financial Institutions Subcommittee approves H.R. 27, providing $15 billion for FSLIC, by a vote of 23–20.

April 1   House Banking Committee reduces FSLIC funding to $5 billion by a vote of 25–24. Forbearance provisions are added to the bill.

April 27   FSLIC files a $540 million civil suit against owners of Vernon S&L in Texas.

April 28   Wright urges House to pass $15 billion bill. GAO circulates letter reporting that FSLIC's current insolvency had grown to $6 billion.

May 5	House votes 153–258 to reject increasing FSLIC's funding above $5 billion. House approves H.R. 27 by a vote of 402–6.
May 14	Senate rejects H.R. 27, rejects an amendment to offer a "clean" FSLIC bill, and approves S. 790 as a substitute measure.
June 25	Conference committee begins.
July 1	Conference committee agrees on an $8.5 billion FSLIC recap and reaches agreement in principle on other issues.
July 21	Reagan announces he will veto FSLIC recap unless the funding limits are raised and other changes are made.
July 29	Conference committee reaches final agreement to provide FSLIC with $10.8 billion and agrees on other measures.
August 3	House approves conference report by voice vote.
August 4	Senate approves conference report by voice vote.
August 10	President Reagan signs the Competitive Equality Banking Act.

Appendix 4
Congressional Voting

This appendix contains details regarding the congressional voting examined in chapter 8. I first present the analytical model, estimating techniques, and statistical results upon which that chapter is based. Next, I provide definitions, sources, and descriptive statistics for the variables used in the analysis. I conclude with a brief summary of one Banking Committee vote in the House of Representatives.

Estimation and Analysis Techniques

I predicted the impact of the thrift business variables, partisan affiliation, and region on each legislator's vote on each of twenty-one roll calls by using logistic regression.[1] Logistic regression closely resembles linear regression, but is more appropriate when the dependent variable is dichotomous rather than continuous. The estimated dependent variable indicates the probability that one of the two outcomes occurred; in this analysis, it gives the probability that a legislator voted "yea." The coefficients indicate the change in the log odds of voting "yea" given a unit change in the independent variable when the other independent variables are held constant. The model used to estimate the probability that a legislator voted "yea" on a given roll call takes the typical logit form:

Equation 1.   The Determinants of Congressional Voting

$$\text{Prob}\left(V_{it}\right) = 1 \Big/ \left(1 + \exp\left(-\left(\beta_0 + \beta_1 P_{it} + \beta_2 C_{it} \right. \right. \right.$$
$$\left. \left. \left. + \beta_3 N_{it} + \beta_4 A_{it} + \beta_5 I_{it} + \beta_6 R_{it}\right)\right)\right)$$

where
V = Voting "yea";
P = Political party (0=Republican, 1=Democrat);
C = Campaign contributions from thrifts;

N = Number of thrifts in the district;
A = Average assets of district thrifts;
I = Average income of district thrifts;
R = Region (0=Non–Sun Belt, 1=Sun Belt);
$\beta_{0\cdots6}$ = Logistic regression coefficients;
i = Individual legislator;
t = Specific roll call.

Some scholars have argued that there is a simultaneous relationship between campaign contributions and voting: contributions influence voting, and voting in turn affects contributions.[2] Although this seems reasonable in general, it seems unlikely that each and every vote affects contributions, and vice versa. The model estimated here assumes that no simultaneous relationship exists between the aggregate indicator of campaign contributions and the individual votes examined. This implies that campaign contributions over the course of the decade were expected to influence individual votes, but that no single vote was believed to affect total campaign contributions.

Estimations were made both with the variables in their "natural" units and transformed into "logarithms."[3] There were few differences in the number or type of significant coefficients using logged and unlogged data. As a result, I used natural units throughout this analysis.

Under certain conditions, data can be "pooled" in various ways to increase sample size, obtain more reliable estimates, and conduct hypothesis tests comparing different periods.[4] In preliminary analyses I pooled data across the House and Senate, within each house over time, and within each chamber in a given year. These analyses showed that the coefficients were not acceptably stable from chamber to chamber, period to period, or vote to vote, and that therefore this technique was statistically inappropriate.[5] This simply means that "one size fits all" is not an accurate statement, and that the size and significance of the coefficients varied for each vote within a single year, over the years, and between the House and the Senate.

Another issue arises in determining which variables are genuinely "significant," in the sense that one can be confident that the statistical relationship between the independent and dependent variables is not spurious. If each independent variable (party, campaign contributions, average thrift assets, income, and numbers of thrifts in the district and region) appears to influence only some votes, then how is it possible to determine whether these variables in general genuinely affected congressional voting?

My approach was as follows. First, I estimated logistic regression coefficients for each individual roll call vote. Then, I designated coefficients from each estimation statistically significant if their t-statistic had a probability of less than 10 percent (i.e., p < .10). This implies that the probability that the coefficient is not actually relevant for that particular vote is less than 10 percent. Next, I obtained the total number of times that each variable was statistically significant over all the votes in each house. The likelihood of obtaining this sum by chance alone could then be calculated by using the binomial probability distribution. The calculated probability indi-

TABLE A4.1

Determinants of Voting on Thrift-Related Legislation in the U.S. House of Representatives, 1979–1989

Vote	Party	Region	S&L Funds	S&L Number	S&L Assets	S&L Income
1979:1	0.31	0.92	−0.04*	−0.21	0.035*	−3.78*
	(0.61)	(0.70)	(0.02)	(0.12)	(0.018)	(2.15)
1982:1	−5.52**	1.58*	−0.03	0.42**	0.000	−1.17**
	(0.75)	(0.70)	(0.02)	(0.13)	(0.00)	(0.38)
1982:2	2.97**	-0.83*	0.03	0.24**	−0.003**	−0.32
	(0.51)	(0.47)	(0.02)	(0.09)	(0.0001)	(0.35)
1987:1	−0.40*	−1.06**	0.01	−0.07*	0.0002	−0.07*
	(0.23)	(0.31)	(0.01	(0.04)	0.0003)	(0.02)
1989:1	−0.83**	−0.79**	0.02*	0.02	0.0000	−0.01
	(0.24)	(0.32)	(0.01)	(0.05)	(0.0000)	(0.01)
1989:2	1.65**	−0.29	0.01	−0.01	−0.0005	0.01
	(0.38)	(0.42)	(0.02)	(0.07)	(0.0004)	(0.01)
1989:3	2.51**	−2.12**	−0.01	−0.06	0.0011**	0.01
	(0.28)	(0.32)	(0.01)	(0.05)	(0.0003)	(0.01)
1989:4	0.63**	−0.46*	−0.04**	0.05	0.0001	0.00
	(0.23)	(0.27)	(0.01)	(0.05)	(0.0001)	(0.01)
1989:5	−4.64**	1.90**	−0.00	0.01	−0.0009*	0.00
	(0.40)	(0.38)	(0.01)	(0.06)	(0.0004)	(0.01)
1989:6	0.25	0.53*	0.07**	−0.09*	−0.0008**	−0.01
	(0.24)	(0.31)	(0.02)	(0.05)	(0.0003)	(0.01)
Sig[b]	8/10	8/10	4/10	4/10	5/10	3/10
Prob[c]	.000	.000	.002	.002	.000	.013

* p < .10; ** p < .01

a. Standard errors are given in parentheses.

b. Number of significant coefficients/number of roll-call votes.

c. Binomial probability.

cates how likely it is that this number of coefficients appeared statistically significant if there was actually no relationship between the variables.[6]

A more complicated problem concerns determining the substantive significance of the independent variables.[7] It is not easy to interpret the relative importance of the variables because the individual coefficients indicate the "log odds" of voting "yea" (as described above), because the variables differ in size and scale, and because the influence varies from vote to vote. To summarize the average impact of the independent variables on congressional voting, I took the following steps. First, I calculated the change in the probability of voting "yea" on each individual vote over a likely range for each independent variable.[8] Second, I took the absolute value of these changes to show the net effect of the independent variables.[9] Third, I calculated the mean and standard deviation of these absolute values for each variable across all votes.

The range used here to estimate the influence of the independent variables encompasses most of the effect that thrift and political factors were likely to have on voting probabilities. Given the nature of the logistic function, very small or very large values of an independent variable will have little impact on a dependent variable, but values within one standard deviation of the mean can have a large effect.

TABLE A4.2

Model Results for Thrift-Related Legislation in the U.S. House of Representatives, 1979–1989

| Vote | Chi-Square | | | Percentage Correctly Predicted | | N |
	Model	Thrift	Political[a]	Model	Base	
1979:1	24.2**	22.0**	2.2	.92	.91	176
1982:1	152.3**	14.6**	137.7**	.90	.63	197
1982:2	66.7**	22.4**	44.3**	.85	.73	198
1987:1	24.1**	15.6**	8.5*	.64	.64	373
1989:1	23.3**	5.4	17.9**	.78	.77	414
1989:2	27.6**	2.5	25.1**	.90	.90	423
1989:3	164.4**	33.8**	131.6**	.77	.51	412
1989:4	27.2**	14.9**	12.3**	.74	.73	415
1989:5	287.0**	13.6**	273.4**	.85	.51	412
1989:6	27.9**	23.9**	4.0	.77	.77	412

* p < .10; ** p < .01

a. **Combines the variables** "political party" and "region."

Tables A4.2 and A4.4 contain six model statistics for each roll call for the House and Senate, respectively. The first column in each table, labeled the model chi-square, describes the goodness of fit of the model for each roll call. It tests the hypothesis that all coefficients except the intercept are

TABLE A4.3

Determinants of Voting on Thrift-Related Legislation in the U.S. Senate, 1979–1989

Vote	Party	Region	S&L Funds	S&L Number	S&L Assets	S&L Income
1979:1	−1.44**	−1.33**	—	0.004	0.01	−0.63
	(0.52)	(0.54)	—	(0.003)	(0.01)	(0.88)
1979:2	−0.42	1.87*	—	−0.006	−0.01	0.66
	(0.51)	(0.57)	—	(0.004)	(0.01)	(1.01)
1979:3	−2.97**	2.54**	—	−0.005	−0.01	1.63
	(1.11)	(1.13)	—	(0.004)	(0.01)	(1.35)
1979:4	0.19	−1.73*	—	0.006	0.05*	−5.01*
	(0.85)	(.96)	—	(0.009)	(0.03)	(2.92)
1987:1	9.12**	−1.16	−0.01	−0.014	−0.00	0.25*
	(2.33)	(1.52)	(0.02)	(0.010)	(0.00)	(.14)
1987:2[a]	−4.05**	—	0.00	−0.011	0.00	−0.23*
	(0.87)	—	(0.01)	(0.009)	(0.00)	(0.11)
1987:3	10.51	−1.56	−0.01	0.041*	0.005	−0.09
	(36.60)	(1.06)	(0.03)	(0.020)	(0.003)	(0.13)
1987:4	−3.58**	1.59*	0.01	−0.014*	−0.001	−0.04
	(0.77)	(0.83)	(0.01)	(0.007)	(0.001)	(0.06)
1989:1	−2.10**	−0.08	0.00	0.038*	−0.000	0.06*
	(0.60)	(0.55)	(0.01)	(0.018)	(0.001)	(0.03)
1989:2	0.00	−0.65	0.014*	0.003	0.001	0.02
	(0.46)	(0.51)	(0.006)	(0.011)	(0.001)	(0.02)
1989:3	−12.74	−0.50	0.01	0.013	0.002*	0.00
	(38.39)	(0.80)	(0.01)	(0.014)	(0.001)	(0.04)
Sig[b]	6/11	5/10	1/7	3/11	2/11	5/11
Prob[c]	.000	.000	.150	.018	.090	.000

* $p < .10$; ** $p < .01$

Note: Standard errors are given in parentheses.

a. Political party and region were highly correlated on this vote. Region was excluded to avoid problems with multicollinearity.

b. Number of significant coefficients/number of roll-call votes.

c. Binomial probability.

TABLE A4.4

Model Results for Thrift-Related Legislation in the U.S. Senate, 1979–1989

| Vote | Chi-Square | | | Percentage Correctly Predicted | | N |
	Model	Thrift	Political[a]	Model	Base	
1979:1	18.0**	5.1	12.9**	.71	.60	95
1979:2	19.7**	5.3	14.4**	.69	.59	88
1979:3	27.3**	3.9	23.4**	.81	.79	84
1979:4	13.0*	6.1	6.9*	.91	.91	85
1987:1	88.8**	6.9*	81.9**	.96	.57	82
1987:2	68.9**	11.1*	57.8**	.88	.61	77
1987:3	29.7**	11.6*	18.1**	.91	.87	78
1987:4	47.0**	5.0	42.0**	.82	.63	88
1989:1	25.1**	13.3*	11.8**	.74	.67	98
1989:2	14.6*	13.6*	1.0	.59	.63	99
1989:3	78.7**	12.5*	66.5**	.90	.62	99

* $p < .10$; ** $p < .01$

a. Combines the variables "political party" and "region."

equal to zero.[10] The larger this number, the greater the likelihood that the model as a whole is useful in predicting voting outcomes.

The second column, called the "thrift chi-square," allows us to test the joint hypothesis that all four thrift variables are equal to zero. This statistic is used to see whether the thrift-related factors considered together influenced congressional voting even if the individual indicators of S&L influence are not significant in a given roll call.[11] If this statistic is not significant, it implies that the legislators' political party and region are the only factors (in the model) that influenced the vote. The third column tests the hypothesis that the political factors (party and region) together influenced voting.

The fourth column describes the percentage of votes "correctly" predicted by the model.[12] This may be compared to the "base" prediction in column five. Rather than assuming that each legislator has a 50–50 chance of voting yea or nay, the base prediction assumes that each representative voted with the majority. This base prediction is a reminder not to overstate how good the model is at correctly predicting votes. If 90 percent of the legislators vote for a proposal, for example, one should be able to predict 90 percent of the votes correctly even if nothing is known about the factors influencing the vote. Finally, the number of cases included in each estimation is given in the sixth column.

This model is useful for understanding congressional voting on thrift-related legislation. It is highly unlikely that the independent variables, considered together, have no impact on voting behavior, as the model chi-squares in tables A4.2 and A4.4 show. The model also correctly predicted an average of 81 percent of the votes, compared to an average of 69 percent for the base model.[13]

The thrift factors usually influenced congressional voting, as the thrift chi-squares demonstrate, though they may have affected the Senate less frequently. In eight out of ten roll calls in the House of Representatives the thrift business variables jointly appear to have affected the votes, and in each of these cases the impact appears highly likely (p < .01). Thrift factors

TABLE A4.5

Variables Used in Roll-Call Voting Analysis, U.S. House of Representatives (mean and standard deviation)

			S&L				
	Party[a]	**Region**[b]	**Funds**[c]	**Number**[d]	**Assets**[e]	**Income**[f]	**Valid Cases**[g]
1979	0.67	0.41	$8.5	9.1	201.2	$1.4	186
			(10.8)	(4.5)	(175.4)	(1.6)	
1982	0.61	0.38	8.9	7.5	288.5	−1.7	237
			(12.3)	(3.6)	(267.1)	(1.1)	
1987	0.60	0.42	8.9	7.2	508.8	−1.8	392
			(12.0)	(3.4)	(476.5)	(7.0)	
1989	0.60	0.43	8.4	6.8	584.4	−4.9	432
			(11.7)	(3.0)	(575.7)	(15.3)	

Note: Standard deviation is given in parentheses.

a. Percentage of representatives affiliated with Democratic party.

b. Percentage of representatives from Sun Belt states.

c. Total campaign contributions from thrift interests per representative, 1981–1990, in thousands of dollars.

d. Number of thrifts per congressional district.

e. Per thrift per congressional district in millions of current dollars.

f. Mean thrift income by state, in millions of dollars.

g. Number of representatives for which complete data were available.

TABLE A4.6

Variables Used in Voting Analysis, U.S. Senate
(mean and standard deviation)

	Party[a]	Region[b]	S&L Funds[c]	S&L Number[d]	S&L Assets[e]	S&L Income[f]	Valid Cases[g]
1979	0.53	0.34	$32.5	73.6	130.1	$0.8	53
			(38.5)	(77.8)	(107.2)	(0.9)	
1987	0.56	0.36	33.7	64.7	387.2	−1.9	88
			(40.2)	(70.2)	(389.7)	(5.4)	
1989	0.55	0.36	31.6	58.6	434.3	−4.5	100
			(38.6)	(61.8)	(434.3)	(14.4)	

Note: Standard deviation is given in parentheses.

a. Percentage of senators affiliated with Democratic party.

b. Percentage of senators from Sun Belt states.

c. Total campaign contributions from thrift interests per senator, 1981–1990, in thousands of dollars.

d. Number of thrifts per state.

e. Mean thrift assets by state, in millions of dollars.

f. Mean thrift income by state, in millions of dollars.

g. Number of senators for which complete data were available.

seem to have influenced fewer votes (six out of eleven) in the Senate, by contrast, and influenced them with less certainty ($p < .10$).

To make the rough estimate concerning the relative importance of thrift-related and political factors on congressional voting, I compared the proportions of the model chi-squares accounted for by each set of factors. The proportions calculated were the sum of the thrift-related (or political) chi-square statistics divided by the sum of the model chi-squares.

The Dependent Variable: Congressional Roll Call Votes
Each "yea" vote was coded 1, each "nay" vote was coded 0, and abstentions, no votes, and absentees were omitted.[14]

House Vote 1, 1979: H.R. 4986 Depository Institutions Deregulation and Monetary Control Act—NOW Accounts Act
As originally considered by the House in 1979, H.R. 4986 only authorized financial institutions to offer interest-bearing checking (NOW) accounts (including automatic transfer from saving to checking accounts); authorized

remote service units (ATM machines) for the withdrawal of funds at S&Ls; and authorized credit unions to offer share draft accounts. H.R. 4986 was considered as a direct response to a court order prohibiting financial institutions from offering NOW accounts and ATM machines unless Congress expressly permitted them.

House Vote 1, 1982: H.R. 6267 Net Worth Guarantee Act— Promissory Note Substitute

This act offered assistance to insolvent or nearly insolvent thrifts in the form of interest-bearing promissory notes to institutions with a net worth below 3 percent of assets. It would have used a sliding scale to make up only a portion of a bank or S&L's losses. In contrast, H.R. 6267 would have guaranteed a thrift's net worth at 2 percent, regardless of the size of its losses. FSLIC would have backed the guarantees by paying them off if a thrift went bankrupt. This was Reagan's alternative to the Democratic proposal, based on a plan suggested by Bank Board Chairman Pratt. It was rejected 155–209.

House Vote 2, 1982: H.R. 6267 Net Worth Guarantee Act— Final Passage

This act guaranteed the net worth of S&Ls, mutual savings banks, and credit unions whose net worth fell below 2 percent, and commercial banks with net worth of less than 4–5 percent. It set up an $8.5 billion Treasury account to back the guarantees and required institutions receiving aid to hold at least 20 percent of their assets in residential real estate and to use at least 60 percent of their net new deposits for home mortgages. It was adopted 272–91.

House Vote 1, 1987: H.R. 27 FSLIC Rescue—$15 Billion Plan

This was an amendment from St. Germain (D-R.I.) to increase the bill's $5 billion, two-year recapitalization borrowing authority to $15 billion over five years. It was rejected 153–258.

House Vote 1, 1989: H.R. 1278 Savings and Loan Restructuring—Goodwill Regulation

This amendment from Hyde (R-Ill.) allowed FDIC or OTS to decide—on a case-by-case basis—whether or not the supervisory goodwill that an S&L carries on its books is based on a valid contract with the government and may therefore continue to be counted toward the thrift's capital requirements. It was rejected 94–326.

House Vote 2, 1989: H.R. 1278 Savings and Loan Restructuring—Civil Penalties

This amendment from Annunzio (D-Ill.) authorized civil penalties of up to $1 million a day for certain criminal offenses involving financial institutions. It was adopted 382–41.

House Vote 3, 1989: H.R. 1278 Savings and Loan Restructuring—Community Lending

Gonzalez (D-Tex.) and Kennedy (D-Mass.) introduced this amendment to require federal regulatory agencies to disclose the ratings and evaluations they give banks and thrifts regarding lending to the communities they serve. It also required mortgage lenders to disclose the number of applications they receive and approve by categories of race, income, and gender. It was adopted 214–200.

House Vote 4, 1989: H.R. 1278 Savings and Loan Restructuring—Junk Bonds

Dorgan (D-N.Dak.) introduced this amendment to prohibit federally insured S&Ls from acquiring or retaining "junk bonds." It was adopted 303–114.

House Vote 5, 1989: H.R. 1278 Savings and Loan Restructuring—Affordable Housing

Bartlett (R-Tex.) introduced this amendment to strike provisions requiring twelve FHLBs to set aside funds for the Affordable Housing Program and the Community Investment Program. It was rejected 206–208.

House Vote 6, 1989: H.R. 1278 Savings and Loan Restructuring—Final Passage

This bill was to reform, recapitalize, and consolidate the federal deposit insurance system in order to enhance the regulatory and enforcement powers of federal financial institutions regulatory powers. It was adopted 320–97.

Senate Vote 1, 1979: H.R. 4986 Banking Regulation—NOW Accounts

Proxmire (D-Wisc.) motioned to table (kill) the Morgan (D-N.C.) substitute to the bill reported by the Senate Banking Committee to authorize depository institutions to offer share drafts, automatic transfer service, and remote service units; increase maximum federal deposit insurance (to $50,000 per individual account); simplify truth-in-lending laws; and temporarily override certain state usury laws. The Morgan substitute omitted Banking Committee provisions to authorize nationwide NOW accounts, phase out interest rate ceilings on time and savings deposits, and decrease the minimum denomination of certificates of deposit with an interest rate tied to that on United States Treasury notes. The motion passed 57–38.

Senate Vote 2, 1979: H.R. 4986 Banking Regulation— NOW Accounts

Morgan (D-N.C.) introduced this amendment to permit states to determine whether to allow interest-bearing NOW checking accounts. It was rejected 37–51.

Senate Vote 3, 1979: H.R. 4986 Banking Regulation— NOW Accounts

Morgan (D-N.C.) introduced this amendment to delete a provision allowing the Federal Reserve to require reserves from nonmember banks. It was adopted 66–18.

Senate Vote 4, 1979: H.R. 4986 Banking Regulation— NOW Accounts

This bill authorized banks, credit unions, and savings and loan associations to offer interest-bearing checking accounts, phase out interest rate ceilings on savings accounts, override state usury limits, and reduce the minimum denominations for "money market" certificates. It passed 76–9.

Senate Vote 1, 1987: S. 790 Competitive Equality Banking Act of 1987—S&L Purchases

This was the Graham (D-Fla.) amendment to the Garn (R-Utah) amendment allowing out-of-state "non-bank banks" to purchase insolvent savings and loans. The Graham amendment limited the authority provided by the Garn amendment to states that explicitly permit out-of-state purchases of failed S&Ls; it was approved 52–42; the Garn amendment was subsequently adopted by voice vote.

Senate Vote 2, 1987: S. 790 Competitive Equality Banking Act of 1987—Non-Bank Banks

Garn (R-Utah) introduced the amendment to strike Titles I and II from the banking bill to eliminate provisions that would ban new "non-bank banks" after March 5, 1987, and to impose a one-year moratorium on the ability of banks to sell securities, real estate, and insurance. It was rejected 35–54.

Senate Vote 3, 1987: S. 790 Competitive Equality Banking Act of 1987—Final Passage

The bill regulated "non-bank banks," imposed a moratorium on certain securities and insurance activities by banks, recapitalized the FSLIC, allowed emergency interstate bank acquisitions, streamlined credit union operations, and regulated consumer check holds. It passed 79–11.

Senate Vote 4, 1987: H.R. 27 FSLIC Rescue—"Clean" FSLIC

Garn (R-Utah) introduced the amendment to strike provisions that would prevent the formation of "non-bank banks" and impose a one-year moratorium on expanded banking powers. The intent of the amendment was to eliminate the most controversial portions of the Senate-passed measure, leaving a "clean" FSLIC bill. It was rejected 37–62.

Senate Vote 1, 1989: S. 774 Savings and Loan Restructuring— RTC Board of Directors

Riegle (D-Mich.) motioned to table (kill) the Kerrey (D-Nebr.) amendment to reconfigure the board of directors of the Resolution Trust Corporation, requiring that seven private citizens be appointed by the president—subject to Senate confirmation—and that the Secretary of the Treasury, the Chairman of the Federal Reserve Board, and the Attorney General serve *ex officio* on the RTC board. The motion was approved 66–32.

Senate Vote 2, 1989: S. 774 Savings and Loan Restructuring— Foreign Deposits

Garn (R-Utah) motioned to table (kill) the Nickles (R-Okla.) amendment to permit the FDIC to insure overseas deposits held by United States banks and savings institutions and to assess deposit insurance premiums on those foreign deposits. The motion was approved 62–37.

Senate Vote 3, 1989: S. 774 Savings and Loan Restructuring— Chairman of the Office of Savings Associations

Riegle (D-Mich.) motioned to table (kill) the Graham (D-Fla.) amendment to require that the current chairman of the FHLBB not continue as chairman of the Office of Savings Associations without being reappointed by the president and confirmed by the Senate. The motion was approved 61–38.

The Independent Variables

Partisan Affiliation

Each legislator's partisan affiliation was coded 0 if the legislator was Republican and 1 if Democrat.[15]

Region

The regional variable used in this analysis divided the country into two regions: the eighteen Sun Belt states and the thirty-two non–Sun Belt states. Sun Belt states were coded "1" and the other states "0." The eighteen Sun Belt states are Alabama, Arizona, Arkansas, California, Colorado, Florida, Georgia, Louisiana, Mississippi, Nevada, New Mexico, North Carolina, Oklahoma, South Carolina, Tennessee, Texas, Utah, and Virginia.

Thrift Campaign Contributions

This is the total amount of campaign contributions received between January 1981 and May 1990 by the members of Congress still serving in 1990, as reported to the Federal Election Commission. Contributions include funds given by thrift PACs and from all individuals identifying themselves as affiliated with S&Ls. Contributions were measured in thousands of current dollars per legislator.[16]

Thrift Size

These are the average assets of FSLIC-insured savings associations in a state or congressional district.[17] The average assets per thrift were calculated by dividing the total savings association assets in a state by the number of thrifts in that state. This estimate was also used as the average thrift assets for each congressional district in the state. Assets were measured in millions of current dollars per thrift.

Thrift Income

This is the average income of FSLIC-insured savings associations in a state or congressional district.[18] The average income per thrift was calculated by dividing the total savings association income in a state by the number of thrifts in that state. This estimate was also used as the average thrift income for each congressional district in the state. Income was measured in millions of current dollars per thrift.

Thrift Numbers

This is the total number of FSLIC-insured savings associations in a state or the estimated number in a congressional district.[19] The estimated number of thrifts per congressional district was calculated by dividing the total number of thrifts in a state by the number of congressional districts.

The variables described below were not included in the final estimations.

Ideology and Partisan Affiliation

I did not include ideology as a separate factor influencing congressional voting because it is closely correlated to partisan affiliation and I expected that regional factors would be more important. In accordance with Grenzke, I calculated an interaction term combining partisan affiliation and ideology for a sample that included the fifty members of the House Banking Committee in 1987. *Ideology* was defined by the *National Journal* in its rating for economic affairs. The correlation between partisan affiliation and the *National Journal* rating was −.86; between partisan affiliation and the interaction term was −.98; between ideology and interaction was .94. Ideology did not systematically influence the logistic regression estimates and was dropped from further consideration.

Multiple Regions

Preliminary analyses included three partially overlapping regions: South, "High Flyer" states, and the rest of the nation. The High Flyer states were those thought to be most aggressive in deregulating state-chartered thrifts and most influenced by thrift industry problems. They were Arizona, Arkansas, California, Colorado, Florida, Louisiana, Nevada, New Mexico, Oklahoma, Texas, and Utah. On most roll calls, the South and High Flyer regions had similar coefficients. Merging them into one region simplified the analysis with no major loss in estimation precision.

Thrift "Importance"

It is theoretically possible that the total "importance" of the thrift business in a political jurisdiction, rather than its individual characteristics (such as the number of thrifts or their size), influences congressional voting. To investigate this possibility, I created a single variable combining the size, number, and "weight" (relative to other businesses) of thrifts in a legislative district. Preliminary estimations using this single indicator of thrift influence were not especially interesting, however.

The House Banking Committee Vote on FSLIC

In a very controversial vote in 1987, a subcommittee of the House Banking Committee had narrowly approved a proposal to provide FSLIC with $15 billion in capital. The next day this vote was overturned by the full committee,

Determinants of Voting by the House Banking Committee on the Neal Amendment, 1987

		S&L			
Party	Region	Funds	Number	Assets	Income
8.66*	4.39	0.13	0.54*	0.00035	0.31
(4.29)	(4.00)	(0.09)	(0.30)	(0.0023)	(0.20)

Chi-Square			Percentage Correctly Predicted		
Model	S&Ls	Political	Model	Base	N
41.9**	19.5**	22.4**	.89	.52	44

* p < .10; ** p < .01

Note: Standard errors are in parentheses.

which, by a one-vote margin, reduced the recapitalization from $15 billion to $5 billion. Congressional critics noted that those voting to reduce FSLIC's funding had received almost twice as much in campaign contributions from the thrift industry in the five previous years as did those who opposed the measure.[20] Table A4.7 shows the results of the logistic regression used to predict the outcomes of this vote, controlling for partisan affiliation, region, thrift campaign contributions, and thrift constituency characteristics.

This vote appears consistent with the results discussed in chapter 8. Both political and thrift-related factors are important. Partisan affiliation and number of constituent thrifts appear to be the factors most likely to have influenced the vote, although campaign contributions, thrift size, thrift profitability, and region may have had an impact. Democrats were much more likely than Republicans to have supported the reduction: Democrats voted "yea" 27–7 and Republicans voted "nay" 17–3.[21] In addition, committee members with more thrifts in their districts were more likely to vote for the reduction than members with fewer thrifts. Recipients of large campaign contributions may also have been more likely to support a smaller recapitalization for FSLIC.

Notes

Chapter 1. Public Spirit and the Thrift Tragedy

1. In this book the terms *savings and loans*, *thrifts*, and *associations* will be used synonymously unless otherwise noted.

2. "Resolving the Savings and Loan Crisis: Billions More and Additional Reforms Needed," statement by Charles A. Bowsher, Comptroller General of the United States, before the Committee on Banking, Housing, and Urban Affairs, U.S. Senate, April 6, 1990.

3. In present-value dollars. Congressional Budget Office, *Resolving the Thrift Crisis* (April 1993), ix.

4. Paul Zane Pilzer with Robert Deitz, *Other People's Money: The Inside Story of the S&L Mess* (New York: Simon and Schuster, 1989), 70.

5. See, for example, U.S. General Accounting Office, "Failed Thrifts: Internal Control Weaknesses Create an Environment Conducive to Fraud, Insider Abuse, and Related Unsafe Practices," GAO/T-AFMD-89-4, March 22, 1989; Resolution Trust Corporation, "Report on the Progress of Investigations of Professional Conduct," 1992.

6. Paulette Thomas, "Fraud Was Only a Small Factor in S&L Losses, Consultant Asserts," *Wall Street Journal*, July 20, 1990; Martin Lowy, *High Rollers: Inside the Savings and Loan Debacle* (New York: Praeger, 1991), 229–37. Thomas cites a study by Bert Ely. Ely and Lowy estimate that fraud accounted for perhaps 3 percent of FSLIC's losses; Barth has argued that fraud made up 10 percent of these losses. James R. Barth, statement before the House Committee on Banking, Finance, and Urban Affairs, April 11, 1990; cited by CBO, *Resolving the Thrift Crisis*, 11.

7. Lowy, *High Rollers*, 229.

8. Michael M. Weinstein, "Is the Peace Dividend at Risk?" *New York Times*, April 15, 1990.

9. "Popular" books about the savings and loan industry's problems include James Ring Adams, *The Big Fix: Inside the S&L Scandal* (New York: John Wiley & Sons, 1989); Kathleen Day, *S&L Hell: The People and the Politics Behind the $1 Trillion Savings and Loan Scandal* (New York: W. W. Norton, 1993); Ned Eichler, *The Thrift Debacle* (Berkeley: University of California Press, 1989); Lowy, *High Rollers*; Martin Mayer, *The Greatest-Ever Bank Robbery: The Collapse*

of the Savings and Loan Industry (New York: Charles Scribner's Sons, 1990); Pilzer and Deitz, *Other People's Money*; Stephen Pizzo, Mary Fricker, and Paul Muolo, *Inside Job: The Looting of America's Savings and Loans* (New York: McGraw-Hill, 1989); Michael Waldman, *Who Robbed America? A Citizen's Guide to the Savings and Loan Scandal* (New York: Random House, 1990); Steven K. Wilmsen, *Silverado: Neil Bush and the Savings and Loan Scandal* (Washington, D.C.: National Press Books, 1991). Lowy's book does not generally blame corrupt politicians.

10. For Wright and St. Germain, see Kathleen Day, "When Hell Sleazes Over: Judgment Day for S&L Slimeballs," *The New Republic*, March 20, 1989; for D'Amato, see Waldman, *Who Robbed America?* 78.

11. Brooks Jackson, *Honest Graft: Big Money and the American Political Process* (New York: Alfred Knopf, 1988); Brooks Jackson, "As Thrift Industry's Troubles and Losses Mounted, Its PACs' Donations to Key Congressmen Surged," *Wall Street Journal*, February 7, 1989, A26.

12. Jane Mentzinger, Jackie G. Howell, and Colleen O'Day, *It's a Wonderful Life: S&L Investments on Capitol Hill* (Washington, D.C.: Common Cause, 1990), 1.

13. The Keating Five Senators were Dennis DeConcini (D-Ariz.), John McCain (R-Ariz.), Alan Cranston (D-Calif.), John Glenn (D-Ohio), and Donald W. Riegle Jr. (D-Mich.). Cranston alone received almost $1 million, most of it given to nonpartisan voter registration organizations. The Senate Ethics Committee criticized all but Cranston for using poor judgment or giving the appearance of being improper; Cranston was rebuked for "improper and repugnant" conduct. Martin Kasindorf, "Senate Rebukes Defiant Cranston," *Newsday*, November 21, 1991, 17.

14. Mentzinger, Howell, and O'Day, *It's a Wonderful Life*, 6. Ralph Nader, founder of Public Citizen, has similar things to say about Congress and campaign finance in his introduction to Waldman, *Who Robbed America?*, xii–xvii.

15. Mayer, *The Greatest-Ever Bank Robbery*, 23, 61.

16. Lowy, *High Rollers*, 59–60.

17. Waldman, *Who Robbed America?* 83.

18. Wilmsen, *Silverado*, 148.

19. Books by scholars include James R. Barth, *The Great Savings and Loan Debacle* (Washington, D.C.: American Enterprise Institute, 1991); R. Dan Brumbaugh Jr., *Thrifts Under Siege: Restoring Order to American Banking* (Cambridge, Mass.: Ballinger Publishing Company, 1988); Edward J. Kane, *The S&L Insurance Mess: How Did It Happen?* (Washington, D.C.: The Urban Institute Press, 1989); and Lawrence White, *The S&L Debacle: Public Policy Lessons for Bank and Thrift Regulation* (New York: Oxford University Press, 1991). All these scholars are economists. One of the few articles on the thrift tragedy by political scientists is Thomas Romer and Barry R. Weingast, "Political Foundations of the Thrift Debacle," in *Politics and Economics in the Eighties*, ed. Alberto Alesina and Geoffrey Carliner (Chicago: University of Chicago Press, 1991), 175–209.

20. William Gorham, in the foreword to Kane, *The S&L Insurance Mess*, xvii.

21. Regarding the thrift industry, see Romer and Weingast, "Political Foundations"; and Kane, *The S&L Insurance Mess*. For the more general case, see Morris P. Fiorina, *Congress: Keystone of the Washington Establishment*, 2nd ed. (New Haven: Yale University Press, 1977).

22. Romer and Weingast, "Political Foundations," 203.

23. Kane, *The S&L Insurance Mess*, esp. chap. 4, "Socially Perverse Incentives Confronting Thrift Regulators." This view is consistent with those presented in Barth, *The Great Savings and Loan Debacle* and Brumbaugh, *Thrifts Under Siege*.

24. Public choice was pioneered by the economist James Buchanan, who won a Nobel Prize for his efforts, and includes classics by Anthony Downs, David Mayhew, Morris P. Fiorina, William A. Niskanen, and George J. Stigler. See James Buchanan and Gordon Tullock, *The Calculus of Consent* (Ann Arbor: University of Michigan Press, 1962); Anthony Downs, *An Economic Theory of Democracy* (New York: Harper & Brothers, 1957); idem, *Inside Bureaucracy* (Boston: Little, Brown, 1966); Fiorina, *Congress: Keystone of the Washington Establishment;* William A. Niskanen Jr., *Bureaucracy and Representative Government* (Chicago: Aldine, 1971); George J. Stigler, "The Theory of Economic Regulation," *Bell Journal of Economics and Management Science* 2 (1971): 3–21. In the social sciences, labelling can be perilous; these scholars do not necessarily call their work "public choice." Romer and Weingast, for example, might consider themselves practitioners of "the new institutionalism." For a general example of this form of the new institutionalism, see Matthew D. McCubbins and Terry Sullivan, *Congress: Structure and Policy* (Cambridge: Cambridge University Press, 1987). Other scholars would attribute the term "new institutionalism" to an entirely different set of scholarly interests. See Elinor Ostrom, "Rational Choice Theory and Institutional Analysis: Toward Complementarity," *American Political Science Review* 85, 1 (March 1991): 237–43.

25. Downs, *An Economic Theory,* 27–28.

26. Romer and Weingast, "Political Foundations," 178, 202.

27. Kane, *The S&L Insurance Mess,* 69.

28. See the review essay by Anne L. Schneider, "Advances in Public Policy," *American Political Science Review,* 84, 3 (September 1990), 951–53.

29. Richard Fenno, *Congressmen in Committees* (Boston: Little, Brown, 1973).

30. See Robert Katzmann, *Regulatory Bureaucracy: The Federal Trade Commission and Antitrust Policy* (Boston: MIT Press, 1980); see also Martha Derthick and Paul J. Quirk, *The Politics of Deregulation* (Washington, D.C.: Brookings, 1985).

31. For a discussion of how politicians manipulate policy agendas to maximize their political credit, see R. Kent Weaver, *Automatic Government: The Politics of Indexation* (Washington, D.C.: Brookings, 1988), 27.

32. Roger Noll, "The Political Foundations of Regulatory Policy," in McCubbins and Sullivan, eds., *Congress,* 464.

33. Nor, apparently, has any other single interest (such as income) been maximized by all these individuals.

34. Steven Kelman, *Making Public Policy* (New York: Basic Books, 1987), 250.

35. Ibid., 253.

36. But see, for example, Brian Barry and Douglas Rae, "Political Evaluation," in *Handbook of Political Science,* ed. Fred I. Greenstein and Nelson W. Polsby (Reading, Mass.: Addison-Wesley, 1975), 1:337–401.

37. See especially James Q. Wilson, *Bureaucracy: What Government Agencies Do and Why They Do It* (New York: Basic Books, 1989), 90–112.

38. Ibid., 97, citing Paul J. Culhane, *Public Lands Politics* (Baltimore: Johns Hopkins University Press, 1981), 232.

39. See Wallace E. Walker, *Changing Organizational Culture: Strategy, Structure, and Professionalism in the U.S. General Accounting Office* (Knoxville: University of Tennessee Press, 1986).

40. Martha Derthick, *Policymaking for Social Security* (Washington, D.C.: Brookings, 1972), 31.

41. See Wilson, *Bureaucracy,* 66–67 for several examples of this.

42. One of the central insights of economic theory is that the public interest is promoted by individuals seeking their own private interests in the market. It has not gone unnoticed that public choice theory, which is based on neoclassical economics, reaches almost exactly the opposite conclusion regarding the outcome of individuals seeking their private interests through politics.

43. Kelman, *Making Public Policy,* 10.

44. Norman J. Ornstein, "The Deficit: A Look at the Bright Side," *New York Times Book Review,* June 3, 1990. Ornstein is reviewing Joseph White and Aaron Wildavsky, *The Deficit and the Public Interest* (Berkeley: University of California Press/Russell Sage Foundation, 1989).

45. Joel D. Aberbach et al., *Bureaucrats and Politicians in Western Democracies* (Cambridge: Harvard University Press, 1981), 94–98. For a more general defense of the U.S. bureaucracy, see Charles T. Goodsell, *The Case for Bureaucracy* (Chatham: Chatham House, 1994).

46. Furthermore, politicians can face penalties when they are seen to be lacking conviction on these issues. President Bush's evolving positions regarding abortion made him suspect to both sides of this issue.

47. Officials can be committed to policy goals or to policy tools. A commitment to goals may on occasion mean that tools are sacrificed. For example, an official committed to "protecting the consumer" may switch from favoring regulation to supporting deregulation if the evidence is convincing that deregulation is more effective.

48. For "government by discussion," see Arthur Maass, *Congress and the Common Good* (New York: Basic Books, 1983). The reader need not imagine I think officials spend most of their time in reflective deliberation. One day visiting Capitol Hill would be enough to destroy that idea. The congressional system as a whole, however, features a fair amount of deliberation in the form of hearings, staff or agency research, floor debate, etc.

49. Kathleen Day, *S&L Hell.*

50. These two kinds of fraud parallel the main types of insider financial misconduct. See Lowy, *High Rollers,* 101–02. Campaign contributions may be legally received under numerous conditions, and therefore do not indicate official misconduct. The literature on the ethical implications of campaign finance is voluminous. For a review, see David B. Magleby and Candice J. Nelson, *The Money Chase: Congressional Campaign Finance Reform* (Washington, D.C.: Brookings, 1990).

51. The most obvious test—what do the officials say motivates them?—is not accepted by all as appropriate. While the public spirit perspective takes the statements of officials seriously, the public choice view does not, since it believes that officials either intentionally or subconsciously use public statements to justify their personal interests. See Kane, *The S&L Insurance Mess,* 68.

52. Fiorina, *Congress: Keystone of the Washington Establishment;* and Terry M. Moe, "The Politics of Bureaucratic Structure," in *Can the Government Govern?,* ed. John E. Chubb and Paul E. Peterson (Washington, D.C.: Brookings, 1989), 267–329.

53. See Martha Derthick, *Agency Under Stress: The Social Security Administration in American Government* (Washington, D.C.: Brookings, 1990), 4.

54. As the history of the Alamo suggests, public spirit need not die even when resource shortages literally prove fatal.

55. For a brief discussion of a theory of representation that includes both specific and public interests, see Maass, *Congress and the Common Good,* 73–74.

56. Interests can be represented in the policy process if they themselves participate or if "proxy advocates" (such as an elected official or interest group) act as their representative. See William T. Gormley, Jr., *Taming the Bureaucracy: Muscles, Prayers, and Other Solutions* (Princeton: Princeton University Press, 1989).

57. See David Braybrooke and Charles E. Lindblom, *A Strategy of Decision: Policy Evaluation as a Social Process* (New York: Free Press, 1963) for a description; and John F. Witte, *The Politics and Development of the Federal Income Tax* (Madison: University of Wisconsin Press, 1985) for an application.

58. See Matthew D. McCubbins and Thomas Schwartz, "Congressional Oversight Overlooked: Police Patrols Versus Fire Alarms," *American Journal of Political Science,* 2, 1 (February 1984): 165–79. McCubbins and Schwartz refer primarily to Congress, though many of their ideas also seem relevant for regulatory agencies. Although these authors do not regard congressional oversight in general as deficient, the public choice view of the thrift tragedy does portray congressional oversight as faulty.

59. See, in particular, Maass, *Congress and the Common Good,* 204–07.

60. Wilson, *Bureaucracy,* 156.

61. See especially Kane, *The S&L Insurance Mess,* on this point.

62. Some scholars also view officials' public statements as facades covering the real purposes. See Murray Edelman, *The Symbolic Uses of Politics* (Urbana: University of Illinois Press, 1964).

63. Day, *S&L Hell,* 10.

Chapter 2. A Brief History of the
Federal Home Loan Bank System

1. The most complete history of the early S&L business is H. Morton Bodfish, *History of Building and Loan in the United States* (Chicago: United States Building and Loan League, 1931). A more abbreviated version is in Leon T. Kendall, *The Savings and Loan Business: Its Purposes, Functions, and Justifications* (Englewood Cliffs, N.J., 1962), a monograph prepared by the United States Savings and Loan League for the Commission on Money and Credit. The first S&L was patterned after British building societies.

2. Kendall, *The Savings and Loan Business*, 5. For a more detailed history of the "Nationals," see Bodfish, *History of Building and Loan*, 100–15.

3. Between 1887 and 1897 the Nationals amassed $250 million in deposits, compared to about $1 billion for the locals. Bodfish, *History of Building and Loan*, 105.

4. Kendall, *The Savings and Loan Business*, 5.

5. Bodfish, *History of Building and Loan*, 114.

6. Kendall, *The Savings and Loan Business*, 5.

7. Bodfish notes that "many prominent men, including bankers, congressmen, treasury officials and cabinet officers, and even one vice president of the United States became involved with the [National] movement. Often, of course, such responsible individuals were hoodwinked and did not know the real character of the organization with which they were connected." Bodfish, *History of Building and Loan*, 104. Politicians are reluctant to be hoodwinked twice.

8. Emphasis added. Representatives of thirteen existing state leagues organized the national league. The rise of the Nationals was, of course, not the only reason for the formation of the league. The 1880s and 1890s were in general a period in which businesses were forming national trade associations.

9. By 1890, a solid majority of Americans no longer lived on farms. Eight of the thirteen million "occupied housing units" in 1890 were defined as "nonfarm." U.S. Bureau of the Census, *Historical Statistics of the United States: Colonial Times to 1970*, part 2 (Washington, D.C.: Government Printing Office, 1975), 646.

10. Ibid., 651.

11. Ibid., 647. Mortgage debt is held by both individuals and institutions.

12. Ruth Werner, "The Federal Home Loan Bank System," *Federal Home Loan Bank Board Journal* 15, 6 (June 1982): 16–19.

13. Kendall, *The Savings and Loan Business*, 141–42. Putting these losses into perspective is not easy. The deposit loss would have been worth about $2 billion in 1990 in inflation-adjusted dollars. An equivalent loss in inflation-adjusted total assets would have represented nearly $50 billion.

14. Ibid., 143.

15. Or about $25 billion in 1990 dollars.

16. Friedman and Schwartz estimate the stock market declined about $85

billion—or $850 billion in 1990 dollars—in value between 1930 and 1933. Milton Friedman and Anna Jacobson Schwartz, *A Monetary History of the United States, 1867–1960* (Princeton: Princeton University Press, 1963), 351.

17. Kendall, *The Savings and Loan Business*, 7.

18. Josephine Hedges Ewalt, *A Business Reborn: The Savings and Loan Story, 1930–1960* (Chicago: American Savings and Loan Institute Press, 1962), 37.

19. Ibid.

20. Federal assistance to thrifts, homeowners, and depositors was part of a much larger reform effort to re-create the nation's financial system. This section describes only the legislation most relevant to the thrift business.

21. Kendall, *The Savings and Loan Business*, 7. All but $2 million of these loans was repaid by 1937.

22. Ewalt, *A Business Reborn*, 50–55.

23. The Bank Board originally had five members appointed for six-year terms. By the 1980s it had three members serving four-year terms.

24. Home Owners Loan Corporation, *Final Report to the Congress of the United States Relating to the Home Owners Loan Corporation*, March 1, 1952, 17.

25. These resources were the HOLC bonds that were exchanged for mortgage loans. The HOLC bonds could then be readily sold for cash. In addition, HOLC deposited over $200 million of its cash in S&Ls. Ewalt, *A Business Reborn*, 46.

26. Furthermore, for the first three years of the loan the borrower had to pay only the interest.

27. Indeed, because HOLC loans were available only to those who were in default on their home mortgages, significant incentives existed for individuals to default on their mortgages in order to refinance with HOLC. As Ewalt argues, "Although the legislation limited the loans to genuinely distressed borrowers, in actual practice many unqualified persons were able to take advantage of this windfall." Ewalt, *A Business Reborn*, 41.

28. HOLC did lose about $350 million (of the $3.1 billion it lent) on mortgages that remained in default. These losses were more than covered by the interest earned by the HOLC on its other loans, minus its financing costs. HOLC, *Final Report to the Congress*, 38.

29. As the National Commission on Financial Institution Reform, Recovery, and Enforcement (NCFIRRE) has pointed out, this was in sharp contrast to federally chartered banks, which could engage in almost any activity not explicitly prohibited by law, so long as "safety and soundness" was maintained. NCFIRRE, *Origins and Causes of the S&L Debacle: A Blueprint for Reform* (Washington, D.C.: Government Printing Office, July 1993), 19.

30. State-chartered S&Ls, if they were FSLIC insured, had to comply with the regulations of both state regulators and FSLIC.

31. H. F. Cellarius, "Building and Loan Associations and Federal Legislation: An Historical Review," in Bodfish, *History of Building and Loan*, 186.

32. See ibid., 214.

33. Theobald argues that "had building and loan managers had an opportunity to vote on it, almost certainly a substantial majority would have been

opposed." A. D. Theobald, *Forty-Five Years on the Up Escalator* (privately printed, 1979), 53.

34. Ewalt, *A Business Reborn*, 75.

35. See ibid., 138–39.

36. Ibid., 92.

37. Ibid., 52.

38. Ibid., 67.

39. Glass wanted to create a "liquidating corporation" which would advance to depositors the funds it was estimated they would receive when the firm was liquidated. Carter H. Golembe, "The Deposit Insurance Legislation of 1933," *Political Science Quarterly*, June 1960.

40. Author's calculations from U.S. Bureau of the Census, *Historical Statistics*, 651.

41. Ibid., 1039.

42. In 1965 there were also about twenty-five hundred state-chartered thrifts, holding $63 billion in assets, insured by the FSLIC. Another seventeen hundred state-chartered S&Ls, with $5 billion in assets, were not insured by FSLIC. U.S. League of Savings Institutions, *Savings Institutions Sourcebook, 1986* (Chicago: USL, 1986), 46.

43. Savings deposits are considered "short term" because they could often be withdrawn at any time without penalty.

44. Savers had more alternatives for two reasons. On the one hand, the number and type of investment possibilities were expanding. On the other, technological improvements made it easier to shift funds among types of investments.

45. Short-term interest rates are defined here as "prime commercial paper, 4–6 months." Savings deposit rates were lower than this. The data series begins in 1890. U.S. Bureau of the Census, *Historical Statistics*, 1001.

46. This figure, by showing the total change in thrift deposits from year to year, understates the actual declines in savings deposits during the periods of rising interest rates. Since these deposits include the interest credited to them, total deposits would grow by the interest rate even if no new deposits were placed. A better measure would be "net new deposits" (new deposits minus new withdrawals). These data are not available for this period.

47. NCFIRRE, *Origins and Causes*, 23.

48. Legislation proposed to allow asset diversification included the Federal Savings Bank Bill of 1965, the Financial Institutions Act of 1973, the Financial Reform Act of 1976, and the Depository Institution Deregulation Act of 1976.

49. Ironically, Representative Fernand St. Germain, who has often been portrayed as the thrift business's best friend, was "unrelenting" in his opposition to ARMs. Norman Strunk and Fred Case, *Where Deregulation Went Wrong: A Look at the Causes Behind Savings and Loan Failures in the 1980s* (Chicago: U.S. League of Savings Institutions, 1988), 46.

50. This preference varies with the level and direction of market interest rates. When rates are low or rising, the preference for fixed-rate loans is higher.

When rates are high or falling, consumers are more favorably disposed towards ARMs.

51. For a discussion of the pros and cons of ARMs see Walter J. Woerheide, *The Savings and Loan Industry: Current Problems and Possible Solutions* (Westport, Conn.: Quorum Books, 1984), chap. 4.

52. For an example of congressional deliberation on this matter, see U.S. House of Representatives, *Adjustable Rate Mortgages: Hearings Before the Subcommittee on Financial Institutions Supervision, Regulation and Insurance of the Committee on Banking, Finance and Urban Affairs*, 97th Cong., 1st sess. (Washington: Government Printing Office, 1981).

53. About the same time the Bank Board authorized S&Ls to make educational loans and investments in urban development projects, while increasing their ability to make loans on apartments. John E. Horne, "Statement," *Federal Home Loan Bank Journal*, April 1982, 79–80.

54. The proportion of thrift assets in mortgage loans of all sorts, for example, had dropped from about 85 percent in 1975 to 82 percent in 1979. U.S. League of Savings Institutions, *Savings Institutions Sourcebook, 1986*, 54.

55. Andrew S. Carron, "The Political Economy of Financial Regulation," in *The Political Economy of Deregulation: Interest Groups in the Regulatory Process*, ed. Roger S. Noll and Bruce M. Owens (Washington, D.C.: American Enterprise Institute, 1983), 69–96.

56. Theobald gives several examples of USL ambivalence. In 1965, the Investments and Mortgage Lending Committee of the USL voted narrowly (eleven ayes, eight nays, and one abstention) to lobby Congress for the ability to make personal and consumer loans. In 1974, the league's legislation program included recommendations *both* to preserve thrifts' traditional role and to expand it to full-service banking. Theobald, *Forty-Five Years*, 224, 250.

57. For example, see Strunk and Case, *Where Deregulation Went Wrong*, 54.

58. U.S. House of Representatives, *Financial Institutions and the Nation's Economy (FINE) "Discussion Principles,"* hearings before the Committee on Banking, Finance, and Urban Affairs, December 1975–January 1976, 1623.

59. See the statements of Norman Strunk, president of the USL, and Garth Marston, acting director of the Bank Board, in *Financial Institutions and the Nation's Economy*, 1623 and 1133. Still others argued that maturity mismatch problems could be reduced by policies other than asset diversification. For example, James Pierce, FINE study director, and Franco Modigliani, Nobel Prize economist, suggested that "interest rate insurance" could adequately protect thrifts from interest rate swings. Statement by Modigliani, *Financial Institutions and the Nation's Economy*, 191.

60. As the NCFIRRE reported, "By virtually any standard, up to the mid-1960s, S&Ls did a superlative job of fulfilling [this] task that Congress had assigned them." NCFIRRE, *Origins and Causes*, 20.

61. The director of the FINE study, for instance, noted simply that the effect of thrift diversification on home mortgage availability was "difficult to predict." Statement by James Pierce in *Financial Institutions and the Nation's Economy*, 6.

62. It is worth noting that the Bank Board had asked Congress for the power to establish rate ceilings several times before, but the S&L business had opposed it and Congress chose not to give them this power. In 1966, however, both the business and the Bank Board agreed that interest rate ceilings were needed.

63. The Bank Board had to act in coordination with the Federal Reserve Board, which set limits for banks. Congress, concluding that cut-throat competition among banks was a main cause of bank failures, had already imposed interest rate ceilings on banks during the Depression.

64. Total deposits continued to increase due to the crediting of interest payments to existing deposits. Net new deposits do not include these interest payments. See Office of Thrift Supervision, *Savings and Home Financing Sourcebook, 1989*, A-13.

65. Congressional Budget Office, *Resolving the Thrift Crisis*, April 1993, 86.

66. Andrew S. Carron, *The Plight of the Thrift Institutions* (Washington, D.C.: Brookings, 1982). Yet as large as the losses were, the true deterioration the business suffered during these years was far greater. For example, the losses were "reported" rather than "real," and the insolvencies were "de jure" rather than "de facto." Real losses, and actual insolvencies, were much greater than the reported numbers indicate. The reason for these understatements are discussed in chapter 6.

67. The political and regulatory responses will merely be outlined here, since the rest of the book examines in detail what government officials did and why they did it.

68. For a typical statement, see *The American Banker*, "'Look-Alike' Financial Institutions of the Future Called a Myth," September 4, 1980, 4. For details about this act, see Thomas F. Gargill and Gillian G. Garcia, *Financial Deregulation and the Monetary Control Act: Historical Perspective and Impact of the 1980 Act* (Stanford, Calif.: Hoover Institution Press, 1982).

69. President Reagan, quoted at the signing ceremony. See "Garn-St. Germain Puts Thrifts Back into Housing Arena," *The American Banker*, August 5, 1983, 17.

70. Several states also ratified laws in the early 1980s to assist thrifts.

71. Thrift failure data from Richard T. Pratt, "Statement," National Commission on Financial Institutions Reform, Recovery, and Enforcement (NCFIRRE), January 29, 1993, 57–58.

72. Andrew S. Carron, *The Rescue of the Thrift Industry: A Staff Paper* (Washington, D.C.: Brookings, 1983).

73. Some observers have suggested that the $10.8 billion was only enough to handle the insolvent thrifts located between downtown Dallas and the DFW airport. Thrift losses were concentrated in Texas.

Chapter 3. The Federal Home Loan Bank Board

1. I will use the acronym FHLBB to refer to the agency as a whole and the term "Bank Board" to denote the agency's board of directors.

2. The FHLBS was dismantled in 1989 by the Financial Institutions Reform, Recovery, and Enforcement Act (FIRREA). The Bank Board was abolished and its functions moved to the newly created Office of Thrift Supervision within the Department of the Treasury; FSLIC merged with FDIC. Thus, although some components of the system (such as the FHLBS) remain in operation, I use the past tense to describe the FHLBS.

3. The Office of the Comptroller of the Currency is responsible for regulating national banks, and the Federal Deposit Insurance Corporation has primary responsibility for regulating state-chartered banks that are not members of the Federal Reserve System. The Fed does have secondary responsibilities for regulating national banks. See Brumbaugh, *Thrifts Under Siege*, 22–23; Andrew S. Carron, *Reforming the Bank Regulatory Structure* (Washington, D.C.: Brookings, 1984).

4. Brumbaugh, *Thrifts Under Siege*, 25.

5. Thomas Marvell, *The Federal Home Loan Bank Board* (New York: Praeger Publishers, 1969), 225, 255.

6. See U.S. Senate, *Financial Institutions Reform, Recovery, and Enforcement Act—Conference Report*, printed in *Congressional Record*, 101st Cong., 1st sess., 3 August 1989, S9895.

7. It is difficult to demonstrate this even when the influence may have been illegal, as the lengthy Senate Ethics Committee hearings on the Keating Five Senators or the Committee on Standards of Official Conduct investigation of House Speaker Jim Wright show. Regarding the Keating Five, see U.S. Senate, *Report of Temporary Special Independent Counsel, Pursuant to Senate Resolution* 202, 13 May 1992. Regarding Wright, see U.S. House of Representatives, Committee on Standards of Official Conduct, *Report of the Special Outside Counsel in the Matter of Speaker James C. Wright, Jr.*, 101 Cong., February 21, 1989.

8. One study of the Fed concluded that the size, length of term, interest composition, and geographic distribution of its membership had an ambiguous influence on the FRS's policy functions and administrative effectiveness. Michael D. Reagan, "The Political Structure of the Federal Reserve System," *American Political Science Review* 55, 1 (March 1961): 64–76.

9. Both the Federal Reserve Board and the Bank Board also had a formal advisory panel. In the FRS, the Federal Advisory Council is composed of twelve members, one from each district. The FAC meets in Washington, D.C., at least four times a year: it confers directly with the Board of Governors on general business conditions and makes recommendations on monetary policy. "It is Federal Reserve tradition that only bankers serve on this Council even though the Federal Reserve Act is silent on this qualification. The majority of FAC members are from very large banks." U.S. House of Representatives, Committee on Banking, Finance, and Urban Affairs, *A Racial, Gender, and Background Profile of the Directors of the Federal Reserve Banks and Branches*, staff report (Washington, D.C.: Government Printing Office, 1990), 14. The Federal Savings and Loan Advisory Council had twenty-four members. Twelve served on

FHLB boards and were elected by them; the other twelve were appointed by the Bank Board to represent the public interest. The FSLAC provided a formal means of communication between the industry and the Bank Board, but it was not considered very important.

10. The classic statement of business influence over regulation through official appointments is found in Marver H. Bernstein, *Regulating Business by Independent Commission* (Princeton: Princeton University Press, 1955), 82; see also Louis Kohlmeier, *The Regulators* (Harper & Row, 1969), 484.

11. Theobald, *Forty-Five Years*, 27, 35.

12. Pizzo, Fricker, and Muolo, *Inside Job*, 16–17.

13. Political scientists who have studied the professional backgrounds and policy preferences of regulatory officials have been led to doubt that the links between them are strong and clear. For an extended discussion of this issue, see Paul J. Quirk, *Industry Influence in Federal Regulatory Agencies* (Princeton: Princeton University Press, 1981); and William T. Gormley, "A Test of the Revolving Door Hypothesis at the F.C.C." *American Journal of Political Science* 23 (November 1979): 665–83. Other scholars have noted the influence of professional training on official behavior. See Katzmann, *Regulatory Bureaucracy*; William T. Gormley, Jr., "Professionalism Within Environmental Bureaucracies: The Policy Implications of Personnel Choices," La Follette Institute Occasional Paper #1 (Madison: Robert La Follette Institute of Public Affairs, 1987).

14. This record is based primarily on statements submitted to the Senate in support of their nominations and on citations printed in the *Washington Post* and *Wall Street Journal*. One interim appointment (Lee Henkel) resigned before the Senate held his confirmation hearings: as a result, his record is based solely on newspaper reports. The Congressional Information Service database did not provide a citation for confirmation hearings for Lawrence White, and therefore his employment record is based on other published sources. I omitted jobs lasting less than a year, and some "first jobs" after college that appeared unrelated to all other employment. I noted memberships on corporate boards, but did not include them in the calculations. An alternative strategy to examining all professional employment would have been to include only the board members' longest or most recent employment. This was the method used by John Woolley. See John T. Woolley, *Monetary Politics: The Federal Reserve and the Politics of Monetary Policy* (Cambridge: Cambridge University Press, 1984), 55. I rejected this method for two reasons. As a theoretical matter, it would seem that individuals' attitudes are shaped by the whole of their professional life and not just certain portions of it. As an empirical matter, several board members had numerous and sometimes overlapping jobs. For example, Robert McKinney was the chairman of a thrift, chairman of a holding company that was parent to an insurance company, and a senior partner in a law firm during the same period. See Mark Rom, "Professional and Educational Background and Foreground of FHLBB Members," unpublished manuscript, 1994, for details on this analysis.

15. Thrift business employment included jobs with individual S&Ls or thrift-related interest groups. Any employment within the FHLBS counted in an-

other category, and any position in other parts of federal or state governments was included in a third. The greatest difficulty lay in distinguishing between the categories of "housing" and "other." I defined housing-related employment rather loosely: it includes developers, realtors, mortgage insurers, participants in the mortgage secondary market, lawyers specializing in representing housing-related clients, and involvement in housing policy. The "other" category includes everything else.

16. Janis and DiPrete also served terms as directors on thrifts' boards (not included in the table).

17. Dalton was the president of the Government National Mortgage Association (an office within the Department of Housing and Urban Development) between 1978 and 1979, and Hovde was the undersecretary of housing and urban development between 1981 and 1983.

18. Woolley, *Monetary Politics*, 56.

19. U.S. House of Representatives, Committee on Interstate and Foreign Commerce, Subcommittee on Oversight and Investigation; and Senate, Committees on Commerce and Government Operations, *Joint Hearings on Regulatory Reform, Volume I: Quality of Regulators*, 94th Cong., 1st sess., 1975, 47.

20. This is admittedly a judgment call. In four of the ten years, one board member had come from the thrift industry while the chairman is listed as having "half" a thrift background. Since neither of these chairmen (McKinney and Gray) is considered to have been especially sympathetic to industry concerns while in office, it seems reasonable to suggest that thrift interests had at best a tenuous majority on the board.

21. Both boards meet only a few times each year and were not considered especially influential.

22. Woolley, *Monetary Politics*, 57. Woolley examined the backgrounds of the thirty-one FRB directors who served between 1955 and 1982. It is also worth nothing that the educational backgrounds of the Bank Board members also varied much more than did those of the Fed. Two individuals holding the Ph.D degree (one in economics, the other in business administration) served on the board, but so did two members apparently without any college degrees. Three lawyers, four with degrees in business administration, and four with undergraduate degrees in fields other than business, served on the Bank Board during this period. Only three members received their degrees (either undergraduate or graduate) at "prestigious" schools. At the Fed, about half the governors came from prestigious schools and about half were economists, with most of the economists holding the Ph.D. degree. For the Fed, see Woolley, *Monetary Politics*, 57–58. The "prestigious" schools are Harvard, Yale, Chicago, Stanford, Columbia, MIT, Cornell, Northwestern, Princeton, Johns Hopkins, Pennsylvania, and Dartmouth. Thomas R. Dye, *Who's Running America?* 3rd ed. (Englewood Cliffs, N.J.: Prentice Hall, 1983).

23. For an account of the importance of expertise in decision making in general, see Hubert L. Dreyfus, *What Computers Still Can't Do* (Cambridge: MIT Press, 1992).

24. John F. Berry, "McKinney Quits FHLBB, Hints of Campaign Role," *Washington Post*, May 3, 1979, C1+.

25. "FHLBB Post," *Washington Post*, July 26, 1979.

26. Ronald Brownstein and Nina Easton, *Reagan's Ruling Class: Portraits of the President's Top 100 Officials* (Washington, D.C.: The Presidential Accountability Group, 1982), 95.

27. Dalton was, like President Carter, a graduate of the U.S. Naval Academy and a nuclear engineer. See "Bank Board Position," *Washington Post*, December 7, 1979; and U.S. Senate, Committee on Banking, Housing, and Urban Affairs, *Nomination of Donald I. Hovde*, 98th Cong., 1st sess., May 24, 1983, 15.

28. McKinney's nomination was the only one of the fifteen that was controversial at the time. Confirmation hearings ran for over three hundred pages, and included a number of statements by groups (such as the NAACP, the AFL-CIO, and Common Cause) opposing McKinney because they perceived he would not help the poor and minorities gain easier access to housing credit. Miller, in contrast, was a member of such organizations as the ACLU, Women's Forum, New York City Mission Society, a fair housing council, and also worked on urban affairs issues for the Ford Foundation. U.S. Senate, Committee on Banking, Housing, and Urban Affairs, *Nomination of Robert H. McKinney*, U.S. Senate, 95th Cong., 1st sess. (Washington, D.C.: Government Printing Office, 1977); U.S. Senate, Committee on Banking, Housing, and Urban Affairs, *Nomination of Anita Miller*, 95th Cong., 2d sess. (Washington, D.C.: Government Printing Office, 1978), 13, 14.

29. Mayer contends that White was recommended by George Benston, the conservative—but apparently too controversial— Democrat the administration had favored. Mayer, *The Greatest-Ever Bank Robbery*, 194. Although White had written several books, none of them concerned finance, housing, or the thrift industry.

30. Woolley, *Monetary Politics*, 51.

31. Quirk, *Industry Influence in Federal Regulatory Agencies*, 45.

32. Donald F. Kettl, *Leadership at the Fed* (New Haven: Yale University Press, 1986), 13–15.

33. For example, Woolley, *Monetary Politics*, 61–64; E. Ray Canterbery, "A New Look at Federal Open Market Voting," *Western Economic Journal* 6 (December 1967): 25–38; and William P. Yohe, "A Study of Federal Open Market Committee Voting, 1955–64," *Southern Economic Journal* 33 (April 1966): 396–405.

34. Nancy L. Ross, "Robert McKinney: A Washington View," *Washington Post*, August 10, 1979, F1+; see also John F. Berry, "McKinney Quits FHLBB, Hints of Campaign Role," *Washington Post*, May 3, 1979, C1+.

35. Ross, "Robert McKinney"; Berry, "McKinney Quits FHLBB."

36. Ross, "Robert McKinney."

37. "Bank Board's Janis is Resigning; GOP Will Control Panel," *Wall Street Journal*, November 25, 1980, 56.

38. The three-person board must have at least one Democratic and one Republican representative, but the president is permitted to designate the chairman.

39. During the 1960s Janis served at the departments of commerce and housing and urban development. Janis had been a real estate developer in Florida and had also served on the board of directors of an S&L for most of the 1970s. In the latter half of the 1970s he served on the board of directors of the National Association of Home Builders (NAHB). He was serving as undersecretary of the Department of Housing and Urban Development when he moved to the Bank Board. U.S. Senate, Committee on Banking, Housing, and Urban Affairs, *Nominations on Jay Janis, John R. Evans, Philip A. Loomis, and R. Robert Russell* (Washington: Government Printing Office, 1980), 96th Cong., 1st sess., September 4, 1979, 44, 50.

40. Pratt was the chief economist for the USL between 1967 and 1969, served on the board of the FHLB of Seattle (as a "public interest director") between 1970 and 1978, and sat on the boards of Home Savings and Loan Association and Western Mortgage Loan Company. Through two consulting firms (Richard T. Pratt, Assoc., and JPS Financial Consultants), Pratt provided consulting services to savings and loan associations, federal agencies, commercial banks, public utility companies, and numerous nonfinancial businesses. See Richard T. Pratt, "Statement," NCFIRRE, January 29, 1993, appendix A; Brownstein and Easton, *Reagan's Ruling Class*, 101.

41. For a discussion of the deregulatory views of economists, see Derthick and Quirk, *The Politics of Deregulation*.

42. Mayer, *The Greatest-Ever Bank Robbery*, 61. Other sources give less emphasis to Pratt's contributions to this measure. The Garn–St. Germain Act is discussed in chaps. 8 and 9.

43. For example, Pratt allowed federally chartered thrifts to write adjustable rate mortgages for the first time and removed the ceiling on the amount of brokered deposits a thrift could hold. Prior to this ruling, thrifts could hold no more than 5 percent of all their liabilities in the form of brokered deposits.

44. Pratt notes that another 516 S&Ls "disappeared" during these years "because of mergers and acquisitions approved, encouraged or arranged by the agency." Pratt, "Statement," NCFIRRE, 57–58.

45. Statement of Richard T. Pratt, Bank Board chairman, to U.S. Senate, Committee on Banking, Housing, and Urban Affairs, "Capital Assistance Act and Deposit Insurance Flexibility Act: Hearings on S. 2531 and S. 2532," 97th Cong., 2nd sess., May 26, 1982, 18.

46. Pratt, "Statement," NCFIRRE, 54–55.

47. For example, until 1980 thrifts were required to maintain a net worth of 5 percent; this was reduced to 4 percent in the fall of 1980 (under Janis) and 3 percent in 1982 (under Pratt). Pratt also expanded the ability of thrifts to count "goodwill" as capital. (When a thrift was sold, the difference between its net tangible assets and the price paid for it is attributed to such intangible assets as its brand name, customer lists, etc., all together called goodwill. Before Pratt,

thrifts had to write goodwill off their books over a ten-year period; Pratt extended this to forty years.) Pratt allowed thrifts to count "appraised equity capital" (i.e., property they owned through foreclosure or direct investment) toward their capital requirements. He also allowed thrifts that sold loans at a loss to write off the loss over the life of the loan rather than taking the loss immediately. The thrifts were allowed to take the loss immediately for the purposes of reducing their income taxes, however.

48. Mayer, for example, concludes that "if you had to pick one individual to blame for what happened to the S&Ls and to some hundreds of billions of taxpayer money, [Pratt] would get the honor without even campaigning." Mayer, *The Greatest-Ever Bank Robbery*, 61. Yet Pratt's Bank Board faced essentially three options. It could have liquidated the thrift business at an enormous cost (perhaps $178 billion in 1981 dollars) to the public. It could have nationalized the business, an act that would have been unprecedented and, almost certainly, hugely expensive. Or it could have attempted to "build a bridge" to allow thrifts time to adjust to the new environment. Pratt chose this last course. Pratt, "Statement," NCFIRRE, 4–9.

49. Jay Janis, "Dealing with Inflation: Ideology vs. Pragmatism," in *Savings and Loan Asset Management under Deregulation*, Federal Home Loan Bank of San Francisco, Proceedings of the Sixth Annual Conference, San Francisco, California, December 8–9, 1980 (San Francisco: Federal Home Loan Bank of San Francisco, n.d.), 11–12.

50. Eichler, *The Thrift Debacle*, 130; see also Mayer, *The Greatest-Ever Bank Robbery*, esp. 57–64 and 66–69.

51. Mayer, *The Greatest-Ever Bank Robbery*, 117. Virtually all observers have described Gray's appointment in similar terms.

52. For example, Gray sought to impose limits on brokered deposits, limit excessive growth, and increase thrift net worth requirements. Gray also doubled the number of FHLBS examiners.

53. Edwin J. Gray, "Keynote Address before the Fifth Annual School of Business Senior Convocation of the Commencement Exercises of California State University, Fresno," May 22, 1993; see also Edwin J. Gray, "Statement," The National Commission on Financial Institution Reform, Recovery, and Enforcement, January 15, 1993.

54. Gray is adamant that the thrift business subverted his efforts to regulate it. Telephone interviews with Gray, February 4, 1993; February 9, 1993.

55. Mayer, *The Greatest-Ever Bank Robbery*, 58.

56. First a city planner in South Dakota, Wall had later worked as Senator Garn's top staffer on the Banking Committee. As the chief Republican staffer on that committee, Wall was (or should have been) well acquainted with the problems the thrift industry faced when he became Bank Board chairman in 1987. Yet Wall lacked both administrative and business experience.

57. Most of FSLIC's losses actually had been incurred—but not recognized—before Wall became chairman, as we shall see in the next two chapters.

58. U.S. General Accounting Office, *Failed Thrifts: Bank Board's 1988 Texas Resolutions*, GAO/GGD-89-59, March 11, 1989. See also William Black, "The Southwest Plan and the 1988 'Resolutions,'" Staff Report No. 3, NCFIRRE.

59. Lowy, *High Rollers*, 204.

60. "Former FHLBB Chairmen Testify on Mortgages," *National Mortgage News*, August 8, 1988, 26. The three chairmen were testifying before the Senate Banking, Housing, and Urban Affairs Committee.

61. Kane states that "the postgovernment career opportunities that have unfolded as a result of distinguished public service for Paul Volcker and Henry Kissinger dramatically exemplify the existence of this [resume enhancement] category of implicit compensation." Kane, *The S&L Insurance Mess*, 107.

62. Ibid., 102.

63. In 1984 the Bank Board had a $70 million operating budget and five hundred employees; FSLIC, which the Bank Board directed, had $1.3 billion in operating income and over one thousand employees. In the private sector, a director of a similarly sized company would have been paid several times the salary of a member of the Bank Board.

64. It is relatively easy to determine what jobs Bank Board members took when they departed office. Private sector salaries are not usually a matter of public record, however, so it is difficult to identify any windfall the members might have received.

65. "Jay Janis Named California S&L Head," *Washington Post*, December 23, 1980, D8; Richard Pratt, "Statement," NCFIRRE, appendix A, 2.

66. It is worth noting that, during the course of his term, Gray apparently was offered positions within the USL and also at Keating's S&L, which would have paid him several times his government salary. He rejected each such offer.

67. These conclusions are based on a name search of the major newspapers indexed in the Lexis/Nexis "ALLNEWS" library. For specific citations, see Rom, "Professional and Educational Background."

Chapter 4. The Federal Home Loan Bank System

1. Federal Home Loan Bank Board, *A Guide to the Federal Home Loan Bank System* (Washington, D.C.: FHLBB, 1987), 35.

2. For the popular view, see Mayer, *The Greatest-Ever Bank Robbery*, 146; for an academic account, see Brumbaugh, *Thrifts Under Siege*, 26–27.

3. Each FHLB has at least fourteen directors. Member thrifts can elect no more than thirteen directors (all of whom must come from the savings and loan industry), and elected directors must outnumber appointed directors by a 4-to-3 ratio.

4. Commercial banks elect both Class A and Class B directors.

5. U.S. House of Representatives, *A Racial, Gender, and Background Profile*, 33.

6. Ibid., 39.

7. Brumbaugh, *Thrifts Under Siege*, 26–27.

8. Kettl shows how the chairman of the Federal Reserve Board has often dominated Fed policy. Kettl, *Leadership at the Fed*.

9. Woolley, *Monetary Politics*, 58–59.

10. Bank Board Chairman Gray also wanted to remove Topeka FHLB Chairman Kermit Mowbray from his position. Since Gray had recently fired the Dallas chairman, he apparently decided that removing Mowbray would create a mutiny among the FHLBs. Wilmsen, *Silverado*, 151.

11. Lincoln and Centrust are discussed at greater length in the appendix to chapter 6.

12. FHLB profits are often large. In 1988 dividends from the FHLBs to member thrifts totaled $1.2 billion, for example, which was about 30 percent of the thrift industry's total profits.

13. For example, U.S. General Accounting Office, "Failed Financial Institutions: Reasons, Costs, Remedies, and Unresolved Issues," GAO/T-AFMD-89-1, January 13, 1989.

14. White, *The S&L Debacle*, 185.

15. Herman E. Krooss and Martin R. Blyn, *A History of Financial Intermediaries* (New York: Random House, 1971); and Kenneth E. Scott, "The Dual Banking System: A Model of Competition in Regulation," *Stanford Law Review* 30 (November 1977): 1–56.

16. Author's calculations from data in GAO, "Failed Financial Institutions." This report examines the thrift resolutions occurring only in 1988, the most expensive single year in the thrift tragedy. The claim that state failures accounted for two-thirds of the total costs of the thrift cleanup appears consistent with other reports. For additional detail, see Mark Carl Rom, "The Thrift Tragedy," Ph.D. diss., University of Wisconsin-Madison, 1992, 40–48.

17. Thrifts, to be sure, will adopt the form of charter they hope will bring them the greatest economic benefits: they *are* in it for the money. The evidence is strong that, in at least some states where state and federal regulations diverge widely, thrifts tend to choose the least expensive charter (though charter switching is relatively rare). See, for example, M. Manfred Fabritius and William Borges, *Saving the Savings and Loan: The U.S. Thrift Industry and the Texas Experience, 1950–1988* (New York: Praeger, 1989), 41–47.

18. One the one hand, some of the most notorious S&L failures (such as Charles Keating's Lincoln and David Paul's CenTrust) involved state-chartered thrifts that gave liberally to members of Congress. On the other, a state legislator with any skill could have enough influence over a federal thrift (through, for example, building codes or state contracts) to secure contributions from it.

19. Woerheide, *The Savings and Loan Industry*, 14.

20. It is not clear that state governments substantially tightened thrift regulations in recent years, but the federal government itself has taken steps to ensure that state rules do not undermine federal rules.

21. "Savings association codes in most states had 'tie-in' clauses which gave state associations the same authority Congress provided the federals." Strunk and Case, *Where Deregulation Went Wrong*, 57.

22. Further, the Texas law forbade the state regulators from prohibiting any loan or investment that federal associations were allowed to make. Fabritius and Borges, *Saving the Savings and Loan*, 46.

23. This section is based primarily on Fabritius and Borges, *Saving the Savings and Loan*.

24. In 1953 there were 77 state and 82 federal thrifts in Texas. In 1978 there were 247 state and 71 federal S&Ls there. Ibid., 41, 75.

25. The FHLBB awarded the commissioner of the Texas S&L department in 1982 for his leadership role in making Texas a model state. This was the only state commissioner so recognized by the FHLBB. Ibid., 74, 81.

26. Between 1979 and 1982 the assets of Texas thrifts grew from $23.8 billion to $35.6 billion, and net worth increased from $1.18 billion to $1.29 billion. Federal thrifts in Texas, meanwhile, had basically stable assets (from $7.7 billion to $7.8 billion) and declining net worth (from $448 million to $308 million). Ibid., 106.

27. Geoff Brouillette, "San Diego S&L to Switch to State Charter; Central Federal First to Convert in the Reverse Direction. Will Others Follow?" *The American Banker*, November 29, 1982, 2.

28. Strunk and Case, *Where Deregulation Went Wrong*, 58.

29. Mayer, quoting the head of the legislative committee of the California S&L League, in *The Greatest-Ever Bank Robbery*, 49.

30. The relative size of state losses is measured as follows. The estimated cost to FSLIC of all S&L failures within a state between 1980 and 1992 is divided by the total S&L assets of the state in 1985; this figure is the numerator. The estimated cost to FSLIC of all S&L failures nationally between 1980 and 1992 is divided by total S&L assets nationally for 1985; this becomes the denominator. Data from Congressional Budget Office, *Resolving the Thrift Crisis*, April 1993, 92–93; U.S. League of Savings Institutions, *Savings Institutions Sourcebook, 1986*, 48.

31. The relevant states and their loss ratios are Arkansas (7.0), Mississippi (5.2), Texas (4.0), New Mexico (3.6), Louisiana (2.3), Colorado (1.7), Arizona (1.3), and Oklahoma (1.1).

32. Wisconsin, Michigan, New Hampshire, Vermont, and Connecticut all had loss ratios of less than 0.2.

33. Some adjoining states had greatly different loss ratios: for example, North Dakota had a loss ratio of 1.8 while South Dakota's loss ratio was 0.3, even though their regulatory systems were probably similar. On the other hand, regional economic factors also contributed to the clustering of high or low loss ratios.

34. Andrew Carron, *Reforming the Bank Regulatory Structure* (Washington, D.C.: Brookings, 1984), 7.

35. Federal Home Loan Bank Board, *A Guide*, 49.

36. GAO, "Failed Financial Institutions," 32.

37. Ibid., 33.

38. Federal Home Loan Bank Board, *A Guide*, 36.

39. In its annual reports, the Bank Board aggregated examinations into three categories: "federal and state-chartered, regular examinations," "federal and state-chartered special examinations," and "state-chartered, joint regular examinations" (conducted with state banking agencies). To estimate the total number of examinations the FHLBB conducted of state-chartered thrifts, I conservatively assumed that only 15 percent of the first two categories focused on state thrifts. Special examinations began in 1984. The data presented in table 4.2 are not comparable to FHLBB data for 1986, and no data were published after that year, though the Bank Board reported a large increase in the total number of examinations. See, for example, Federal Home Loan Bank Board, *1984 Annual Report* (Washington, D.C.: FHLBB, 1984), 30–31.

40. But note the defense of Bank Board enforcement activity given by Pratt, "Statement" and Gray, "Statement" both in NCFIRRE.

41. GAO, "Failed Financial Institutions," 32. As we shall see in the next chapter, there was substantial uncertainty about how the Bank Board should use its authority.

42. James R. Barth, Philip F. Bartholomew, and Michael G. Bradley, "The Determinants of Thrift Resolution Costs," Research Paper no. 89-03, Office of the Chief Economist, Office of Thrift Supervision, November 1989; James R. Barth, Philip F. Bartholomew, and Carol J. Labich, "Moral Hazard and the Thrift Crisis: An Analysis of 1988 Resolutions," in Federal Reserve Bank of Chicago, *Banking System Risk: Charting a New Course* (Chicago, 1989), 344–84; GAO, "Failed Financial Institutions," 60.

43. Congressional action on this issue is considered in more detail in chapter 9.

44. White, *The S&L Debacle,* 141.

45. Barth, Bartholomew, and Bradley, "The Determinants of Thrift Resolution Costs."

46. See for example Mayer, *The Greatest-Ever Bank Robbery,* 249–59; Pilzer and Deitz, *Other People's Money,* 203–32; Waldman, *Who Robbed America,* 83–90.

47. For example, Mayer reports that "for calendar 1989, Perelman's new First Gibraltar reported payments from the government of $461 million and net profits to Perelman (all tax-free) of $129 million. Wow!" *The Greatest-Ever Bank Robbery,* 256.

48. A third way—assistance to the existing owners—is possible but rarely used. For an analytical description of this net worth hole, see appendix 1.

49. White argues that sales are less expensive than liquidations because sales put the assets in private hands and liquidations allow bureaucrats to manage the assets. This is not correct. In both cases bureaucrats must strike deals with the private sector regarding the price of the assets.

50. Cohen and Freier, *The Federal Home Loan Bank System,* 11.

51. Asessing the value of assets might entail determining the correct price of "a loan in arrears on a partially completed suburban Texas shopping center or office complex that was also tied up in litigation" (White, *The S&L Debacle,* 158).

52. FSLIC, and the public, would hear that it had underpriced the assets each time some buyer sold them for a large profit.

53. See especially GAO, *Failed Thrifts*, 158–60.

54. That is, if the covered assets were sold for less than their book value, FSLIC would make up the difference.

55. White, *The S&L Debacle*, 159.

56. The purchaser did not have "complete" incentives to maximize the value of the covered assets. If the purchaser concluded that it was not possible to sell the assets for more than their book value, the purchaser had no incentive to minimize the loss because FSLIC would bear all of it.

57. FSLIC actually received warrants which it could convert into (usually) 20 percent of the stock of the new thrift. These warrants would increase in value if the stock prospered, so when FSLIC sold them its net costs would be reduced.

58. The GAO goes on to say that liquidations "*may* have been more economical had substantial cash been available to FSLIC. . . . It is possible that FSLIC *may* have been able to make better deals [by excluding] some of the most insolvent thrifts" (my emphasis). GAO, *Failed Thrifts*, 8.

59. Lowy continues: "My guess—and it is a pure guess—is that the FSLIC spent between $10 and $15 billion more than it would have had to spend if it had the cash to do the job right. That would mean that the cost was 20 percent or 25 percent more than it might have been." Lowy, *High Rollers*, 217.

60. Mayer, *The Greatest-Ever Bank Robbery*, 258.

61. For example, George J. Benston and George G. Kaufman, "Understanding the Savings-and-Loan Debacle," *The Public Interest* 99 (spring 1990): 79–95; Strunk and Case, *Where Deregulation Went Wrong*; and Kane, *The S&L Insurance Mess*.

62. Note, however, that public officials might also be thought to have incentives for "empire building" (i.e., hiring larger staffs than necessary). The individual incentives of public officials would thus seem to be consistent with hiring too few or too many bureaucrats.

63. This problem is not unique to the federal work force. The impact of staff size, salaries, and turnover on performance in the private sector is also subject to debate.

64. Although Kane argues that "in the federal service today, top officials accept below-market salaries for their period of government service," one might contend that the federal service indeed pays at-market salaries once implicit compensation is included. Kane, *The S&L Insurance Mess*, 106.

65. An equilibrium in the attractiveness of two jobs can be maintained if the explicit compensation for one goes down and its implicit compensation increases.

66. Accountants were chosen as the basis for comparison in the private sector because, although the Bank Board hired individuals with varied backgrounds, it was, for obvious reasons, especially interested in those with education in finance. The comparisons are limited to starting level salaries because I was un-

able to find average salaries for mid- and senior-level accountants. At any rate, comparing public and private sector salaries for mid- and senior-level positions may be more difficult (as the gaps between explicit salaries grow larger) and less meaningful (because implicit compensation must be very important for those who choose to work at higher-level government jobs). The federal government normally hires college graduates at the GS-5 or GS-7 level within the civil service, so both levels are included here; until 1985, Bank Board staff were under the civil service. Beginning in 1985, salaries are for Bank Board examiners hired by the district banks; these examiners were exempt from civil service salary restrictions. Salaries for accountants are for job offers made to graduates by approximately two hundred companies. The year 1977 was arbitrarily chosen as the initial data point because it was the earliest year in the data source and the data for that year appear consistent with the next few years. The year 1985 was chosen to end the series because the Bank Board essentially moved to private sector salaries for its examination staff at that time by transferring them out of the civil service system.

67. The removal of examiners from civil service restrictions allowed their explicit salaries to equal those in the private sector in 1985.

68. Federal Home Loan Bank Board, *1984 Annual Report*, 29.

69. Pilzer and Deitz, *Other People's Money*, 163.

70. Data may not be strictly comparable. The turnover rate for FHLBB examiners, those in the private sector, and those in banking and finance is calculated based on the number of terminations divided by average annual employment figures; the rate for the federal government is twelve times the monthly rate of separations.

71. Kane and White use similar measures. Kane, *The S&L Insurance Mess*, 101; and White, *The S&L Debacle*, 88–89.

72. The Bank Board's records show that larger thrifts required more working days but fewer working days per dollar. For example, in 1984 a thrift with under $10 million in assets took 16.2 working days but 2.3 days per million assets to examine; a thrift with more than $500 million in assets averaged 96.3 days to examine, or 0.1 days per $1 million. Federal Home Loan Bank Board, *1984 Annual Report*, 31.

73. To make the relevant comparisons, examiner-to-asset, examiner-to-institution, employee-to-asset, and employee-to-institution indices were created for the years 1979–1987. Although these years were chosen somewhat arbitrarily on the basis of readily available data, they allow for pre- and post-deregulation trends to be examined. The data include the number of field examiners in the FHLBS; the combined number of field examiners for the OCC, FDIC, and FRS; the total number of employees in the bank and thrift industries; the level of assets in federally insured banks and thrifts, and the total number of federally insured bank or thrift institutions. There are three different types of federal bank examiners. The Office of the Comptroller of the Currency, in the treasury department, is the primary examiner of national banks; the Federal Reserve is the primary examiner of state banks that are members of the Federal Reserve System; and the

FDIC is the primary examiner of state-chartered banks that do not belong to the FRS but are FDIC insured. State agencies have secondary responsibilities for state-chartered, federally insured banks and thrifts. See Brumbaugh, *Thrifts Under Siege*, 22. Data on the number of state examiners were unavailable. First ratios were calculated and then indices were created using 1979 as the reference year. As with any index, choice of reference year is at least in part arbitrary; it is the shape of the lines, and not their intersection at the reference year, that is important. The year 1979 seemed to be useful as a reference year, however, because it was probably the last year that the indices were more or less in equilibrium, prior to the turmoil of the 1980s.

74. For example, the standard deviation of the change in the examiner-to-asset ratio was 14 percent for thrifts and 6 percent for banks.

75. Statement of L. Linton Bowman, in U.S. Congress, House Committee on Banking, Finance, and Urban Affairs, *Financial Condition of the Federal Savings and Loan Corporation and the Federal Deposit Insurance Corporation at Year-End 1988*, Field Hearings, San Antonio, Texas, March 1989, 70.

76. Mayer, *The Greatest-Ever Bank Robbery*, 299. These issues are examined more thoroughly in the next chapter.

77. U.S. Congress, House Subcommittee of the Committee on Government Operations, *Federal Regulation of Direct Investments by Savings and Loans and Banks; and Condition of the Federal Deposit Insurance Funds*, 99th Cong., 1st sess., February 1985, 15.

78. *War On Waste: President's Private Sector Survey on Cost Control* (New York: Macmillan, 1984).

79. Federal Home Loan Bank Board, *1984 Annual Report*, 69.

80. Pizzo, Fricker, and Muolo, *Inside Job*, 268–69.

81. Ibid., 269.

82. The Bank Board did have oversight over the district banks, however.

83. Kane, like most economists, is critical of politicians' willingness to take spending items off the budget, and recommends that all expenses of the federal government be aggregated into one unified budget.

84. Pizzo, Fricker, and Muolo, *Inside Job*, 268–69.

Chapter 5. The Bank Board and the Thrift Business

1. Return on average assets is defined as the net after-tax income divided by average assets (net of "loans in process"). U.S. League of Savings Institutions, *Savings Institutions Sourcebook, 1983* (Chicago: USL, 1983), 40.

2. The estimates Kane and Brumbaugh make include only the effect of interest rate variations on asset values. After 1984 interest rates had a smaller impact on thrift industry asset values, and the worth of individual investments became much more important. It is difficult to make aggregate estimates about the market value of these investments. Kane stops his estimations in 1983, and Brumbaugh discontinues his in 1984. See Kane, *The S&L Insurance Mess*, 76.

3. The difference between GAAP and RAP will be discussed later in this chapter. For now, it is enough to know that both accounting systems were virtually identical until after 1982.

4. Eugene Bardach and Robert A. Kagan, *Going by the Book: The Problem of Regulatory Unreasonableness* (Philadelphia: Temple University Press, 1982).

5. Closer scrutiny could begin when RAP net worth fell below 3 percent.

6. Unless it could merge the insolvent thrift with another and provide the merger partner with a variety of assets (such as "goodwill," tax breaks, or IOUs) for which FSLIC did not actually have to pay.

7. These costs assume that all the money is taken directly from general revenues and spent at once, thus ignoring financing costs. They closely resemble "present discounted value" costs.

8. Pratt has testified that the cost of liquidating the thrift industry in 1981 would have been $178 billion (or $350 billion in 1990 dollars). Pratt, "Statement," NCFIRRE, 4. Moreover, the costs presented in the text understate what it would have cost to actually eliminate only the insolvent S&Ls from the business. For example, these estimates do not include the administrative costs of processing and selling such a huge volume of assets, nor do they take into account how much selling them would further depress the market.

9. Carron, *The Plight of the Thrift Institutions*, 19–20. Carron himself had estimated the market value net worth of the thrift industry as minus $17.5 billion in 1980 and minus $44.1 billion as of June 30, 1981.

10. Federal Home Loan Bank Board, *Federal Home Loan Bank Board Journal, Annual Report 1982* 16, 4 (April 1983): 4.

11. See especially Congressional Budget Office, "The Costs of Forbearance During the Thrift Crisis," unpublished staff memorandum, June 1991.

12. Between 1950 and 1979, 114 thrifts had failed. About 70 percent of the thrift resolutions between 1980 and 1982 were "supervisory mergers" in which FSLIC provided no financial assistance, but the merger proceeded under its direction. The remaining resolutions involved liquidations, assisted mergers, or other financial assistance. Brumbaugh, *Thrifts Under Siege*, 68.

13. Including Net Worth Certificates and Income Capital Certificates. Brumbaugh, *Thrifts Under Siege*, 44–45.

14. Pilzer and Deitz, *Other People's Money*, 74–75.

15. Pizzo, Fricker and Muolo, *Inside Job*, 13.

16. Mayer, *The Greatest-Ever Bank Robbery*, 68–70.

17. White, *The S&L Debacle*, 82.

18. For example, RAP allowed S&Ls to count subordinated debt as net worth. Subordinated debt is a loan that "in the event of bankruptcy, will not be repaid until other unsecured debt has been repaid. As a consequence of being subordinated, it often is wiped out or loses most of its value if the issuer becomes bankrupt." Lowy, *High Rollers*, 298. Subordinated debt is not covered by deposit insurance.

19. Mayer, *The Greatest-Ever Bank Robbery*, 70.

20. This should worry those who want to rely on market value accounting to provide more accurate estimates of the thrift business's real net worth.

21. White, *The S&L Debacle*, 83. In fact, these assets could have a market value if thrifts were allowed to sell losses for tax purposes.

22. This is the main reason why the thrift industry had a very large negative market net worth, as shown in table 5.1.

23. Industry RAP net worth was 1.21 percent higher than GAAP net worth in 1985 and 1.15 percent higher in 1986. Brumbaugh, *Thrifts Under Seige*, 45.

24. The standards were even more permissive than this because they allowed thrifts to average net worth and liabilities over five years and because newly chartered thrifts had twenty years to comply. This meant that thrifts could grow rapidly over a short period and still comply with the rule.

25. Almost 75 percent of thrift industry assets were in thrifts that had GAAP net worth of less than 5 percent in 1982. Brumbaugh, *Thrifts Under Siege*, 49. Perhaps another 15 percent of industry assets were in thrifts with less than 5 percent RAP net worth.

26. White, *The S&L Debacle*, 82.

27. Ibid., 87.

28. Later in this chapter we will examine the extent to which the Bank Board was able to set and enforce clear standards and will assess the degree to which FSLIC's losses could have been reduced had violators been caught and stopped sooner.

29. Assets for these thrifts grew from $141 billion to $283 billion during this period. Seventy-four of the 637 thrifts grew by over 400 percent. The 637 thrifts were those filing financial reports in both 1982 and 1985 that FSLIC had sold, liquidated, or predicted would fail. White, *The S&L Debacle*, 100–01.

30. Ibid., 113. White discusses some of these studies 114–15.

31. Remember, however, that by 1982 FSLIC was almost certain to suffer enormous losses.

32. U.S. League of Savings Institutions, *Savings Institutions Sourcebook, 1987* (Chicago: USL, 1987), 27. See also figure 5.1.

33. White, *The S&L Debacle*, 125.

34. Mayer, *The Greatest-Ever Bank Robbery*, 106.

35. Lowy, *High Rollers*, 62. As Lowy puts it, "Growing . . . was what *everyone* was telling S&L managements to do" (my emphasis).

36. See, for example, Mayer, *The Greatest-Ever Bank Robbery*, 80–88.

37. Actually, selling assets at a loss will not cut the net worth ratio unless the ratio of the loss to the asset is larger than the existing net worth ratio.

38. Remember, if the thrift industry had sold all its assets in 1982 it would have been over $70 billion in the hole.

39. An unfortunate series of events made problems worse. Bank Board Chairman Pratt left in April 1983. Edwin Gray became Bank Board chairman on May 1, and Don Hovde also joined the board in May. Gray had been appointed to the board in December 1982, and Hovde was confirmed by the Senate in June 1982. The third member of the board, Jamie Jackson, began serving his term only at the beginning of 1982. In other words, at the very peak of thrift business growth, the Bank Board was new on the job.

40. Chapters 7 and 8 describe some of the background, and the congressional involvement, regarding these issues.

41. For examples of rapidly growing thrifts that were insolvent or nearly so, see the FHLBB staff memorandum by William Schilling, "Examples of Insured Institutions with Rapid Growth and/or Direct Investments," December 10, 1984, in *Federal Regulation of Direct Investments by Savings and Loans and Banks*, 299–309.

42. See Joseph A. McKenzie, "Analysis of Service Corporation Investment and Direct Real Estate Investment by FSLIC-Insured Savings Institutions," Federal Home Loan Bank Board, November 16, 1984, 310–31; George J. Benston, "Direct Investments by Savings and Loan Associations: Return and Risk," 505–71; both in *Federal Regulation of Direct Investments*.

43. U.S. Congress, House of Representatives, *Federal Regulation of Brokered Deposits*, 17.

44. *Savings Institutions*, December 1984.

45. Lowy, *High Rollers*, 77. Later, Lowy goes even further: "In fact, on an industry-wide basis, if we took loan fees out of S&L income for the years 1983 through 1987, we would wipe out *all* of the reported earnings of the industry." Lowy, *High Rollers*, 81.

46. This discussion relies heavily on Lowy, *High Rollers*, chap. 6, "Permissive Loan Fee Accounting—The Linchpin," 77–85.

47. Ibid., 78.

48. The riskiness of loans is lower than for investments because, should the borrower become bankrupt, lenders have precedence over investors for the borrower's assets. The potential yield for investors is higher than for lenders, however, because the investor can share in the appreciation of the borrower's assets, while a lender does not.

49. For example, an investment in a shopping center could become profitable either when it was sold or when tenants started paying rent.

50. Lowy, *High Rollers*, 78–79, italics in the original.

51. The AICPA is the national association of CPAs and the most important private group promulgating standards for S&L auditing.

52. *Journal of Accountancy*, November 1983; cited in Lowy, *High Rollers*, 79 (Lowy's italics).

53. "The authoritative AICPA *Auditing and Accounting Guide for Savings and Loan Associations* didn't even mention ADC loans" in 1983. Lowy, *High Rollers*, 79.

54. Empire Savings and Loan failed in 1984, and Empire had made a huge number of ADC loans. U.S. House of Representatives, Committee on Government Operations, *Federal Home Loan Bank Board Supervision and Failure of Empire Savings and Loan Association of Mesquite, Texas*, 6 August 1984.

55. Lowy, *High Rollers*, 80–81.

56. The corollary of this problem is that loan loss reserves are always too big when you don't need them, and never big enough when you do. FSLIC's own experience validates this corollary.

57. Lowy notes further that, although the AICPA *Industry Audit Guide for Audits of Banks* "is far more stringent on the subject of loan losses, as anyone who reads the newspapers knows, when a bank's loans go bad, there still are never enough reserves." Lowy, *High Rollers*, 83.

58. As Lowy interprets this guide, S&Ls could count as income fees equal to the costs of originating the loan plus the other fees if the loan was sold to another firm. Lowy, *High Rollers*, 81.

59. Unless the loan was sold, at which time the fees could be recorded as income.

60. U.S. General Accounting Office, CPA *Audit Quality: Failures of CPA Audits to Identify and Report Significant Savings and Loan Problems*, GAO/AFMD-89-45, February 1989.

61. The third criteria for selection that GAO used was that the accounting firms did not question the extent of the loan losses.

62. GAO, CPA *Audit Quality*, 1.

63. Ibid., 9.

64. Ibid.

65. Stephanie Strom, "Accounting Firm Settles Federal Auditing Charges," *New York Times*, August 10, 1994, D1. The firms involved included Ernst & Young ($400 million), Deloitte Haskins & Sells ($312 million), KPMG Peat Marwick ($186 million), and Arthur Anderson & Co. ($82 million).

66. See, in particular, Lowy, *High Rollers*, chap. 8; Brumbaugh, *Thrifts Under Siege*, 74–76; Kane, *The S&L Insurance Mess*.

67. Those who want to allow regulators to impose regulations even if they lack convincing evidence to support them would have to be willing to accept rules such as those limiting brokered deposits.

68. U.S. General Accounting Office, *Wrongdoing, Fraud Main Factor in Thrift Industry Crisis*, GAO/T-AFMD-89-4, March 22, 1989, 13–14.

69. Mayer, *The World's Greatest-Ever Bank Robbery*, 64. Mayer also claims that after the Garn–St. Germain Act was adopted, the Bank Board did not even take the time to design regulations to implement the law: instead, the board "announced omnibus memoranda, telling the S&Ls and their lawyers that they could make their own readings of the law and get going and the Bank Board would trail along later to okay what they did." Ibid., 95.

70. For a thrift not meeting its net worth requirement, the annual growth rate was limited to the interest credited to depositors accounts. Thrifts meeting their net worth requirements could grow up to 25 percent annually without regulatory permission, and faster than that if they received such permission.

71. The ability to make such investments was linked to net worth.

72. As on so many points, the data are not crystal clear. As White puts it, 609 thrifts that the Bank Board disposed of between 1986 and 1989 were in operation both at year-end 1985 and year-end 1987 (that is, they had been neither liquidated nor sold during these two years). This group of 609 thrifts grew on average by only 5 percent a year between 1985 and 1987, with more than half of

them shrinking in size. The ones that grew, White argues, still were reporting adequate net worth during this period. White, *The S&L Debacle*, 132–33.

Lowy, in contrast, examined the 177 thrift failures that he judged to be the most expensive to FSLIC. Of these thrifts, 63 were "nasty little fast growers" in Texas. These NLFG thrifts grew by about 57 percent between the end of 1984 (not 1985) and 1987, more than 18 percent a year on average. Seventeen of these thrifts grew by over 20 percent in 1985, 4 grew by more than that amount in 1986, as did 5 in 1987. Lowy does not discuss the net worth of these firms during this period. Lowy, *High Rollers*, 230, 232.

73. Estimates by Bert Ely contained in Thomas, "Fraud Was Only a Small Factor in S&L Losses" and by Martin Lowy and Maryann Schembri in Lowy, *High Rollers*, 229–37.

74. For example, Ely estimates total present value costs (i.e., those excluding interest on debt) for FSLIC's losses to be $147 billion, while Lowy looks at a sample of thrift failures that are estimated to have a present value cost of $83 billion.

Chapter 6. Congress Before Deregulation

1. U.S. Congress, House of Representatives, Committee on Banking, Hearings, November 13, 1989, 8, cited by Mayer, *The Greatest-Ever Bank Robbery*, 32.

2. Braybrooke and Lindblom, *A Strategy of Decision*, 83.

3. The best stories are found in Day, *S&L Hell*; Mayer, *The Greatest-Ever Bank Robbery*; and Pizzo, Fricker, and Muolo, *Inside Job*.

4. In chapter 8 I do look at the influence of constituents and ideologies on congressional voting.

5. What if a legislator has good public reasons for supporting a policy (for example, because it is good for the people) but bad private reasons (for example, it especially favors his family)? Unless the private reasons are illegal (his family receives kickbacks) or patently private (it helps only his family), it seems fair to take the public statements seriously. Of course, good policies can be made for bad reasons, and good reasons do not necessarily produce good policies. But here we are interested in the quality of the reasons given for the policies.

6. Of course, asset, liability, and deposit insurance are not entirely distinct issues. The kinds of liabilities a firm offers will influence the types of assets it holds, for example, while the deposit insurer will be concerned with both assets and liabilities.

7. U.S. League of Savings Institutions, *'82 Savings and Loan Sourcebook*, (Chicago: USL, 1982), 21.

8. Thrifts also received tax advantages for holding at least 82 percent of their portfolio in "qualified assets," primarily home mortgages.

9. The mean difference between costs and returns was 1.5 percent.

10. Woerheide, *The Savings and Loan Industry*, 139.

11. In addition, interest rate ceilings were supposed to reduce "unfair" competition between depository institutions in different parts of the country.

During the 1960s, S&Ls in western states (primarily California) were paying much higher interest rates than eastern S&Ls and banks, and were therefore attracting funds that otherwise would have remained in the East. Western S&Ls could be more aggressive both because the West was growing faster (and so had greater demand for home mortgages) and because relatively small portions of their portfolios were tied up in low-yielding mortgages. Scott Winningham and Donald G. Hagan, "Regulation Q: A Historical Perspective," *Economic Review*, April 1980, Federal Reserve Bank of Kansas City, 10–16.

12. To attract funds, thrifts were allowed to offer slightly higher interest rates on deposits than banks offered. See Edward J. Kane, "Short-Changing the Small Saver: Federal Government Discrimination Against Small Savers During the Vietnam War," *Journal of Money, Credit, and Banking*, November 1970, 513–22; and Dwight Jaffee and Kenneth Rosen, "The Changing Liability Structure of Savings and Loan Associations," *Journal of the American Real Estate and Urban Economics Association*, Spring 1980, 39.

13. When the Federal Reserve raised market interest rates above the Regulation Q ceilings, the supply of funds to thrifts and banks fell, and they were less able to extend credit.

14. See Carron, *The Plight of the Thrift Institutions*, 13–14.

15. For a discussion of the literature, see Woerheide, *The Savings and Loan Industry*, 139–42.

16. See Dwight Jaffee, "Eliminating Deposit Rate Ceilings," *Federal Home Loan Bank Board Journal*, August 1973.

17. See Thomas F. Cargill and Gillian G. Garcia, *Financial Deregulation and Monetary Control: Historical Perspective and the Impact of the 1980 Act* (Stanford: Hoover Institution Press, 1982); and Kerry Cooper and Donald R. Fraser, *Banking Deregulation and the New Competition in Financial Services* (Cambridge: Ballinger, 1984).

18. Large savers had a variety of safe investments, such as Treasury securities, that would earn market rates.

19. Interest rates on three-month Treasury bills were around 11 percent and passbook savings accounts were limited to 5 percent.

20. The housing industry was convinced that interest rate ceilings were essential to its continued prosperity, expert analysis notwithstanding. The National Association of Home Builders (NAHB) and the National Association of Realtors (NAR) lobbied vigorously against interest rate deregulation, claiming that it "will lead to an unprecedented increase in interest rates for home mortgages which could put costs, finally, beyond the ability of people to own their own homes." U.S. Congress, *Congressional Record*, 96th Cong., 1st sess., October 31, 1979, 30285. Academic economists tended to disagree with this assessment.

21. Thrifts could still pay .25 percent higher interest rates on these MMCs than could banks.

22. Jaffee and Rosen estimated that, without the MMCs, the thrift industry would have had a deposit outflow of about $24 billion in 1979. Jaffee and Rosen, "The Changing Liability Structure of Savings and Loan Associations," 39.

23. Profitability, as measured by retained earnings as a percentage of average total assets, fell from 0.84 percent in 1978 to 0.14 percent in 1980. Carron, *The Plight of the Thrift Institutions*, 12.

24. This proposal was part of S. 1347, the Depository Institutions Deregulation Act of 1979.

25. Including U.S. Congress, House of Representatives, Subcommittee of the Committee on Government Operations, *Interest Rate Regulation on Small Savings Accounts*, Hearings, 96th Cong., 1st sess.; U.S. Congress, Senate, Committee on Banking, Housing and Urban Affairs, Subcommittee on Financial Institutions, *Equity for the Small Saver*, Hearings on S. Con. Res. 5, 96th Cong., 1st sess.

26. See, for example, Charles Clotfelter and Charles Liberman, "On the Redistributive Impact of Federal Interest Rate Ceilings," *Journal of Finance* (March 1978): 199–213; David H. Pyle, "Interest Rate Ceilings and Net Worth Losses by Savers," in Kenneth E. Boulding and Thomas Frederick Wilson, eds., *Redistribution through the Financial System* (New York: Praeger, 1978), 87–101; and Bruce W. Morgan, "Ceilings on Interest Rates, the Saving Public and Housing Finance," in U.S. Senate *Equity for the Small Saver*, 175.

27. Testimony was given by such groups as the American Association of Retired Persons (AARP), the National Retired Teachers Association (NRTA), the Gray Panthers, the Consumers Union, National Organization for Women (NOW), and Public Advocates. "Political Support for Home Buyers Shifts in Face of Outcry from Small Savers," *Savings and Loan News*, May 1979, 35.

28. Statement of Robert Gnaizda, Public Advocates, Inc., in U.S. Senate, *Equity for the Small Saver*, 6.

29. U.S. Congress, *Congressional Record*, October 31, 1979, 30286.

30. Ibid., October 31, 1979, 30311. The U.S. League of Savings Institutions (USL), National Association of Realtors (NAR), and National Association of Homebuilders (NAB) all provided similar statements.

31. U.S. Congress, *Congressional Record*, October 31, 1979, 30314.

32. Ibid., 30312.

33. The Comptroller of the Currency was a nonvoting member.

34. "Broad Banking Deregulation Bill Approved," *1980 CQ Almanac*, 277.

35. Carron, *The Rescue of the Thrift Industry*, 4–5. Thrifts relied more heavily on borrowings from the Federal Home Loan Banks, on other wholesale borrowings, and on longer-term certificates limited by Regulation Q, which still paid comparatively high rates.

36. Carron, *The Rescue of the Thrift Industry*, 3.

37. Carron, *The Plight of the Thrift Institutions*, 56–58.

38. U.S. Congress, House of Representatives, Committee on Banking, Finance, and Urban Affairs, Subcommittee on Financial Institutions Supervision, Regulation and Insurance, *Oversight Hearings on Depository Institutions Deregulation Committee*, Hearing, 96th Cong., 2nd sess., July 2, August 26, 1980; U.S. Congress, House of Representatives, Committee on Banking, Finance, and Urban Affairs, *Depository Institutions Deregulation Committee*,

Hearing, 96th Cong., 2nd sess., August 5, 1980; U.S. Congress, House of Representatives, Committee on Banking, Finance, and Urban Affairs, Subcommittee on General Oversight and Regulation, *Oversight Hearing on the Depository Institutions Deregulation Committee*, Hearing, 97th Cong., 1st sess., November 18, 1981.

39. Statement by Richard Pratt, U.S. Congress, House of Representatives, *Oversight Hearing*, 1982, 7.

40. Statement of Edwin J. Brooks, U.S. League of Savings Institutions, in U.S. Senate, Committee on Banking, Housing, and Urban Affairs, *Financial Institutions Restructuring and Services Act of 1981*, Hearings, 97th Cong., 1st sess., 448.

41. Carron, *The Plight of the Thrift Institutions*, 59–60.

42. Pamela Fessler, "Savings and Loan Aid Package Boosts Powers of Banks, Thrifts," *Congressional Quarterly*, October 2, 1982, 2424.

43. Including *The Report of the President's Commission on Financial Structure and Regulation* (Washington, D.C.: Government Printing Office, 1970); U.S. Congress, House of Representatives, Committee on Banking, Currency, and Housing, Subcommittee on Financial Institutions Supervision, Regulation and Insurance, *Financial Institutions and the Nation's Economy* (FINE), Hearings, 94th Cong., 1st and 2nd sess.; and *The Report of the President's Commission on Housing* (Washington, D.C.:Government Printing Office, 1982).

44. Statement by Andrew Carron in U.S. Congress, Senate, Committee on Banking, Housing, and Urban Affairs, *Capital Assistance Act and Deposit Insurance Flexibility Act*, Hearings, 97th Cong., 2nd sess., 395; see also Carron, *The Plight of the Thrift Institutions*, 65.

45. Carron in U.S. Congress, Senate, *Capital Assistance Act*, 395.

46. Ibid., 399.

47. Testimony by Comptroller of the Currency C. Todd Conover in U.S. Congress, Senate, *Capital Assistance Act*, 399.

48. Testimony by Roger Mehle in U.S. Congress, Senate, *Capital Assistance Act*, 159.

49. DIDMCA also broadened federal thrifts' abilities to make home mortgage loans by permitting them to make residential real estate loans without geographic restriction. It replaced the existing $75,000 limit on residential mortgage loans with a sliding scale allowing thrifts to make loans for a certain percentage of the value of the property. For example, thrifts could make loans of up to 66.7 percent of the appraised value of unimproved real estate and up to 90 percent of the appraised value of improved real estate.

50. The interagency task force was composed of the White House Domestic Policy Staff, the Department of the Treasury, the Department of Housing and Urban Development, the FHLBB, the Federal Reserve, the FDIC, the Comptroller of the Currency, and the National Credit Union Administration in 1980. Department of the Treasury, *The Report of the Interagency Task Force on Thrift Institutions*, (Washington, D.C.: Government Printing Office, 1980), 57.

51. Department of the Treasury, *The Report of the Interagency Task Force*, 61–62.

52. Nontraditional assets included commercial mortgage loans, land loans, commercial loans, consumer loans, and direct equity investments. More than half of the total came from commercial mortgage loans. James R. Barth, Philip F. Bartholomew, and Carol J. Labich, "Moral Hazard and the Thrift Crisis: An Analysis of the 1988 Resolutions," *Banking System Risk: Charting a New Course* (Chicago: Federal Reserve Bank of Chicago, 1989), 344–84.

53. Robert Masterson, chairman of the National Association of Mutual Savings Banks, in "Thrift Institutions Seek Congressional Aid," *Congressional Quarterly*, April 17, 1982, 849.

54. Texas-chartered thrifts held about 3–5 percentage points less in mortgages and mortgage-backed securities than did federally chartered thrifts in Texas in 1981 and 1982. Since asset definitions changed in 1982, the data from these years do not lend themselves to exact comparison. Federal Home Loan Bank Board, *Combined Financial Statements: FSLIC-Insured Thrifts, 1981*, 81; *Combined Financial Statements, 1982*, 81.

55. Federal Home Loan Bank Board, *Combined Financial Statements, 1981*, 81; *Combined Financial Statements, 1982*, 81.

56. Direct investments had to be made through a "service corporation" subsidiary of the thrift.

57. California, for example, permitted state-chartered thrifts to invest 100 percent of their assets in service corporations or in commercial real estate.

58. See, for example, Carron, *The Rescue of the Thrift Industry*; Cooper and Fraser, *Banking Deregulation*.

59. At the time, this change was noted without comment as one of the "other provisions" in DIDMCA by *1980 Congressional Quarterly Almanac*, 277.

60. Waldman, *Who Robbed America*, 23. Mayer, in contrast, writes that it was the big California S&Ls insisting that insurance coverage be raised to $100,000, and that "Senator Alan Cranston carried their water to the table." Mayer, *The Greatest-Ever Bank Robbery*, 93–94. For the most detailed account, see Day, *S&L Hell*, 61–66.

61. Pizzo, Fricker, and Muolo write that "regulators later said that this may have been the most costly mistake made in deregulating the thrift industry." Pizzo, Fricker, and Muolo, *Inside Job*, 11. However, at least one regulator, former Bank Board member Lawrence White, called the expansion of deposit insurance "a sensible step" and even recommended *universal* deposit insurance coverage. White, *The S&L Debacle*, 75, 235–37.

62. Congress had also doubled insurance coverage from $5,000 to $10,000 in 1950.

63. "U.S. League Sets Legislative Goals," *Savings & Loan News*, April 1978, 76.

64. Office of Thrift Supervision, *Savings and Home Financing Sourcebook*, 1989, A-24.

65. Banks that are "too big to fail" are almost always handled through purchase and assumption.

66. Cooper and Fraser, *Banking Deregulation*, 169.

67. For pre-DIDMCA discussions of 100-percent deposit insurance, see Robert E. Barnett, Paul M. Horvitz, and Stanley C. Silverberg, "Deposit Insurance: The Present System and Some Alternatives," *Banking Law Journal* (April 1977): 304–32; and Gary Leff, "Should Federal Deposit Insurance Be 100 Percent?" *Bankers Magazine* (Summer 1976): 23–30. For a recent defense of universal deposit insurance coverage, see White, *The S&L Debacle*, 235–37.

68. Steven S. Smith, *Call to Order: Floor Politics in the House and Senate* (Washington, D.C.: Brookings, 1989), 202.

Chapter 7. Congress After Deregulation

1. The 637 thrifts were those filing financial reports in both 1982 and 1985 that FSLIC had sold, liquidated, or predicted would fail. White, *The S&L Debacle*, 100–01.

2. This section is based primarily on House of Representatives, Committee on Government Operations, *Federal Regulation of Brokered Deposits in Problem Banks and Savings Institutions*, Report, U.S. House of Representatives, 98th Cong., 2nd sess. (Washington, D.C.: Government Printing Office, 1984).

3. "Brokered Deposits," FDIC and FHLBB advance notice of proposed rule making, *Federal Register*, November 1, 1983, 50339–41.

4. U.S. House of Representatives, *Federal Regulation of Brokered Deposits*, 5.

5. Mayer suggests that the USL favored the proposal because the FHLBB already had the authority to reimpose the pre-1981 limits on brokered deposits, while FDIC had no similar power. The USL thus worried that banks would have greater access to deposits than would thrifts. Mayer, *The Greatest-Ever Bank Robbery*, 135.

6. U.S. House of Representatives, Committee on Government Operations, Commerce, Consumer, and Monetary Affairs Subcommittee, *Proposed Restrictions on Money Brokers*, Hearings, 98th Cong., 2nd sess., March 14, 1984.

7. See *FAIC Securities Inc. v. U.S.*, 595 F. Supp. 73 (1984), 753 F. 2d. 166 (1985), 762 F. 2d. 352 (1985); cited by White, *The S&L Debacle*, 142n. 5. White notes that "a modest limitation on the use of brokered deposits—no more than 5 percent of deposits by thrifts that were below their minimum net worth requirement—remained." *The S&L Debacle*, 142.

8. Bills to limit brokered deposits are listed in U.S. House of Representatives, *Federal Regulation of Brokered Deposits*, 3. FIRREA forbids any bank or thrift that is not meeting its net worth requirements from accepting any brokered deposits unless they received a waiver from FDIC, but places no restrictions on those thrifts in compliance with the requirements. M. Maureen Murphy, "FIRREA: The Financial Institutions Reform, Recovery, and Enforcement Act of 1989: A Summary," Congressional Research Service, August 28, 1989, 7.

9. See Rom, "The Thrift Tragedy," for a list of these documents.

10. U.S. House of Representatives, *Federal Regulation of Brokered Deposits*, 31.

11. Ibid.

12. Because these data depict only a "snapshot" of the thrifts' condition, it is possible that the rapidly growing nonproblem thrifts did become problems later. I have not seen data concerning the eventual condition of these thrifts.

13. "Brokered Deposits: Limitations Applicable to Institutions with Low Net Worth," Federal Home Loan Bank Board interim final rule, *Federal Register*, April 2, 1984, 13012-4; clarified in *Federal Register*, April 30, 1984, 18282-3. The rule was reissued in final form in "Brokered Deposits: Limitations Applicable to Institutions with Low Net Worth," Federal Home Loan Bank Board final rule, *Federal Register*, February 7, 1985, 5232-4.

14. U.S. House of Representatives, Committee on Government Operations, *Federal Regulation of Brokered Deposits: A Follow-Up Report*, 99th Cong., 2nd sess. (Washington, D.C.: Government Printing Office, 1986), 13.

15. Ibid., 18.

16. Thrifts with less net worth than required could have growth equal to the interest credited to depositors' accounts—in other words, they could not have net new deposits. Thrifts were in general required to have at least 3 percent net worth according to regulatory accounting principles.

17. *Savings Institutions*, December 1984.

18. Statement by Edwin Gray in U.S. House of Representatives, *Federal Regulation of Direct Investments by Savings and Loans and Banks; and Condition of the Federal Deposit Insurance Funds*, 14.

19. The rule was first proposed in May 1984, issued in final form in January 1985, and implemented in March 1985.

20. U.S. House of Representatives, *Federal Regulation of Direct Investments By Savings and Loan Associations*, 5–8.

21. U.S. House of Representatives, *Federal Regulation of Direct Investments by Savings and Loans and Banks*.

22. As it turns out, there was not even a consensus concerning direct investments within the Bank Board. Although Chairman Gray proposed the regulations, his chief economist James Barth opposed them. Mayer, *The Greatest-Ever Bank Robbery*, 139.

23. Mayer, quoting Robert Sahadi, in *The Greatest-Ever Bank Robbery*, 139.

24. Federal Home Loan Bank Board, "Regulation of Direct Investments by Insured Institutions," proposed rule, *Federal Register*, 12 CFR Part 563, January 31, 1985. See also Daniel Quinn et al., "Possible Regulations of the FHLBB to Limit Direct Investment of State Chartered, Federally Insured Savings Associations," SRI International, December 1984; John Crockett, Clifford Fry, and Paul Horvitz, "Equity Participation in Real Estate by Savings and Loans: Implications for Profitability and Risk" (n.d.); both in U.S. House of Representatives, *Federal Regulation of Direct Investments*.

25. Benston, "Direct Investments by Savings and Loan Associations: Return and Risk," in U.S. House of Representatives, *Federal Regulation of Direct Investments*, 505–72, quotation on 544; Benston, "A Review and Critique of the FHLBB's Economic Support for Rules Restricting Direct Investment and Growth," in U.S. House of Representatives, *Federal Regulation of Direct Investments*, 584–713.

26. U.S. House of Representatives, *Federal Regulation of Direct Investments*, 834–35.

27. Ibid., 859–65.

28. U.S. House of Representatives, Committee on Banking, Finance, and Urban Affairs, Subcommittee on Financial Institutions Supervision, Regulation and Insurance, *The Federal Home Loan Bank Board's Proposed Direct Investment Regulation*, Hearing, 99th Cong., 1st sess. (Washington, D.C.: Government Printing Office, 1985).

29. Ibid., 2.

30. Statement by Edwin Gray, U.S. House of Representatives, *The Federal Home Loan Bank Board's Proposed Direct Investment Regulation*.

31. U.S. House of Representatives, Committee on Government Operations, *Federal Regulation of Direct Investments by Savings and Loan Associations*, report, 99th Cong., 1st sess. (Washington, D.C.: Government Printing Office, 1985).

32. Ibid., 32.

33. Ibid., 32, 22.

34. Ibid., 13.

35. Ibid., 14.

36. Furthermore, there was no compelling data showing that FSLIC must ever run large deficits. This distinguishes FSLIC from, say, Social Security. Social Security also never ran deficits during its first several decades, but there was ironclad actuarial evidence that it would, given its existing benefit levels and changing demographics. When there is solid evidence of impending deficits for particular programs, Congress can act to fix the problem. See Paul Light, *Artful Work: The Politics of Social Security Reform* (New York: Random House, 1985).

37. Woerheide, *The Savings and Loan Industry*, 171–72.

38. Kane, *The S&L Insurance Mess*, 9.

39. Pizzo, Fricker, and Muolo, *Inside Job*, 285. The same theme, with different quotations, appears in Mayer, *The Greatest-Ever Bank Robbery*, 158–59; and Pilzer, *Other People's Money*, 199.

40. Federal Home Loan Bank Board, *1987 Annual Report* (Washington, D.C.: FHLBB, 1984), 30. The Bank Board had authority under the National Housing Act to levy a "special assessment" of up to an additional 1/8 of 1 percent of deposits per year.

41. For an S&L with $100 million in insured deposits, the special assessment cost it an additional $125,000 per year.

42. See Brumbaugh, *Thrifts Under Siege*, 108–10. At the time, a thrift could convert charters by paying FSLIC an exit fee worth two years of premiums.

43. Of course, no insurance premium can perfectly resolve issues involving equity. Flat rate premiums make all firms pay equal amounts but do not force these firms to make equal contributions for the risks they create. Variable rate premiums may make all firms pay equally according to the risks they create but do not charge them all equal amounts. For an insightful discussion of the various meanings of equity, see Douglas Rae, *Equalities* (New Haven: Yale University Press, 1982).

44. Thrift premiums were then scheduled to decline to 18 cents per $100 in 1994 and 15 cents in 1998. Insurance premiums were also raised for banks from 8.33 cents to 15.0 cents per $100 dollars of deposits.

45. The FHLBs are required to contribute slightly more than $2 billion of their net worth in 1989 and 1990, and to contribute $300 million of their profits annually. White, *The S&L Debacle*, 178.

46. Pilzer and Deitz, *Other People's Money*, 198.

47. Mayer, *The Greatest-Ever Bank Robbery*, 232.

48. Waldman, *Who Robbed America?* 67.

49. Adams, *The Big Fix*, 47.

50. Pilzer, *Other People's Money*, 199.

51. Adams, *The Big Fix*, 47.

52. Waldman, *Who Robbed America?*, 71.

53. Appendix 3 contains a brief political chronology of FSLIC's recap.

54. Steve Blakely, "Fight Brews Over Bailing Out Ailing Savings Insurance Fund," *Congressional Quarterly Weekly Report*, January 24, 1987, 152.

55. White, *The S&L Debacle*, 138.

56. Steve Blakely, "Panel Approves S&L Bailout That Meets CBO Objections," *Congressional Quarterly Weekly Report*, July 19, 1986, 1612.

57. Steve Blakely, "Panel Votes Bare-Bones Bill to Aid FSLIC, Troubled Banks," *Congressional Quarterly Weekly Report*, August 16, 1986, 1893.

58. A loophole in federal law allowed non-bank banks (those that accepted deposits or made commercial loans, but not both) to avoid federal banking regulations.

59. Steve Blakely, "Prospects Dim for Legislation to Aid Ailing Thrift Industry," *Congressional Quarterly Weekly Report*, March 8, 1986, 553.

60. Blakely, "Panel Votes Bare-Bones Bill," 1893.

61. Steve Blakely, "Congress' Inaction on Banks Complicates Regulators' Job," *Congressional Quarterly Weekly Report*, October 25, 1986, 2684.

62. Two Senators, Phil Gramm (R-Tex.) and William Armstrong (R-Colo.) then also threatened to filibuster if the Senate bill included either of these consumer or housing provisions.

63. Quoted in Blakely, "Congress Inaction," 2684.

64. U.S. House of Representatives, Committee on Standards of Official Conduct, *Report of the Special Outside Counsel in the Matter of Speaker James C. Wright, Jr.*, 100th Cong., February 21, 1989. This source is called the "Phelan report" after the special outside counsel who conducted the investigation.

65. White, *The S&L Debacle*, 138–39.

66. Proxmire's proposal would have banned all non-bank banks created after July 1, 1983—which means that huge firms such as Sears and Merrill Lynch would have had to give up their limited-service banks.

67. Steve Blakely, "Proxmire Offers Comprehensive Banking Bill," *Congressional Quarterly Weekly Report*, February 21, 1987, 331.

68. Steve Blakely, "Senate Rejects the House Plan to Rescue S&L Insurance Fund," *Congressional Quarterly Weekly Report*, May 16, 1987, 1002.

69. U.S. House of Representatives, Committee on Banking, Finance, and Urban Affairs, *Federal Savings and Loan Insurance Corporation Recapitalization Act of 1987*, Committee Report Together with Additional and Dissenting Views, 100th Cong., 1st sess., Report 100-62, April 22, 1987, 28.

70. U.S. House of Representatives, Committee on Banking, Finance, and Urban Affairs, *Federal Savings and Loan Insurance Corporation Recapitalization Act*, Hearings, 100th Cong., 1st sess., (Washington, D.C.: Government Printing Office, 1987), 430. Barnard continued—undoubtedly to his later regret—that "in Texas, people are especially concerned over situations like Vernon Savings & Loan and Independent American Savings and Loan." These two S&Ls turned out to be among the industry's most spectacular failures. Vernon's failure cost FSLIC approximately $1.3 billion; it has been widely reported that an incredible 96 percent of Vernon's loans were delinquent. FSLIC filed a $540 million civil suit against the owners and directors of Vernon, and CEO Woody F. Lemons was eventually sentenced to thirty years in prison for bank fraud. In Barnard's defense, at the time he made these comments Vernon boasted a clean statement from the Arthur Young accounting firm, supported by Sandra Johnigan, who supervised the Arthur Young Dallas office and chaired the S&L committee of the American Institute of Certified Public Accountants. Mayer, *The Greatest-Ever Bank Robbery*, 241.

71. "State Ponders Suit Over Federal Thrift Regulations," United Press International, January 28, 1987.

72. In particular, Tom Gaubert, who was closely affiliated with Independent American, was the finance chairman of the Democratic Congressional Campaign Committee.

73. U.S. House of Representatives, *Federal Savings and Loan Insurance Corporation Recapitalization Act of 1987*, Report, 28.

74. Blakely, "Fight Brews," 152.

75. U.S. League of Savings Institutions, Report of the Task Force on FSLIC Issues, in U.S. House of Representatives, *Federal Savings and Loan Insurance Corporation Recapitalization Act*, 168.

76. RAP-insolvent thrifts are those that had negative net worth according to the "regulatory accounting principles" used at the time by the FSLIC. There were 351 RAP-insolvent thrifts with $99.1 billion in assets nationwide; 109 of them had $39.2 billion in assets in Texas. White, *The S&L Debacle*, 151.

77. In March 1988, there were 148 solvent and 130 insolvent Texas thrifts. Short and Gunther, "The Thrift Situation," 2.

78. The South consists of Alabama, Arkansas, Florida, Georgia, Louisiana, Mississippi, Oklahoma, Tennessee, and Texas. Arkansas, Louisiana, Oklahoma, and Texas constitute the Southwest. Data from Frank Russell Company and the U.S. Department of Energy, as cited by White, *The S&L Debacle*, 111.

79. See in particular Congressional Budget Office, "The Cost of Forbearance."

80. Federal regulators, however, have not once and for all rejected forbearance for failing banks and thrifts, and at least one former critic of this approach continues to have an open mind. Robert Litan, a Brookings Institution economist who has long favored quick shutdowns of troubled banks, said that "three years ago, people would have said [forbearance for banks] is totally crazy, but now people have become aware there are significant costs to just shutting them down." Jerry Knight and Sue Schmidt, "Bank Regulators Consider Radical Shift on Cleanup," *Washington Post*, June 11, 1991.

81. U.S. General Accounting Office, *Thrift Industry: Cost to FSLIC of Delaying Action on Insolvent Institutions*, September 1986.

82. GAO apparently anticipated that 100 of the 467 thrifts would regain solvency during that period. Ibid., 3.

83. Ibid., 13. Furthermore, FSLIC obviously incurred no liquidation costs for the 52 thrifts that regained solvency between 1982 and 1985.

84. One key assumption is that the thrifts had no asset changes between 1985 and 1987, so that they could not increase the riskiness of their portfolios.

85. Of course, there are various opinions concerning future asset values. But almost everyone believed that most assets declined sharply in value once FSLIC owned them, because the government is not seen as a good landlord. The policy implications of this were unfortunately not clear. Some concluded that FSLIC should do everything possible to keep thrifts operating and in private hands, whether through forbearance, mergers, or some other form of assistance. Others concluded FSLIC should quickly liquidate all properties. The ultimate costs of each method were highly uncertain.

86. Complaints were attributed, at least in part, to the massive hiring of new examiners and their inadequate training after the Bank Board transferred its examination force to the district banks. The number of examiners grew from about thirteen hundred to about thirty-three hundred between 1984 and 1987. These transfers are described in more detail in chapter 4. Phelan report, 209–12.

87. The forbearance clauses were apparently added to the bill primarily at the insistence of Texas lawmakers. Steve Blakely, "House Sides with S&L Lobby on Rescue of Insurance Fund," *Congressional Quarterly Weekly Report*, May 9, 1987, 925.

88. See the analysis of this vote in appendix 4.

89. Doug Barnard (D-Ga.) and Marcy Kaptur (D-Ohio) also switched their votes. Steve Blakely, "Panel Approves $5 Billion FSLIC Rescue Plan," *Congressional Quarterly Weekly Report*, April 4, 1987, 636.

90. Particularly by Waldman, *Who Robbed America?* 68–69.

91. U.S. House of Representatives, *Savings and Loan Corporation Recapitalization Act of 1987*, Report.

92. Ibid., 25, 26.

93. Ibid., 102, 104, 105.

94. Blakely, "House Sides," 924. The day before the vote, the FSLIC had filed a $540 million suit against the owners of Vernon S&L, one of the most notorious Texas thrifts. Wright had personally intervened before the Bank Board on Vernon's behalf. Pizzo, Fricker, and Muolo, *Inside Job*, 222–26.

95. Supporters of the $5 billion proposal included House Majority Whip Tony Coelho (D-Calif.), Minority Whip Trent Lott (R-Miss.), Democratic Congressional Campaign Committee Chairman Beryl Anthony (D-Ark.), and National Republican Congressional Committee Chairman Guy Vander Jagt (R-Mich.).

96. Blakely, "Senate Rejects," 1002.

97. Those who question the wisdom of one conference committee raising FSLIC's insurance coverage (see the previous chapter) might think differently about another conference committee's decision to raise FSLIC's borrowing authority.

98. Although, in Mayer's view, "the decision to deregulate by cooperation of the five separate bank, thrift, and credit-union regulatory agencies produced an incredible mass of new regulations expressing the need to compromise the views of separate bureaucratic empires." Mayer, *The Greatest-Ever Bank Robbery*, 94.

99. I have not discussed junk bonds because they raised similar issues but were much less important than direct investments for the thrift tragedy. For example, just two S&Ls held about half of the merely $15 billion in junk bonds held by the entire thrift business. For a discussion, see Lowy, *High Rollers*, 155–59.

100. The delays should not be compared to some hypothetical, instantaneous, and thus fantastical enactment. FSLIC's refinancing might be more usefully compared to any actual legislature's handling of any other complex and controversial issue.

101. See Mathew D. McCubbins and Thomas Schwartz, "Congressional Oversight Overlooked: Police Patrols versus Fire Alarms," in McCubbins and Sullivan, *Congress: Structure and Policy*, 426–40.

102. The NCFIRRE drew the opposite conclusion regarding congressional oversight. The commission notes that "academic witnesses raised warning signals time and time again . . . warn[ing] that unless action was taken to correct the situation, major taxpayer expense was inevitable. These voice were drowned out by the louder and more potent ones of industry lobbyists and even regulators who insisted that while there may be problems, matters were under control." These conclusions ignore the issues (such as direct investments) when the regulators were right and the academics wrong. On the whole, it is not clear that academics gave better advice to Congress than did the Bank Board. NCFIRRE, *Origins and Causes*, 73–74.

103. For the importance of complexity and salience, see William T. Gormley, Jr., "Regulatory Issue Networks in a Federal System," *Polity* 18, 4 (Summer 1986): 595–620.

Chapter 8. Congressional Voting

1. Public choice scholars did not, of course, originate the idea that politicians can be bought, or even that they are primarily motivated by electoral concerns. The most prominent statement of the electoral motivations of members of Congress is in David Mayhew, *Congress: The Electoral Connection* (New Haven: Yale University Press, 1974). A statement of particular relevance to the thrift tragedy is in Romer and Weingast, "Political Foundations."

2. See especially Waldman, *Who Robbed America?*; Mentzinger, Howell, and O'Day, *It's a Wonderful Life*; Jackson, *Honest Graft*, esp. chap. 14; Kane, *The S&L Insurance Mess*, 51–52.

3. Waldman, *Who Robbed America?*, 60.

4. Mentzinger, Howell, and O'Day, *It's a Wonderful Life*. This estimate is conservative because it counts only donors identifying themselves as connected with an S&L on Federal Election Commission disclosure forms.

5. As quoted by Pizzo, Fricker, and Muolo, *Inside Job*, 295.

6. Of course, one might argue that it is politically most advantageous simply to choose a position and stick with it despite fluctuations in public support for it. Such a decision comes close to becoming what is known as a policy commitment.

7. Democratic theorists have long debated whether, and under what conditions, elected officials should substitute their judgment for the will of their constituents. For a brief discussion, see Maass, *Congress and the Common Good*, 73–74.

8. As long as the money is handled legally. Accepting illegal contributions—bribes—cannot be justified from the public spirit perspective.

9. For an example of a study that focuses on key votes, see John R. Wright, "PACs, Contributions, and Roll Calls," *American Political Science Review* 79, 2 (June 1985): 400–14. For the use of voting indices, see Janet M. Grenzke, "Shopping the Congressional Supermarket: The Currency Is Complex," *American Journal of Political Science* 33 (1980): 1–24.

10. Partisan factors, for example, are often especially important on key votes, where they may dominate all other effects.

11. Welch, for example, finds that campaign contributions from the dairy industry influenced one close vote on dairy price supports. Since Welch does not test the model on another close vote on these supports which immediately preceded the final vote, the reader is left to wonder if the results are similar. W. P. Welch, "Campaign Contributions and Legislative Voting: Milk Money and Dairy Price Supports," *Western Political Quarterly* 35, 4 (December 1982): 478–95.

12. In Grenzke's study of twenty-nine voting indices, for example, the *only* factor apparently influencing voting was a combination of a legislator's party and ideology.

13. Of course some matters, like the confirmation of presidential appointees or ratification of treaties, are handled by the Senate alone.

14. Welch, "Campaign Contributions and Legislative Voting"; Wright, "PACs, Contributions, and Roll Calls"; Grenzke, "PACs and the Congressional Supermarket." Welch also uses the size of the dairy industry (as measured by gross sales) in the congressional district as an indicator of dairy influence on congressional voting.

15. Romer and Weingast, "Political Foundations."

16. This issue is discussed in greater depth in appendix 4 and chapter 7.

17. The authors identify six variables that are likely to influence voting: the member's party, ideology, membership on the Banking Committee, campaign contributions from the thrift industry, the number of "weak" thrifts in the district, and the number of "strong" thrifts in the district.

18. Their results are puzzling or problematic for several reasons. Campaign contributions have no identifiable impact; this may be due to the fact that the authors lump together funds received from the U.S. League of Savings Institutions and the National Council of Savings Institutions, even though the USL opposed the amendment and the NCSI favored it. Representatives with more healthy thrifts in their district were also more likely to oppose the amendment, even though these thrifts were less affected by it; representatives with more weak thrifts in their district tended to support the amendment, even though these thrifts were most threatened by it. The clearest structural variable, committee membership, is statistically significant but perplexing. Romer and Weingast argue that committees rarely bring bills to the floor unless they have the votes for passage, and that committee members will follow their chairman there. Within the committee, St. Germain had actually favored the $5 billion limit, but was able to find only a one-vote majority (25–24) to back him. St. Germain had completely reversed his official position by proposing the floor amendment, but the amendment lost. Romer and Weingast, "Political Foundations," 197–200.

19. I excluded from the analysis laws affecting the financial condition of the S&L industry but not as their main intent, because of the difficulty in linking thrift interests to congressional votes. The Deficit Reduction Act of 1984 and the Tax Reform Act of 1986 fall into this category. I also excluded legislation primarily affecting depository institutions, but not their financial condition. The Bank Bribery Amendments Act and the Money Laundering Act, both of 1986, fall into this category.

20. The data for the Senate include four roll calls for DIDMCA and CEBA, three for FIRREA, and one for Garn–St. Germain. The House data include one roll call for DIDMCA, two for Garn–St. Germain, one for CEBA, and six for FIRREA. Brief descriptions of each roll call are provided in appendix 4.

21. The vote with the least amount of variation included in the study had 91 percent of the votes cast on one side.

22. Both quotations are from Bruce C. Wolpe, *Lobbying Congress: How the System Works* (Washington, D.C.: Congressional Quarterly, 1990), 86.

23. For an example of research that shows little impact, see Grenzke, "Shopping the Congressional Supermarket," 1–24; Wright, "PACs, Contributions, and Roll Calls," 400–14. For the minority view, see James B. Kau and Paul H. Rubin, *Congressmen, Constituents, and Contributors: Determinants of Roll Call Voting in the House of Representatives* (Boston: Martinus Nijhoff, 1982).

24. As satirist Dave Barry summarizes the situation, politicians "did NOT sell out the public trust. . . . We know this because they said so, and they are supported by the following complete transcript. Charles Keating: Here's $1 million. Senators: What for? Keating: No reason! I'm handing out large sums of money at random! I must be a complete moron! Senators: Oh, okay." Dave Barry, "Oops! There Goes Another Zillion Bucks," *Washington Post Magazine*, June 10, 1990, 60.

25. See for example Grenzke, "PACs and the Congressional Supermarket"; Welch, "Campaign Contributions and Legislative Voting"; Wright, "PACs, Contributions, and Roll Calls." Grenzke does hypothesize that campaign contributions could influence voting outcomes during the next two legislative sessions.

26. Data were readily available only for those members of Congress still in office in 1990.

27. For example, would a legislator who received $20,000 from the thrift industry over the decade (or $4,000 per election) be more or less likely to vote the contributors' preferences than a one-term legislator who received $5,000 in contributions (or $5,000 per election)? Legislators with the highest total contributions would also have the highest average contributions if they served during the entire period.

28. To investigate the possibility that those in Congress in 1990 differed systematically from those who had served earlier, I estimated the coefficients for each roll call in 1979, 1982, and 1987 twice, once with the contributions variable included and once with it omitted. If the coefficients from both estimations were similar in direction, size, and significance, I used the results from the estimation that included campaign contributions, even though doing so reduced the number of cases. All House votes in 1979, 1982, and 1987 fell into this pattern. Difference of means t-tests comparing the group for which I had campaign finance data to the group for which such data were missing also supported these results. In general, these two categories did not differ regarding the mean value of the other variables. If the results were dissimilar, as they were for the Senate in 1979, I used the coefficients from the estimation which excluded campaign contributions. Results of both estimations for the House and Senate are presented in appendix 4.

29. One obvious solution—disaggregating contributions into different categories according to the characteristics of the contributors—is not very practical. Multiple, overlapping contributor categories (such as small, rapidly growing, and profitable thrifts) could be easily defined but linked to campaign contributions only with great difficulty.

30. They were also politically "conservative" in their attempts to use the political system to maintain the status quo. This status quo was "liberal" in that it involved heavy doses of government intervention into the markets.

31. The measure of variation used here is the standard deviation.

32. For example, failing thrifts often had to pay relatively high interest rates to attract deposits, driving the interest rates up for their competitors as well. If the failing thrifts were declared insolvent by the regulators, their competitors could enjoy lower interest rates. As a result, solvent thrifts benefited economically when their insolvent peers were shut down. See Genie D. Short and Jeffery W. Gunther, "The Texas Thrift Situation: Implications for the Texas Financial Industry," Federal Reserve Bank of Dallas, September 1988. The differences in political goals among differing portions of the thrift industry—and in particular between the National Council of Savings Institutions and the U.S. League of Savings Institutions—on specific issues were noted in the previous chapter.

33. See appendix 4 for a more detailed discussion of these indicators.

34. Estimations that include separate indicators of a representative's ideology and political party often face the statistical problem of multicollinearity. To address this problem, Grenzke used an interactive term combining ideology and partisanship in her study. I created and used such a term in some preliminary analyses, but it did not appear to improve the estimations obtained using partisan affiliation alone. For further details, see appendix 4 and Grenzke, "PACs and the Congressional Supermarket."

35. Conservatives might typically be more "probusiness" than liberals, but support for the thrifts could entail restrictions on other businesses, greater government involvement in commerce, or more deficit spending, for example, all actions conservatives usually oppose. Liberals might in general be less probusiness than conservatives, but might be more eager to assist thrifts, since they do such things as promote housing and provide employment.

36. A list of the states in each category and a discussion of alternative regional groupings is included in appendix 4.

37. Estimates were obtained through logistic regression. This technique determines whether legislators were more likely to have voted for (or against) the proposal based upon their partisanship, region, and thrift constituency.

38. The two roll calls in which thrift-related factors had no apparent impact on votes involved the treatment of goodwill and civil penalties for criminal activities in thrifts.

39. This statement should be qualified by the reminder that thrift industry campaign contributions were excluded from the estimated votes in the Senate in 1979.

40. Interestingly, the two votes in the House in which party and regional factors seem to have played no role were the votes for final passage of legislation.

41. These votes included vote 2 in 1982 and votes 4 and 7 in 1989. See appendix 4.

42. See tables A4.1 and A4.3.

43. In the Banking Committee, Republicans opposed an amendment to reduce FSLIC's recapitalization from $15 to $5 billion by a vote of 17 to 3; Democrats supported this amendment 27-7.

44. On vote 1 in 1979 and votes 2 and 4 in 1987. See appendix 4.

45. The terms larger and smaller, and greater and fewer, refer to levels one standard deviation above and below the mean values for each variable. For example, a legislator who received a large amount in campaign contributions from the thrift business (that is, an amount that put the legislator one standard deviation above the mean) would be on average 8 percent more likely to vote for (or against) a bill than a legislator who received a small amount in campaign contributions (that is, an amount one standard deviation below the mean).

46. In other words, it is as likely that each factor will have an effect equaling its mean plus or minus one standard deviation.

Chapter 9. Concluding Words

1. In present-value dollars. Congressional Budget Office, *Resolving the Thrift Crisis,* April 1993, ix.

2. Office of Management and Budget, *Historical Tables,* 39–46.

3. For example, in 1988 the "tax expenditures" on this provision were $19.9 billion. Joseph A. Pechman, *Federal Tax Policy,* 5th ed. (Washington, D.C.: Brookings, 1988), 359. The large federal spending on the mortgage interest deduction is especially noteworthy given that the long-term, fixed-rate home mortgage loans made by S&Ls during the 1970s and 1980s were a leading financial cause of the thrift tragedy. In essence, the federal government subsidized these mortgages twice: once through the mortgage deduction, once through deposit insurance payments.

4. These tax losses cost the federal government an estimated $130 billion in 1992. General Accounting Office report cited in *Newsday,* May 19, 1994.

5. Office of Management and Budget, *Historical Tables,* 39–46.

6. For that matter, various observers have also argued that the federal government spends far too much on defense, income security, and health care.

7. White and Wildavsky, *The Deficit and the Public Interest.*

8. Although there is an insurance cap of $100,000 per account, multiple accounts can be established to insure additional funds. Millionaires who truly wanted to receive federal deposit insurance for all their deposits could probably obtain it.

9. This point is accentuated because accounts at failed thrifts also tended to be larger on average than those in solvent S&Ls.

10. It can sometimes be difficult to see who receives the benefits of a deposit insurance payment. Consider the following example. An individual makes an insured deposit of $100 at a thrift. The thrift lends this $100 to a developer and receives fees for doing so. The developer spends the $100 to build a shopping center; in doing so, he must purchase land and pay architects, lawyers, contractors, and laborers—and the developer himself receives money. The shopping center goes bust, the developer defaults on the loan, the thrift takes possession of the shopping center, and the thrift goes bankrupt. FSLIC arranges for a second thrift to take over the failed thrift and its assets. Because the failed

thrift has a $100 liability (the deposit) but only, say, a $50 asset (the shopping center) FSLIC must give the new thrift $50 to bring the value of its assets up to the level of its liabilities. Who exactly is FSLIC paying?

11. Benjamin I. Page, *Who Gets What From Government* (Berkeley: University of California Press, 1983), 132. Page cites Charles L. Schultze, *The Distribution of Farm Subsidies: Who Gets the Benefits* (Washington, D.C.: Brookings, 1971). Although Schultze's book is now two decades old, little has changed regarding farm subsidies. For an update, see Clifton B. Luttrell, *The High Cost of Farm Welfare* (Washington, D.C.: Cato Institute, 1989).

12. Page, *Who Gets What*, 80. Page cites Henry J. Aaron, *Shelter and Subsidies: Who Benefits from Federal Housing Policies* (Washington, D.C.: Brookings, 1972). There is no reason to believe that the distribution of housing subsidies has become more equitable since then.

13. The distributional effects depend on "how the borrowed money is spent (i.e., the distributional impact of the whole federal budget) and upon the incidence of taxes that borrowing replaces" as well as the effect of government borrowing on inflation and real interest rates. Page, *Who Gets What*, 134.

14. Congressional Budget Office, *The Economic Effects*.

15. According to the model CBO used, GNP was depressed by as much as 0.7 percent (in 1990) from its expected value due to thrift industry losses. CBO acknowledges that its estimates are illustrative rather than definitive, and that "losses in GNP could be much smaller or larger than these figures indicate." Congressional Budget Office, *The Economic Effects*, xi, 36.

16. Ibid., 26.

17. Indeed, the typical conservative critique is that government spending in general diverts funds away from more productive uses. Critics on the left have suggested that the private sector may also be judged to have channelled investment into inefficient and sometimes worthless projects.

18. Luttrell, *The High Cost of Farm Welfare*, 123–24.

19. Barry P. Bosworth, Andrew S. Carron, and Elisabeth H. Rhyne, *The Economics of Federal Credit Programs* (Washington, D.C.: Brookings, 1987), 75, citing Office of Management and Budget, *Special Analyses, Budget of the United States, Fiscal Year 1984*, F-1.

20. The chief victims were those not actually covered by deposit insurance, such as the primarily elderly individuals who, thinking they were insured, bought $200 million in bonds from Keating's S&L shortly before it collapsed.

21. Just as most analysts have focused on the financial causes of the thrift tragedy, most proposals have emphasized financial reforms. See, for example, NCFIRRE; Lowy, *High Rollers*; White, *The S&L Debacle*; and Kane, *The S&L Insurance Mess*.

22. There is a paradox here. If self-interest is all-important, then how can public choice scholars identify the public good that is to be the goal of the reform?

23. Elections do sometimes so degenerate.

24. The answer, of course, is that we can't. The response to this is that individual voters must provide the impetus for reform. Alas, it is almost never in

the self-interest of individual voters to promote such reforms, since the real and immediate cost of self-involvement is typically greater than the potential future benefits.

25. Why proponents of public choice would even advocate political reform is somewhat of a mystery. Presumably, the purpose of reform is to enhance the general good. This implies that the reformers grant themselves a vision of the public interest (unless they want change only to benefit themselves?) while denying that politicians have such beliefs.

26. For sensible proposals for congressional reform not arising from the thrift tragedy, see Thomas E. Mann and Norman J. Ornstein, *Renewing Congress: A First Report* (Washington, D.C.: American Enterprise Institute for Public Policy Research and Brookings, 1992); Mann and Ornstein, *Renewing Congress: A Second Report* (Washington, D.C.: American Enterprise Institute for Public Policy Research and Brookings, 1993).

27. Especially Waldman, *Who Robbed America?*

28. Campaign finance reform can have benefits other than improved policy making. See David B. Magleby and Candice Johnson, *The Money Chase: Congressional Campaign Finance Reform*, (Washington, D.C.: Brookings, 1990).

29. Kane, *The S&L Insurance Mess*, 162.

30. Ibid.

31. Ibid.

32. The idea that all the government's implicit obligations should be included in the budget raises other interesting issues. For example, should the government report the implicit increase in its likely Medicaid expenditures if pre- and neonatal care for poor women is not fully funded?

33. House Banking Committee Chairman Fernand St. Germain, the legislator perhaps most cozy with the thrift industry, was not reelected in an election where his personal corruption weighed heavily against him. A handful of other politicians linked to thrift industry scandals (Jim Wright, Tony Coelho, and Alan Cranston, for example) have either resigned from office or retired before again facing the electorate. In none of these cases was the thrift industry the legislator's only political or personal problem, however.

34. See especially Barth, *The Great S&L Debacle*, chap. 4; and White, *The S&L Debacle*, chap. 9, for descriptions of FIRREA. Besides altering the bureaucratic aspects of the FHLBS, FIRREA also changed policies toward thrift asset and liability powers.

35. The treasury department also contained the Office of the Comptroller of the Currency, which was responsible for chartering and regulating national banks.

36. The FDIC administers the Savings Association Insurance Fund (SAIF), the Bank Insurance Fund (BIF), and the Resolution Trust Corporation (RTC), which is responsible for disposing of the S&Ls taken over by the government after January 1, 1989. The FDIC maintains separate accounts for the S&L and bank insurance funds.

37. The FHFB has five members: the Secretary of Housing and Urban Development and four other appointed members.

38. See chapter 3 for a discussion of this issue.

39. Barth, *The Great S&L Debacle*, 80; White, *The S&L Debacle*, 182.

40. In previous chapters I indeed argued that the structural aspects of the FHLBS were not a main cause of FSCIC's losses.

41. The one exception was Ed Gray, who had never held an administrative position in government until appointed to the board. In contrast, all but one Federal Reserve Board chairman since its inception have served two full four-year terms. See chapter 3.

42. But see Moe's argument about interest group attention to administrative structure in Terry M. Moe, "The Politics of Bureaucratic Structure," in *Can the Government Govern?*, ed. John Chubb and Paul E. Peterson (Washington, D.C.: Brookings Institution, 1989), 267–329.

43. As far as I know, only one other author has suggested a similar reform. As Lowy puts it, "We can't afford weak, political appointments to bank regulatory positions. Technocrats do the job best." Lowy notes that his view is biased because he is a self-proclaimed technocrat "with 25 years experience in thrift institution law, management, and regulation." Because I am an academic, my support for regulatory expertise is, clearly, not self-interested. Yet because I believe that we should treat skeptically the regulatory recommendations of inexperienced academics, perhaps my support for this proposal should be discounted (Lowy, *High Rollers*, 282, and book jacket).

44. For example, Kane, *The S&L Insurance Mess*; Benston and Kaufman, "Understanding the Savings-and-Loan Debacle."

Appendix 1. The Thrift Business

1. In practice other assets might include cash, other securities (e.g., bonds), ownership interests in subsidiaries or other enterprises, and direct ownership of real estate.

2. Again, a real thrift's liabilities might also include bonds or other forms of debt.

Appendix 2. Thrift Failure Case Studies

1. This section is based primarily on U.S. Congress, House of Representatives, Committee on Banking, Finance and Urban Affairs, "Hearing on CenTrust Savings and Loan Association," 101st Cong., 2nd sess., March 26, 1990. See also Myra MacPherson, "The Banker's Toppled Tower: In Miami, the Spectacular Fall of David Paul and His CenTrust S&L," *Washington Post*, March 19, 1990; Lowy, *High Rollers*, 152–54.

2. Testimony of Ash Williams Jr., assistant comptroller, State of Florida, and Lawrence Fuchs, deputy comptroller, State of Florida, *CenTrust Hearings*, 2.

3. David Dahl, "Gifts to State's Universities are Falling Short of Pledges," *St. Petersburg Times*, September 23, 1991, 1; Dahl, "Florida Lawmakers Com-

plained in '87 on Behalf of Thrifts," *St. Petersburg Times*, March 29, 1990, 8; Dahl, "CenTrust Chief was Big Giver Politically," *St. Petersburg Times*, February 10, 1990, 1.

4. "Supervisory History of Centrust Bank, A State Savings Bank," in *CenTrust Hearings*.

5. Testimony of Williams and Fuchs, *CenTrust Hearings*, 4.

6. Full examinations began on June 26, 1984; July 11, 1986; January 11, 1988; and May 31, 1989. Special limited examinations commenced on July 26, 1985; August 2, 1985; and September 27, 1985. "Supervisory History of CenTrust Bank," *CenTrust Hearings*.

7. Statement by Ryan and Richmond, *CenTrust Hearings*.

8. Ibid., 10.

9. Ibid., 5.

10. Deloitte Haskins & Sells, in the latest public record of its audits of CenTrust, found that the thrift's financial statements, including reported net income and equity, were in accordance with GAAP during 1987 and 1988. *Moody's Bank and Finance Manual*, 1990 edition, 1:79.

11. Statement by Ryan and Richmond, *CenTrust Hearings*, 11. In giving unqualified approval of Centrust's financial statements, the outside auditors also did not discover a series of asset "flips" between CenTrust and Lincoln Savings, with the two thrifts selling assets back and forth and each registering profits on the transactions. Regulators happened to detect these transactions because they were auditing Lincoln Savings at the same time. Both thrifts were making these transactions through Drexel, with neither thrift recording the ultimate purchaser on its own books. Deloitte Haskins & Sells finally resigned its account with CenTrust in 1988 after disputes with the thrift, and Price Waterhouse performed the 1989 audit. Neither firm required CenTrust to recognize the losses from its securities trading, though Price Waterhouse did include a statement of these losses in its year-end 1989 audit, after CenTrust's deterioration was already widely recognized.

12. Paul fought the law all the way. Before he was convicted of embezzlement, he was already serving an eighteen-month sentence for contempt of court because he refused to produce subpoenaed documents. He had also sued the RTC, claiming it owed him millions of dollars for letting the value of his home deteriorate after the regulators seized it. See "David Paul May Get 22 Years," *Problem Asset Reporter*, April 18, 1994, 12; "Ex-CenTrust Chairman Pleads Guilty to Fraud," *Problem Asset Reporter*, February 21, 1994, 15.

13. This section is based largely on FDIC v. Ernst & Young and Arthur Young and Company, U.S. District Court, Northern District of Texas, March 1, 1990.

14. Bruce Ingersoll, "Bank Board Seizes Western Savings, Alleging Speculative Lending Practices," *Wall Street Journal*, September 15, 1986, 8.

15. Arthur Young and Company was purchased by the accounting firm of Ernst & Whinney in 1989.

16. FDIC v. Ernst & Young, 11.

17. Ingersoll, "Bank Board Seizes Western Savings."

18. FDIC v. Ernst & Young, 27.

19. *Wall Street Journal*, September 15, 1986, 8; and *Wall Street Journal*, September 24, 1986, 26. Woods's request for a temporary restraining order to prevent the regulators from liquidating Western was rejected. *Wall Street Journal*, October 2, 1986, 41.

20. FDIC *v. Ernst & Young*, 21.

21. Ibid., 24.

22. The FDIC's arguments about the auditors were rejected by a district court and this decision was upheld by Fifth Circuit Court. Judge Jerre Williams essentially argued that, since Woods and Western did not rely on Arthur Young's audits (because they knew the true financial condition of the thrift), the accountants could not be held responsible for Western's losses. "Lack of Reliance on Audit Precludes Negligence Claim on Failed S&L's Behalf," *BNA Banking Daily*, September 3, 1992.

23. Most of this information about Silverado comes from Wilmsen, *Silverado* and Lowy, *High Rollers*.

24. Lowy, *High Rollers*, 143.

25. Wilmsen, *Silverado*, 54, 152.

26. "As long as they could get an appraiser to say the land was worth what [Silverado] paid for it—not too difficult—nobody would object." Lowy, *High Rollers*, 142.

27. Pooling loans and selling securities backed by the loans were legitimate financial innovations that had become hugely popular during the 1980s.

28. Wilmsen argues that the regulators actually wanted to impose a cease and desist order on Silverado. A C&D order can be enforced in court, but it requires higher standards of proof. At the last minute, Kermit Mowbray, president of the Topeka FHLB, allegedly told the regulators to drop the C&D in favor the weaker supervisory agreement. Wilmsen, *Silverado*, 154.

29. Lowy, *High Rollers*, 143.

30. Wilmsen, *Silverado*, 168–71.

31. Wilmsen reports that, even when the regulators came in to take over the thrift, "some Silverado employees were near hysterical. Many had no idea the thrift was in trouble." Ibid., 185.

32. Publicity about Silverado has focused on Neil Bush, who made the foolish mistake of serving on Silverado's board of directors without having a clear understanding of the phrase "conflict of interest."

33. Hedging strategies attempt to protect an investor from price swings. For thrifts, these strategies were efforts to reduce the effect of rising or falling interest rates.

34. *Franklin Savings Assoc. v. Director*, Case No. 90-4054-S D. KS. Saffels, J., 5 September 1990.

35. The Supreme Court declined to hear the case. Dan Margolies, "Court Awards Franklin Savings $11.2 Million Tax Refund," *Kansas City Business Journal*, September 24, 1993, 5.

36. Franklin's assets declined from $11 billion to $3 billion after the RTC takeover.

37. The background for this section is provided by Lowy, *High Rollers,* 146–52; and Pizzo, Fricker, and Muolo, *Inside Job,* 293–96.

38. Greenspan's letter is reprinted in Mayer, *The Greatest-Ever Bank Robbery,* 324–26. The purpose of this letter was to ask that Lincoln be granted an exemption from a new FHLBS rule limiting thrift direct investments to 10 percent of their assets. Greenspan and many others had testified against this rule. U.S. House of Representatives, Committee on Government Operations, *Federal Regulation of Direct Investments by Savings and Loans and Banks; and the Condition of the Federal Deposit Insurance Funds,* Hearings, February 1985.

39. The three large accounting firms that worked for Lincoln were sued by the holders of Lincoln's bonds. All settled out of court, with Ernst & Young (successor to Arthur Young) paying $63 million, Arthur Anderson paying $30 million, and Deloitte & Touche (successor to Touche Ross) paying $7.5 million. While each firm denied any wrongdoing, a report by a federally appointed auditor, Kenneth Leventhal & Co., concluded that "seldom in our experience as accountants have we encountered a more egregious example of the misapplication of generally accepted accounting principles." "Lincoln Savings: An Amazing Tale," *Economist,* August 26, 1989, 66.

40. Matt Yancey, "Keating: Regulators Arbitrary. Former Head of S&L Contests U.S. Figures," *Washington Post,* April 12, 1990; see also Paul Duke, Jr., "Keating Estimates Lincoln S&L Had $500 Million Value," *Wall Street Journal,* April 11, 1990. Examples of disputed asset values include:

Appraised Value (in $millions)

Asset	Lincoln	Regulators
Interest in Phoenician Hotel, Ariz.	$170	$99
Uplands development, Tex.	$101	$30

41. *Lincoln Savings and Loan Assoc. v. M. Danny Wall,* Consolidated Civil Action Nos. 89-1318 and 89-1323, August 2, 1990.

42. "Lincoln Savings: Amazing Tale"; "Lincoln Savings and the Fifth Amendment: 'Nuff Said," *Economist,* November 25, 1989, 95; Pizzo, Fricker, and Muolo, *Inside Job,* 293–96.

43. Lowy, *High Rollers,* 148. No independent commentators have disputed this conclusion.

44. Paul was active in community groups and sat on boards of various hospitals and other organizations. From early in his career Wise was hailed as a civic leader and he moved up swiftly in business and political circles. Fleischer was a CPA with a magna cum laude J.D. degree from Harvard. Keating had served on President Nixon's Federal Commission on Obscenity and Pornography and had chaired John Connally's unsuccessful campaign for president.

Appendix 3: A Brief Political History of Refinancing FSLIC

1. This history is based on Mark Rom, "The Thrift Tragedy."

Appendix 4: Congressional Voting

1. The logistic regression program used was SPSS-PC+ version 3.1.

2. Grenzke, "PACs and the Congressional Supermarket," Henry Chappell, "Campaign Contributions and Congressional Voting: A Simultaneous Probit-Tobit Model," *Review of Economics and Statistics* 64 (1982):77–83; Allen Wilhite and John Theilmann, "Labor Contributions and Labor Legislation: A Simultaneous Logit Approach," *Public Choice* 53 (1987): 267–76.

3. Preference for logged or unlogged data depends on expectations about marginal relationships, precision of the coefficients, and overall goodness of fit for the model. Eric A. Hanushek and John E. Jackson, *Statistical Methods for Social Scientists* (New York: Academic Press, 1977), 100–01.

4. For an example, see Lois W. Sayrs, *Pooled Time Series Analysis*, Sage University Paper Series in Quantitative Applications in the Social Sciences, 07-070 (Beverly Hills: Sage, 1989).

5. See Hanushek and Jackson, *Statistical Methods for Social Scientists*, 128.

6. For example, there is only a 1.3 percent chance that three of ten coefficients estimated from independent samples will be statistically significant at the .10 level if there is no actual relationship between the variables. In short, it is not very likely that one would get so many significant coefficients simply by chance.

7. For a discussion of this point, see William Kruskal and Ruth Majors, "Concepts of Relative Importance in Recent Scientific Literature," *The American Statistician* 43, 1 (February 1989): 2–6.

8. The values used in making these estimations varied between one standard deviation above and below the mean for each variable except party and region; for these variables, both values (0 and 1) were used. I estimated one voting probability by substituting the low value (one standard deviation below the mean) for each variable into the model containing estimated coefficients and mean values of all other variables; I calculated the second probability by replacing the low value with the high value (one standard deviation above the mean). The difference between the two probabilities was considered to be the effect of that independent variable. The means and standard deviations for each variable are found in this appendix.

9. If legislators receiving large amounts of S&L campaign contributions are 30 percent more likely (.30) than those receiving small amounts to vote "yea" on one roll call and 30 percent less likely (−.30) to vote "yea" on another one, the "average" effect of contributions on voting "yea" is zero. By taking absolute values, I demonstrated that the average effect on voting probabilities is 30 percent.

10. This statistic is often presented in tables as "−2 log L." This term approximately follows a chi-square distribution, where the degrees of freedom

equals the number of coefficients estimated. Since the expression "–2 log L" is not as commonly understood as the term "model chi-square," I have used the latter term. See John H. Aldrich and Forrest D. Nelson, *Linear Probability, Logit, and Probit Models* (Beverly Hills: Sage Publications, 1984), 55.

11. It is calculated by subtracting the model chi-square of the estimation in which the thrift-related variables are omitted from the model from the model chi-square in which all variables are included. See Aldrich and Nelson, *Linear Probability*, 59–60.

12. If the predicted vote score is greater than .50, the legislator is assumed to have voted for the proposal; if less than .50, against the proposal. Predicted votes are then compared to actual votes. Predicted vote scores have some well-known weaknesses as a measure of how well a logit model works, as do all other goodness-of-fit statistics. See Aldrich and Nelson, *Linear Probability*, 55–58.

13. The percentage correctly predicted based on the model had a standard deviation of 9 percent, compared to 11 percent for the base model.

14. For data sources on congressional voting and a discussion of the omitted votes, see Rom, "The Thrift Tragedy."

15. *Congressional Quarterly Weekly Report*, various issues.

16. Common Cause, "It's a Wonderful Life," and Common Cause, unpublished data, 1990.

17. Federal Home Loan Bank Board, *Combined Financial Statements, FSLIC-Insured Institutions*, 1979, 1982, 1987, and 1988.

18. Ibid.

19. Ibid.

20. Waldman, *Who Robbed America?*, 69.

21. At the time, Democratic House Speaker Wright supported the reduction, while President Reagan wanted to provide FSLIC with the full amount. Wright later (half-heartedly) supported full funding on the House floor.

Index